Mass Atrocities, Risk and Resilience

Mass Atrocities, Risk and Resilience

Rethinking Prevention

Edited by

Stephen McLoughlin

BRILL
NIJHOFF

LEIDEN | BOSTON

Cover illustration: "Mud and Wattle Facade – Bahir Dar – Ethiopia" by Adam Jones, 2013.

Mass atrocities, risk and resilience : rethinking prevention / edited by Stephen McLoughlin.
pages cm
Includes bibliographical references and index.
ISBN 978-90-04-29986-3 (pbk. : alk. paper) -- ISBN 978-90-04-29987-0 (e-book) 1. Atrocities--Prevention. 2. Crimes against humanity--Prevention. I. McLoughlin, Stephen, editor.

HV6322.M38 2015
364.4--dc23

2015019148

This publication has been typeset in the multilingual "Brill" typeface. With over 5,100 characters covering Latin, IPA, Greek, and Cyrillic, this typeface is especially suitable for use in the humanities. For more information, please see www.brill.com/brill-typeface.

ISBN 978-90-04-29986-3 (paperback)
ISBN 978-90-04-29987-0 (e-book)

Originally published, in part, as Volume 6, No. 4 (2014) of Brill Nijhoff's journal, *Global Responsibility to Protect*.

This book is printed on acid-free paper.

Contents

Acknowledgements

I would like to thank the Australian Research Council, for funding research for two chapters in this book: 'Iran 1998–2008: insight on the containment of risk,' by Sara E. Davies, and 'Azerbaijan 1998–2008: Ceasefire, stalemate and simmering tensions,' by Stephen McLoughlin. The Australian Research Council's funding also supported my PhD research, during which time I developed an interest in 'Risk and Resilience' to mass atrocities, and became conscious of the need to broaden research into negative cases. I am also grateful to the editors of the journal, *Global Responsibility to Protect* – Alex J. Bellamy, Sara E. Davies and Luke Glanville, who invited me to edit a special edition on 'Risk and Resilience to Mass Atrocities.' Five chapters in this book were originally published as part of that edition: 'The Next "Spring" is Certain to Come – and Certain to be Missed: Deficits in conflict prevention and research' by Witold Mucha; 'Who is the subject of atrocities prevention?' by Bridget Conley-Zilkic; 'Rethinking the Structural Prevention of Mass Atrocities,' by Stephen McLoughlin; 'International Affinity and the Prevention of Genocide: Implications for R2P,' by Manus I. Midlarsky; and 'Rethinking Approaches to Prevention under the Responsibility to Protect: Agency and Empowerment within Vulnerable Populations,' by Deborah Mayersen.

List of Table and Figures

Table

Figures

About the Authors

Bridget Conley-Zilkic
is the Research Director of the World Peace Foundation and Assistant Research Professor at Tufts University's The Fletcher School. She is currently leading WPF's project, How Mass Atrocities End, which studies cross-case patterns of decline in large-scale assaults against civilians. She previously worked as Research Director for the U.S. Holocaust Memorial Museum's Committee on Conscience, where she led the Museum's research and projects on contemporary threats of genocide, including curating an interactive installation *From Memory to Action: Meeting the Challenge of Genocide Today.*

Sara. E. Davies
is an ARC Future Fellow, Australian Centre for Health Law Research, QUT and Program Manager, Prevention of Mass Atrocities, Asia Pacific Centre for Responsibility to Protect. Sara has (co)authored *Disease Diplomacy* (2015), *Global Politics of Health* (2010) and *Legitimising Rejection* (2007). She is co-editor of Responsibility to Protect and Women, Peace and Security (Brill 2013) and co-editor of the journal *Global Responsibility to Protect.*

Deborah Mayersen
is a Vice-Chancellor's Postdoctoral Research Fellow at the Institute for Social Transformation Research, University of Wollongong. Deborah is an historian, and her research interests are in comparative genocide studies. Her most recent publications include *On the Path to Genocide: Armenia and Rwanda Reexamined* (Berghahn Books, 2014) and *Genocide and Mass Atrocities in Asia: Legacies and Prevention* (co-edited with Annie Pohlman, Routledge, 2013).

Stephen McLoughlin
is a Research Fellow at the Griffith Asia Institute and Centre for Governance and Public Policy, at Griffith University. His research interests include mass atrocities early warning, structural prevention of mass atrocities, ethnic conflict in post-communist states, and the responsibility to protect. His current research is focused on understanding local and national sources of resilience, and how these play a protective role in states at risk of future atrocities. He is the author of the book, *The Structural Prevention of Mass Atrocities: Understanding Risk and Resilience* (Routledge, 2014).

Manus I. Midlarsky
is the Moses and Annuta Back Professor of International Peace and Conflict Resolution at Rutgers University, New Brunswick and Director of the Center for the Study of Mass Violence. He most recently published the *Origins of Political Extremism: Mass Violence in the Twentieth Century and Beyond* (Cambridge University Press, 2011) and *The Killing Trap: Genocide in the Twentieth Century* (Cambridge University Press, 2005). He also published the edited volume *Handbook of War Studies III: The Intrastate Dimension* (University of Michigan Press, 2009), the third in this Handbooks series. In 2011, the original *Handbook of War Studies* was reissued in the Routledge Revival Series, as have *The Onset of World War* and *The Internationalization of Communal Strife* been reissued in 2014. He has served as a consultant to the governments of the United States, Canada, and the Netherlands.

Witold Mucha
is a political scientist with a development policy background in the Andean region and Central Africa. Based at the Institute for Advanced Study in the Humanities (KWI) in Essen, Germany, his field of interest is peace and conflict studies with a focus on escalation and de-escalation processes in internal armed conflict, transnational political mobilisation, and securitisation theory.

Michael Walls
is a Senior Lecturer at UCL's Development Planning Unit (DPU) and Course Director for the MSc in Development Administration and Planning. For some twelve years, his research has focused on the Somali Horn of Africa, and most particularly on the evolving political settlements in Somaliland and Puntland. As well as undertaking research on state formation and political representation, he has been a part of the coordination team for international election observations to Somaliland elections in 2005, 2010 and 2012. Michael remains actively involved in a number of Somali-related groups, including the Anglo-Somali Society, Somaliland Focus (UK) and Kayd Somali Arts and Culture Ltd.

INTRODUCTION

Exploring Risk and Resilience: Implications for Comparative Genocide Studies, and Mass Atrocity Prevention

Stephen McLoughlin

1 Introduction

Two innovations have recently emerged in the scholarly and policy literature on mass atrocities. One is the developing interest amongst scholars in why such violent phenomena *do not* occur in places where risk is present. The second is related to long-term prevention. Typically framed as the identification and amelioration of the 'root causes' of potential violence, the concept has recently broadened in scope to recognise and incorporate national sources of resilience. These two innovations are connected – a better understanding of why mass atrocities do not occur inevitably yields insights into ways that local and national actors build resilience and mitigate risk.

The contributions in this book explore the relationship between 'risk and resilience' in relation to mass atrocities. Such a relationship considers the question, what do local and national actors already do to protect their populations from genocide, crimes against humanity, ethnic cleansing and war crimes? This question has implications for the scholarship within comparative genocide studies, as well as the research into the prevention of such violence, both by scholars and policy makers. Likewise, the contributions in this book can be divided into two broad areas: critiques of prevention, both in relation to mass atrocities specifically, as well as to civil wars more generally; and investigations of negative cases – cases where the risk of mass atrocities existed, but such violence was avoided.

2 Comparative Genocide Studies and the Dearth of Negative Cases

Scholars investigating the preconditions and causal paths of genocide and other mass atrocities have typically focussed on positive cases. In methodological terms, the common approach for genocide scholars has been to compare past cases of mass violence, to identify common antecedents, and to make

 | DOI 10.1163/9789004299870_002

theoretical claims on the basis of such antecedents.[1] Such research has made great progress in uncloaking the dynamics behind some of the worst episodes of systematic violence perpetrated against populations. Due to the diversity of academic disciplines involved in such research, as well as the variation of phenomena under scrutiny, it is inevitable that there is some differentiation in methods and conclusions. Despite this, some broad similarities can be made. For the most part, such root causes were local in character, embedded in identity, patterns of social relations, and the behaviour and actions of political elites and institutions. Poverty and inequality also play a strong role. Yet many scholars stress that the existence of such root causes in and of themselves do not make mass atrocities inevitable. At best, these 'causes' have a correlation with violent outcomes – while they do not indicate an inevitable path to violence, such violence rarely, if ever, occurs in their absence. Moreover, such preconditions exist far more frequently than the violent phenomena they are commonly associated with.[2] While there are situations where the risk associated with mass atrocities can escalate, particularly if provoked by instability or upheaval, more often than not such preconditions can exist without leading to such violence.

However, a major limitation in such studies is they overlook the myriad cases where such preconditions exist *without* ever manifesting in the perpetration of mass atrocities. While any example of such violence is an aberration, in truth mass atrocities are rare phenomena that do not occur in most countries most of the time.[3] The general implications for an over-dependence on positive cases are well known. Rebecca Emigh, for instance, argues that "a focus on positive cases can perpetuate the stereotype that the outcome is inevitable…"[4] Scott Straus considers how this affects research amongst genocide scholars. He argues that the tendency within comparative genocide studies to focus overwhelmingly on positive cases leads to a "frequency mismatch: most theory

---

1 Stephen McLoughlin and Deborah Mayersen, 'Reconsidering Root Causes: A New Framework for the Prevention of Genocide and Mass Atrocities' in Bert Engelaere, Stephan Parmentier, Jacques Haers and Barbara Segaert (eds.), *Genocide, Risk and Resilience: An Interdisciplinary Approach* (Basingstoke: Palgrave, 2013).

2 Scott Straus, 'Retreating from the Brink: Theorizing Mass Violence and the Dynamics of Restraint,' *Perspectives on Politics* 10/2: 343–362 (2012).

3 Andrea Bartoli, Tetsushi Ogata and Gregory H. Stanton, 'Emerging Paradigms in Genocide Prevention,' *Genocide Prevention* (Bern: Federal Department of Foreign Affairs, Confederation of Switzerland, 2009), p. 21.

4 Rebecca Jean Emigh, 'The Power of Negative Thinking: The Use of Negative Case Methodology in the Development of Sociological Theory,' *Theory and Society* 26: 649–684 (1997), p. 658.

posits causal factors that are much more common than the outcome."[5] If, as Straus argues, these causal factors are far more common than the outcome of genocide – or other related violence – what other outcomes are possible? What possible scenarios are there that such causal factors exist in the absence of violence more generally? A better understanding of these scenarios surely yields insights for prevention – if there a number of cases where such causal factors (or risk factors) have been managed relatively well over time, then there exist countries and communities that have effectively prevented mass atrocities.

3 Insights for Prevention

Clearly such research has positive implications for understanding and advocating preventive strategies. Scholarship on the long-term prevention of mass atrocities – and conflict more generally – has, until recently, been limited by focus on causes. Structural (long-term) prevention has been defined as the identification and amelioration of root causes.[6] Such a framing necessitates preventive action be premised on an understanding of *causes*, in places that have not experienced violent outcomes. In other words, it applies the trajectories of cases where violence *has* occurred, onto places where such violence *has not* occurred.[7] It assumes that the existence of 'root causes' necessitates an inevitable path to violence, if such causes are not addressed. Preventive policy then becomes a means of addressing potential 'root causes', which, if left unguarded, will presumably escalate towards violence. The fact that these 'root causes' – or preconditions – can exist without necessarily manifesting into violent outcomes has, until recently, not been acknowledged in policy reports and academic writings on prevention.

This broad tendency to focus on the causes of mass atrocities – at the expense of negative cases – has resulted in many scholars of genocide and other mass atrocities devoting little time to considering how insights from their research might be translated into preventive strategies. What little space is given to prevention can be categorised into two broad areas: diagnosing root causes, and direct prevention. Some scholars of genocide and other mass atrocities identified the diagnosis of root causes as the most significant step towards

5 Scott Straus, 'Retreating from the Brink,' p. 343.

6 David Hamburg, and Cyrus R Vance, *Preventing Deadly Conflict – Final Report* (Washington DC: Carnegie Commission on Preventing Deadly Conflict, 1997).

7 See Bridget Conley-Zilkic's chapter in this book.

prevention. Ben Kiernan, for example, argued that the most significant strategy for long term prevention was simply the identification of their causes – the 'cure' for genocide, he argued was found in naming its causes.[8] For Robert Melson, the identification of the causes of genocide and other mass atrocities "might help in laying the groundwork for more informed philosophical and normative discussions."[9] For Jacques Semelin, such work was the responsibility of social scientists – "the responsibility to know and make known."[10] However, where such philosophical discussions and knowledge might lead is not explained.

The most common preventive strategies recommended by genocide scholars were those that could be categorised as direct prevention. Michael Mann, for instance, stressed the need to apply numerous "powerful geopolitical restraining influences", such as better arms control, and a more robust international reaction to regional conflicts.[11] Kuper argues for the importance of the UN as a preventive actor, but cautioned that it needed to develop this capacity through the institutional translation of its "ceaseless manufacture of normative documents."[12] Illustrating how this could happen, he identifies the consensus on the mandate of the High Commissioner for Human Rights in 1982 as one step forward.[13] Helen Fein recommends public censure of states where the perpetration of atrocities seemed likely. She uses the example of the international Baha'i community's successful public international campaign in the early 1980s as an illustration of how a public campaign can work.[14]

While these scholars have certainly advanced our understanding of the causes of genocide and other mass atrocities, corresponding suggestions for prevention prioritise the role international actors, overlooking what local and national actors are already doing to mitigate risk. In order to have insights into such domestic processes of risk mitigation, more research is needed on why such violence *does not* occur. In other words, the field of comparative genocide studies needs to incorporate more research into negative cases.

---

8 Ben Kiernan, *Blood and Soil: A World History of Genocide and Extermination from Sparta to Darfur* (Melbourne: Melbourne University Press, 2007), p. 606.

9 Robert Melson, *Revolution and Genocide: On the Origins of the Armenian Genocide and the Holocaust* (Chicago: University of Chicago Press, 1992), p. 257.

10 Jacques Semelin, *Purify and Destroy: The Political Uses of Massacre and Genocide* (London: C. Hurst & Co, 2007), p. 372.

11 Mann 2005, 535–526.

12 Leo Kuper, *The Prevention of Genocide* (New Haven, CT: Yale University Press, 1985), p. 210.

13 Kuper, *Prevention of Genocide*, p. 214.

14 Helen Fein, 'Accounting for Genocide after 1945: Theories and Some Findings,' *International Journal on Group Rights* 1: 79–106 (1993), p. 102.

4 A Renewed Interest in Negative Cases

While scholars of comparative genocide studies have generally overlooked negative cases in theorizing the causes of genocide and other mass atrocities, there have been some exceptions. Cumulatively, these studies have utilized negative cases in two ways: by examining why very high risk countries step back from the brink of mass violence, and by examining long-term processes of risk mitigation in places of moderate risk.

The first to highlight the value of examining nations that displayed risk but no atrocities was Leo Kuper, through his analysis of South African under Apartheid, and Northern Ireland.[15] Two and a half decades later, Manus Midlarsky investigated why both Finland and Bulgaria were able to avoid surrendering their Jewish populations during the Second World War. He identified an 'absence of loss' in these countries – that is, the absence of 'the combustible mix of territorial loss, threatening ethno-religious identity, and class conflict.'[16] More recently, two publications proposed analyses that compared one positive with one negative case, in order to better understand why genocide occurred in some places but not in others. Deborah Mayersen and Stephen McLoughlin compared Rwanda and Botswana, pointing out that they shared fairly similar histories, yet Botswana's moderate level of risk never escalated, despite enduring widespread poverty, especially before the extraction of diamonds in the early 1970s. Scott Straus' 2012 comparison of Rwanda in 1994 and Côte d'Ivoire in 2010/11 sought to better understand why it is that some countries 'retreat from the brink' of genocide.[17] Finally, Stephen McLoughlin's 2014 book, *The Structural Prevention of Mass Atrocities,* provides an in-depth analysis of three countries that displayed moderate risk associated with mass atrocities (Botswana, Zambia and Tanzania), in order to better understand long-term processes of risk mitigation.[18]

These studies provide important insights for both direct and structural prevention. They highlight that the international community has an important role to play even when countries are on the verge of committing widespread

---

15 Leo Kuper, *Genocide: Its Political Use in the Twentieth Century* (New Haven, CT: Yale University Press, 1981).

16 Manus Midlarsky, *The Killing Trap: Genocide in the Twentieth Century* (Cambridge: Cambridge University Press, 2005), pp. 325, 330. See also Mcloughlin and Mayersen, 'Reconsidering Root Causes.'

17 Scott Straus, 'Retreating from the Brink.'

18 Stephen McLoughlin, *The Structural Prevention of Mass Atrocities* (Oxon: Routledge, 2014).

and systematic atrocities against their populations. For instance, in 2011, The Security Council resolution 1975, which authorised the United Nations Operation in Côte d'Ivoire (UNOCI) to "use all necessary means" in protecting people from the government-driven violence against protestors in Côte d'Ivoire illustrates this. The descent into civil war, and the escalation of violence was stalled when a contingent of peacekeeping forces, together with French military assistance, helped precipitate the defeat of Laurent Gbagbo and his army, halting the escalation of violence against civilians.[19] This, of course, was an extreme measure, considered after all other attempts at diplomacy had failed.

Perhaps the most useful insights for prevention arise from the more causally ambiguous cases. It is far more difficult to justify the inclusion of negative cases in places where risk is moderate (and hence the association with mass atrocities is more challenging to establish), but such cases have the most to offer in terms of prevention. They yield insights into locally and nationally-driven processes of risk mitigation over periods of years and decades. The study of negative cases in relation to mass atrocities is not without its challenges – the methodological challenge in terms of case selection is to justify the association with the non-occurrence of a violent event. How does the researcher prove that certain processes were responsible for the outcome of a non-event? This is a question that many of the contributions in this volume seek to answer.

5 Risk, Resilience and the Responsibility to Protect

These questions are of central concern to the emerging norm of the Responsibility to Protect (R2P). That R2P rests on the premise that the primary responsibility of protection lies with states themselves was established at the 2005 World Summit, where member states endorsed the notion each state held the primary responsibility in protecting their populations from genocide, war crimes, crimes against humanity and ethnic cleansing (mass atrocities), and that this entailed the prevention of such crimes. Further unpacking this commitment, Secretary-General Ban Ki-moon identified three pillars: the first pillar entailed the state's own responsibility to protect its populations from atrocity crimes; the second pillar related to international assistance to help states fulfil this responsibility; the third pillar involved the international responsibility to act (on a case-by-case basis) in situations where states

19 Alex J. Bellamy and Paul D. Williams, 'The New Politics of Protection? Côte d'Ivoire, Libya and the Responsibility to Protect', *International Affairs* 87/4: 825–850 (2011), pp. 834–836.

'manifestly failed' in their responsibility to protect.[20] Despite this, to date there has been very little research exploring the ways that such responsibility is carried out, particularly in places where risk is present.

This lacuna has not gone entirely unnoticed in policy circles. In the Secretary General's 2009 inaugural report on R2P, *Implementing the Responsibility to Protect,* he acknowledged that "more research and analysis are needed on why one society plunges into mass violence while its neighbours remain relatively stable…"[21] Writing about the broader phenomenon of mass political violence, the Human Security Report Project pointed out that the causes of war attract far greater interest than the causes of peace.[22] Amongst policy documents, one significant exception to this apparent lack of interest is the Secretary-General's 2013 report, *Responsibility to Protect: State Responsibility and Prevention.* The report contains two innovations. First, it stresses that no country is entirely absent of risk associated with mass atrocities. As the Secretary-General says, "no state can consider itself immune to the risk of atrocity crimes."[23] Therefore, *every* country has a responsibility in managing, or mitigating challenges associated with such risk. Second, the national sources of resilience that it identifies as having preventive value, are, in and of themselves, beneficial for fostering social cohesion and strengthening stability. Thus, such preventive strategies have currency well beyond the purpose of preventing atrocity crimes. In the report, the Secretary-General offers a frame of reference for understanding state-initiated processes of risk mitigation. While earlier approaches to long term, or structural prevention are characterised by the identification and amelioration of root causes, this report broadens the lens by identifying not only risk factors, but also national sources of resilience. The report argues that an understanding of state responsibility in R2P needs to be premised on ways that each state manages risk over time. The report provides a lens on ways that risk is managed by identifying six ways that states build national resilience, including constitutional reform, democracy, codifying mass atrocity crimes, security sector reform, strategies that address inequalities, and – where appropriate – transitional justice mechanisms.[24] By identifying these domestic sources of

---

20 Ban Ki-moon, *Implementing the Responsibility to Protect: Report of the Secretary-General,* A/63/677, 12 January 2009.

21 Ibid, pp. 10–11.

22 Human Security Report Project. *Human Security Report 2009/2010: The Causes of Peace and the Shrinking Costs of War* (New York: Oxford University Press, 2011), p. 52.

23 Ban Ki-moon, *Responsibility to Protect: State Responsibility and Prevention,* A/67/929-S/2013/399, 9 July 2013, p. 7.

24 Ban Ki-moon, *State Responsibility and Prevention,* pp. 3–11.

resilience and the value they have in mitigating risk, the report overcomes the tendency in the broader academic literature to make distinctions between prevention actors (usually external actors) and prevention recipients (potential victims). These distinctions are problematic, as Bridget Conley-Zilkic's article in this edition argues. The report breaks new ground by offering a framework for identifying and tracing the measures and strategies that states themselves adopt to manage risk factors over time. It does this based on the assumption that states themselves are the primary preventive actors. This does not rule out the need for international actors to contribute to prevention – often assistance is needed to strengthen the capacity to deal with such challenges.[25] It is clear that any internationally-generated approaches to prevention need to be based on a thorough understanding of local and national processes of risk mitigation.

6 Contributions

By pointing out that risk, by itself, is not adequate to explain the causes of mass atrocities, the report echoes the findings of many genocide scholars who argue that the link between long term risk and the perpetration of mass atrocities is tenuous at best. Yet many early warning mechanisms still tend to base their assessments on risk alone, rather than the complex arrange of factors that comprise the relationship between risk and resilience, as Witold Mucha points out in this book. Moreover, very little attention is given to negative cases – where genocide and other atrocities *did not* occur, despite the presence of risk. Manus Midlarsky and Deborah Mayersen, conduct explorations of why such atrocities were averted in historical cases, and in doing so, provide insights on how both local and state actors can resist the path to such violence. Complementing these analyses, Michael Walls, Sara Davies and Stephen McLoughlin investigate more recent cases to understand how that places with very high levels of risk – the territory of Somaliland (after 1991), Iran and Azerbaijan (between 1998 and 2008) – avoided the perpetration of mass atrocities Investigating negative cases is an essential component of prevention, as it helps to give clarity to the Secretary-General's question of why it is that atrocities that are committed in some places, but not in others.

The first three chapters of this book explore some of the conceptual challenges in relation to prevention. The first, by Witold Mucha, takes a critical look at the construction of 'crisis knowledge' that is used to generate conflict

25 See Ban Ki-moon, *Fulfilling our Collective Responsibility: International Assistance and the Responsibility to Protect*, A/68/946-S/2014/449, 11 July 2014, p. 3.

and mass atrocities early warning. He analyses four early warning tools – the World Bank greed/grievance model, the Political Instability Task Force, the Failed States Index, and the International Crisis Group's investigative approach. Pointing out that the Arab Spring took both policymakers and academics by surprise, he argues that this is because of the belief in the stability of authoritarian regimes. Mucha's analysis of these tools shows that prevention research contains biases that can then have an influence on the way that policymakers make assessments of risk. He then argues that large-scale violence can be better anticipate by incorporating negative cases into existing frames of analysis.

In the second chapter, Bridget Conley-Zilkic presents a critique of common conceptions of the 'subject' of atrocities. She points out that within the scholarship investigating the causes of genocide and atrocities, a range of names for the subject of such violence "are treated as if they are synonymous: ethnic, national, racial and religious groups; populations; civilians; perpetrators; victims, bystanders and rescuers." She argues that there are important distinctions between these different vocabularies, distinctions that have an impact on how preventive efforts are devised. Her article explores these distinctions by analysing three major conceptual vocabularies deployed in the scholarship: 'victim', 'groupness', and 'civilian or population'. Conley-Zilkic's analysis demonstrates how these terms become more problematic the further away from their original context they are used. This is particularly significant for prevention, which typically anticipates not only potential violence, but also potential 'victim' groups prior to any victimization. She argues that a new prevention agenda, which challenges current representations of 'subjects', is needed. Her paper considers some possible ways forward for such an agenda. She considers such notions as 'resilience' and 'inhibiting factors', as ways of understanding how negative cases with risk avoid atrocities. By doing so, she explores alternatives that use a different vocabulary, ones that correspond more effectively to prevention.

In the third chapter, Stephen McLoughlin also argues for the need to consider insights from negative cases in his critique of the concept of structural prevention. Tracing the evolution of the concept, as articulated in UN reports and academic texts, McLoughlin points out that the common framing of structural prevention – the identification and addressing of the root causes of potential deadly violence – is limited in two key ways. First, it leaves open the possibility that the identification of root causes assumes a linear path to an inevitable violent outcome. The tendency in the academic literature to refer to phases of conflict, from long-term risk, to periods of gestation, to escalation and violence reinforces this assumption. The second limitation is that the identification of these root cause, and their corresponding preventive strategies, are largely determined and enacted by external actors. McLoughlin argues that these limitations fail to take into account the findings in the scholarship on genocide and other forms of mass violence, that the existence of long-term risk factors (or 'root causes') have a tenuous causal link with the perpetration of such violence. Observing that such risk exists in many countries, without escalating to mass atrocities, McLoughlin argues that prevention should be premised on understanding such local and national processes of risk mitigation. In this article, he proposes a framework for understanding the role that sources of resilience have in mitigating the long-term risk of mass atrocities, and argues for the need to build on such experience as a basis of prevention.

The second part of the book contains contributions from scholars that explore the question of why genocide and other atrocities do not occur through in-depth analyses of negative cases. Manus Midlarsky provides a compelling account of historical cases where genocide did not eventuate where all the indicators suggested otherwise. These cases include the Ottoman Greeks prior to and during World War One, and Jews in Eastern Europe. The key intervening variable in these cases is the existence of affinity groups in neighbouring countries. He argues the existence of 'highly placed Soviet Jews' had a protective effect on the treatment of Jews in Eastern Europe prior to the 1941 German invasion of the Soviet Union. Similarly, the Greeks in the Ottoman Empire benefitted from the neighbouring Greek state, which had been growing in size and strength as the Ottoman Empire endured territorial losses. Targeting Greeks in the empire risked provoking yet another opponent. This protection was further consolidated by 'indirect' affinity, through the great powers of Great Britain, France and Russia, which had previously supported Greek independence. Midlarsky also considers two further cases, focussing on potential victimizers: late eighteenth century Poland, and the British in Ireland from 1916 to 1921.

Deborah Mayersen utilizes both positive and negative cases to argue that often it is vulnerable populations themselves that develop strategies to reduce the risk of atrocities, or ensure that at least some members avoid falling victim. Mayersen argues that the notion of mass atrocity prevention, found in the Responsibility to Protect, as well as other key policy documents, is focussed on the level of the state, overlooking the agency that persecuted groups have. The concept itself assumes that a population in need of protection is ostensibly unable to protect itself. She challenges this assumption by investigating how vulnerable populations have used their own agency to a) prevent genocide and other atrocities from being perpetrated in the first place; and b) to prevent at least some of the persecuted group from being targeted in cases where atrocities are already being committed. The two negative case studies she considers are the Yemenite Jewry between 1900 and 1950, and the Bahá'í religious minority in Iran after the 1979 revolution. In both these cases each group were able to use their agency to reduce their susceptibility to such violence. In the two positive cases – German and Austrian Jews under Nazi rule, she demonstrates how they were 'intensely active in attempting to reduce their risk of experiencing mass atrocities.' Given the dearth of options available, protection here took the form of mass emigration. Mayersen points out that emigration in these cases was not a simple matter of crossing borders and getting on boats, but occurred in the midst of profound obstacles, including a Nazi-imposed 'flight tax', not to mention the difficulty of securing asylum in other countries.

Michael Walls' contribution examines how and why Somaliland has managed to establish and maintain 'order and agreed systems of governance.' Somaliland stands in stark contrast to its neighbour, Somalia, where two and a half decades of periodic armed conflict and mass atrocities continue. Following the collapse of Siad Barre's regime, Somalia's northern province seceded in May 1991, declaring a restoration of sovereignty to the former state of Somaliland, which had existed for five days, between independence from Great Britain and union with Somalia in 1960. Somaliland has forged an extended period of relative peace and stability, despite the fact its statehood is not internationally recognised. Countering the common belief that the former Republic of Somalia is 'the quintessential failed state', Walls details the strategies that a variety of actors and stakeholders implemented between 1991 and 1997 – amidst sporadic conflict – to establish a constitution which established 'a commitment to electoral democracy and a strong electoral wing.' Since 1997, Somaliland has maintained a relatively stable and peaceful democratic state. While challenges remain, Somaliland's period of effective peacebuilding and subsequent statebuilding is a testament to its ability to manage crises and deepen legimtimacy. In doing so, as Walls argues, 'we find the basis for an argument around the prevention of atrocity.'

Sara Davies, in her chapter, 'Iran 1998–2008: Insight on the containment of risk,' investigates how and why Iran avoided the perpetration of mass atrocities in the same decade. Iran contains many features associated with the high risk of mass atrocities, including the absence of democratic institutions, a weak and unstable economy, and a history of human rights violations against religious, ethnic and political minority groups. Davies argues that this high level of risk was counter-balanced by the fragmenting nature of Iran's political system. This, Davies argues, 'provides an essential if delicate power balance' that accommodates all political actors, thus providing incentives for all to preserve the status quo.

Finally, Stephen McLoughlin's chapter, 'Azerbaijan 1998–2008: Ceasefire, stalemate and simmering tensions,' explores why it is that this country – which contains very high levels of risk – managed to avoid mass atrocities in the decade between 1998 and 2008. Azerbaijan is a post-Soviet state that has endured more than a century of tensions and occasional armed conflict, between the dominant ethnic Azeris and the minority ethnic Armenians. Under Soviet rule, territorial dispute over Nagorno Karabakh was left unresolved. Following the collapse of the Soviet Union in 1991, tension between the two identity groups escalated, in Azerbaijan and Armenia, both newly independent. This lead to an all-out war from 1992 to 1994, with Armenian militia groups (backed by the Armenian army) wresting control of substantial amounts of Azerbaijan's territory, including Nagorno-Karabakh. McLoughlin argues that tensions between the two countries persisted through the period 1998 to 2008, and at times threatened to re-escalate to war. Yet Azerbaijan managed to avert conflict and potential atrocities in this period as a result of three factors: the advent of a more stable regime, which managed to avoid the kind of upheaval of the early 1990s that had previously precipitated conflict; economic growth and increased trade; and the mediation efforts of the OSCE-led peacekeepers along the ceasefire line.

Taken together, these contributions elucidate – both conceptually and empirically – the myriad ways that the risk of mass atrocities can be mitigated over time. This knowledge allows for a greater appreciation of the role that local and national actors play in preventing such crimes. Given that 'prevention begins at home',[26] understanding such dynamics offers a valuable starting point for implementing policies and strategies that aid in the peaceful management of diversity and the fostering of long term stability in the face of challenges associated with risk.

---

26 Ban Ki-moon, *Implementing the Responsibility to Protect*, p. 10.

PART 1

Conceptual Approaches to Prevention

CHAPTER 1

The Next 'Spring' is Certain to Come – and Certain to be Missed: Deficits in Conflict Prevention and Research

Witold Mucha
Institute for Advanced Study in the Humanities (KWI), Essen, Germany
witold.mucha@kwi-nrw.de

Abstract

The Arab Spring took policymakers and academics by surprise. The starting point, the scope, nor the impact had been seen coming. This was primarily because of academics' irrevocable belief in the stabilising power of authoritarian regimes. In light of this failing, the article will critically discuss the production of crisis knowledge on the basis of four major early warning tools. These are World Bank's greed/grievance model, the predictive model by the Political Instability Task Force, the risk and capacity approach applied by the Failed States Index, and the International Crisis Group. The article will add to the debate in two ways. First, the analysis will show that prevention research can be biased in ways that crucially influence policymakers' assessment of states at risk. Second, the article will argue in favour of a complementary perspective that includes the analysis of conflicts that do not erupt into large-scale violence against all odds (so-called 'negative cases').

Keywords

conflict – crisis – early warning – prevention – risk – violence

Introduction

Failing to anticipate the beginning, scope, and different paths of the Arab Spring demonstrated the academic community's deficits in assessing countries

I would like to thank Stephen McLoughlin and the anonymous reviewers for their helpful comments on earlier drafts of this article.

 | DOI 10.1163/9789004299870_003

at risk. While policymakers from Washington to London took much stick for missing the revolutionary tide, scholars were largely exempted.[1] More than three years after the first regime was toppled in Tunisia, it seems that neither have academics admitted this failure nor has the conventional belief in the stability of authoritarian regimes been questioned.[2] Missing the upheavals in Ukraine in early 2014 substantiate that the Arab Spring was not a one-time only episode in this regard.[3] Against this backdrop, the article will analyse the deficits in conflict prevention and research. The latter will be of particular interest as it is the author's assumption that many of the prevailing deficits are related to the production and transfer of scholarly expertise and policy recommendations. Pinpointing these shortcomings will help to understand that missing the genesis and escalation of intrastate large-scale violence, be it armed conflict, mass atrocity, or both, is because of very similar normative, conceptual, and political mistakes.[4] The article will be divided into four sections. First, the evolution of the concept of conflict prevention will be introduced on the basis of prominent works by the Carnegie Commission and pioneers such as Goldstone or Marshall. Second, four of the most popular early warning systems will be

1 Uri Dadush and Michele Dunne, 'American and European Responses to the Arab Spring: What's the Big Idea?', *The Washington Quarterly*, 34/4: 131–145 (2011), p. 132; Gregory Gause III, 'Why Middle East Studies Missed the Arab Spring', *Foreign Affairs*, 90/4: 81–90 (2011), p. 81; Eva Bellin, 'Reconsidering the Robustness of Authoritarianism in the Middle East: Lessons from the Arab Spring', *Comparative Politics*, 44/2: 127–149 (2012), p. 128.

2 Bellin, 'Reconsidering the Robustness of Authoritarianism in the Middle East', p. 128.

3 Anastasyia Ryabchuk, 'Right Revolution? Hopes and Perils of the Euromaidan Protests in Ukraine', *Debatte: Journal of Contemporary Central and Eastern Europe*, 22/1: 127–134 (2014.).

4 Acknowledging the different objectives and thus need for contextualized approaches of early warning tools to prevent mass atrocities on the one hand and armed conflict on the other, this article does not focus on these distinctions. In many armed conflicts (mass) atrocities are committed. Recent civil war in Syria is one of the darkest examples in this regard. However, the present analysis is about the deficits of knowledge transfer in generally preventing the eruption of large-scale violence. This broad analytical lens allows for comparing diverse conflict situations, be they driven by radicalized protest movements or experienced rebel groups fighting the state. For an excellent discussion on the variances and parallels of preventive measures against mass atrocity and armed conflict see Alex J. Bellamy, *Mass Atrocities and Armed Conflict: Links, Distinctions, and Implications for the Responsibility to Prevent*. Policy Analysis Brief (Muscatine: The Stanley Foundation, 2011). See also Benjamin E. Goldsmith, Charles R. Butcher, Dimitri Semenovich, and Arcot Sowmya, 'Forecasting the onset of genocide and politicide: Annual out-of-sample forecasts on a global dataset, 1988–2003', *Journal of Peace Research*, 50/4: 437–452 (2013); Benjamin E. Goldsmith, Dimitri Semenovich, and Arcot Sowmya, 'Political Instability and Genocide. Comparing causes in Asia and the Pacific and globally' in Deborah Mayersen and Annie Pohlman (eds.), *Genocide and Mass Atrocities in Asia: Legacies and prevention* (New York: Routledge, 2013).

presented that at least implicitly claim predictive capability over crisis situations. These are World Bank's greed/grievance model, the predictive model by the Political Instability Task Force (PITF), the risk and capacity approach applied by the Failed States Index (FSI), and the International Crisis Group (ICG) which is based on intelligence and investigative research. Each tool will be empirically put to test with the cases of Egypt, Libya, Syria, Tunisia, and Yemen after the beginning of uprisings in early 2011. Thereafter, the most relevant critique will be discussed. At last, suggestions will be made of how to improve the existing conflict prevention architecture – both in terms of policy-making and crisis knowledge production.

The Concept of Conflict Prevention

The debate on conflict prevention is historically rooted in the prevention of interstate wars. In former times, traditional diplomacy, rules, or power demonstrations were major means to prevent attacks by potential enemies.[5] This changed after the experiences with the First and Second World War when the League of Nations (1920) and the United Nations (UN) (1945) were established. These two organisations heralded the beginning of a collectively interpreted prevention approach that was meant to inhibit a Third World War.[6] However, in the context of Cold War the ability and willingness of policymakers to prevent intrastate conflicts by these very organisations was constrained. Some of the conflicts were even added fuel by waging geostrategic proxy wars. Armed conflicts in Afghanistan (1979–1989) and Vietnam (1964–1975) have been mentioned most in this respect.[7] This prevention logic changed with the end of Cold War. In particular, UN General Secretary Boutros-Ghali's 'Agenda for Peace' (1992) opened up a new perspective on conflict prevention: the claim that all conflicts in the world should and could be prevented.[8] Based on four operational levels (preventive diplomacy, peace

5 Susan Pedersen, 'Back to the League of Nations', *The American Historical Review*, 112/4: 1091–1117 (2007), p. 1116; Alice Ackermann, 'The Idea and Practice of Conflict Prevention', *Journal of Peace Research*, 40/3: 339–347 (2003), p. 340.

6 Pedersen, 'Back to the League of Nations', p. 1116; Ackermann, 'The Idea and Practice of Conflict Prevention', p. 340.

7 Milton Bearden, 'Afghanistan, Graveyard of Empires', *Foreign Affairs*, 80/6: 17–30 (2001); Stathis N. Kalyvas and Laia Balcells, 'International System and Technologies of Rebellion: How the End of the Cold War Shaped Internal Conflict', *American Political Science Review*, 104/3: 415–429 (2010), p. 418.

8 Boutros Boutrous Ghali, 'An Agenda for Peace. Preventive Diplomacy, Peacemaking and Peace-keeping', *International Relations*, 11/3: 201–218 (1992), p. 201.

enforcement, peacekeeping, and postconflict peacebuilding), the approach was welcome by the international community in the early 1990s.[9] However, failed preventions in former Yugoslavia or Rwanda quickly dampened the enthusiasm.[10] More than two decades after the 'Agenda for Peace' was declared, the international conflict prevention architecture still faces major challenges. Armed conflicts in Darfur in 2003 or the Central African Republic since 2012 speak volume of that.[11]

In the late 1990s, scholars and policymakers agreed that preventive measures were to be launched in three phases.[12] According to the Carnegie Commission, it was thereby vital that any prevention measure would include the postconflict period. In the first phase, it is all about preventing the eruption of violence (primary prevention). In the second phase, measures are taken to curtail the scope and intensity of ongoing escalation processes (secondary prevention). In the third and last phase, the major objective is to prevent the re-escalation of violent clashes that have been already settled (tertiary prevention).[13] In light of this dynamic escalation logic, two different prevention imperatives are discussed: the operational and the structural prevention. While the first is related to short and middle term measures to prevent violent conflict (i.e. political and military means), structural prevention means actions that tackle the background conditions of societies. This is the attempt to lower the risk of collective violence before it is triggered in the first place. Basically, these are development projects and economy programs.[14] Some scholars relate the structural perspective to the notion of systemic prevention. This perspective is in line with the long term focus of measures. However, it is not one

9 Thomas G. Weiss Jr., 'New Challenges for UN Military Operations: Implementing an Agenda for Peace', *The Washington Quarterly*, 16/1: 51–66 (1993), p. 52.

10 David Chandler, 'The People-Centred Approach to Peace Operations: The New UN Agenda', *International Peacekeeping*, 8/1: 1–9 (2001), p. 1.

11 Paul D. Williams and Alex J. Bellamy, 'The Responsibility to Protect and the Crisis in Darfur', *Security Dialogue*, 36/1: 27–47 (2005), p. 29; Scott Straus, 'Darfur and the Genocide Debate', *Foreign Affairs*, 84/1: 123–133 (2005), p. 123; Lisa Hultman, Jacob Kathman, and Megan Shannon, 'United Nations Peacekeeping and Civilian Protection in Civil War', *American Journal of Political Science*, 57/4: 875–891 (2013), p. 882.

12 Carnegie Commission on Preventing Deadly Conflict, *Preventing Deadly Conflict. Final Report with Executive Summary* (Washington D.C.: Carnegie Corporation, 1997), p. xviii.

13 Ibid.

14 Michael S. Lund, 'Conflict Prevention: Theory in Pursuit of Policy and Practice', in Jacob Bercovitch, Victor Kremenyuk, and William Zartman (eds.), *The Sage Handbook of Conflict Resolution* (London: SAGE Publications, 2009), pp. 289–290.

country or region only that is targeted. The argument rather goes that conflict prevention needs to take into account the global level where systemic risk factors need to be dealt with. For instance, an unequal world trade regime that discriminates against countries of the Global South is most often mentioned in this regard.[15] The distinction between operational and structural/systemic prevention is related to the different definitions of conflict prevention. Scholars working on structural prevention make use of a broad definition:

> (...) [Actions] or policies that address deeper societal conditions that generate conflicts between interests and/or the institutional, procedural and policy deficits or capacities that determine whether competing interests are channelled and mutually adjusted peacefully. These more basic factors make up the environment within which contending actors operate and thus policies toward them can create constraints or opportunities that shape what the actors do. Diverse examples are reducing gross regional disparities in living standards, reforming exploitative agricultural policies, and building effective governing institutions.[16]

Sanctions, development aid, and structural adjustment policies are also considered as structural measures of conflict prevention.[17] The broad understanding of prevention also refers to the scope (i.e. global, regional, national, local) and the involved stakeholders (i.e. governmental and non-governmental organizations).[18] In contrast to this perspective, research on early warning is based on a rather narrow understanding. The argument goes that tensions need to be contained before escalating into armed violent conflict. As such, conflict prevention is not synonymous with early warning – although, the terms are often used that way. Early warning systems are a complementary part of the overarching prevention architecture. These are used to identify growing tensions that might lead to armed conflict on a time-sensitive and actor- or event-focused basis.[19] However, in contrast to conflict prevention, early warning is not expected to deliver policy recommendations. This task (i.e. conflict prevention) falls to the

15 Barnett R. Rubin and Bruce D. Jones, 'Prevention of Violent Conflict: Tasks and Challenges for the United Nations', *Global Governance*, 13/3: 391–408 (2007), p. 403.

16 Michael S. Lund, 'Conflict Prevention', p. 290.

17 Rubin and Jones, 'Prevention of Violent Conflict', p. 401.

18 Ibid, pp. 400–402.

19 Herbert Wulf and Tobias Debiel, *Conflict Warning and Response Mechanisms: Tools for Enhancing the Effectiveness of Regional Organisations? A Comparative Study of the AU, ECOWAS, IGAD, ASEAN/ARF and PIF* (London: Development Studies Institute, 2009), p. 4.

respective political decision-making units such as state departments that make use of expertise provided by think tanks (i.e. early warning). Given the focus of this article on knowledge production, the following section will primarily deal with early warning tools.

Early Warning Architecture

During the last couple of years, a number of studies were published that deal with early warning.[20] In order to differentiate the variety of material, this section will present early warning tools on the basis of four overarching

TABLE 1 *Deaths during protests and clashes between opposition and government forces*[21]

Country	Number killed, minimum	Period of unrest
Syria[22]	160.000[23]	Mar 2011 – ongoing
Libya[24]	30.000	Feb 2011 – Oct 2011
Egypt[25]	3.000	Jan 2011 – Sep 2013
Yemen[26]	2.000	Feb 2011 – Mar 2012
Tunisia[27]	219	Dec 2010 – Jan 2011

20 Monty G. Marshall, *Fragility, Instability, and the Failure of States. Assessing Sources of Systemic Risk* (New York: Center for Preventive, 2008); Jack A. Goldstone, Robert H. Bates, David L. Epstein, Ted Robert Gurr, Michael B. Lustik, Monty G. Marshall, Jay Ulfelder, and Mark Woodward, 'A Global Forecasting Model of Political Instability', *American Journal of Political Science*, 54/1: 190–208 (2010).

21 Own illustration based on The Economist 2011, 'The Arab Spring Death Toll, The Price of Protest, So far', http://www.economist.com/blogs/dailychart/2011/07/arab-spring-death-toll, accessed 4 June 2014.

22 In March 2011, anti-regime protest began in Syria's southern city of Deraa. Given the continued violent state response, the once peaceful uprising evolved into an increasingly sectarian armed conflict. An excellent overview is given by Raymond Hinnebusch, 'Syria: from 'authoritarian upgrading' to revolution?', *International Affairs*, 88/1: 95–113 (2012).

23 This number was confirmed by different local and international monitoring groups at the time of writing this article in May 2014. See Anne Barnard, 'Syria Death Toll Reported to Rise by 10,000 in Less Than 2 Months', *New York Times*, 19 May 2014.

24 Libya's uprising began in February 2011 after security forces in the eastern city of Benghazi opened fire on protesters. In March 2011, after the UN Security Council authorised 'all

categories. First, causal models will be introduced that claim to identify factors that trigger violent conflict. Second, forecasting models will be presented. These claim to predict the eruption of large-scale violence for a specific time horizon. Closely related third, so-called risk and performance approaches will be discussed. With the help of rankings, scholars reveal the vulnerability of states at risk. And last, intelligence and investigative research will be presented. Each of these four will be empirically tested against popular uprisings in the context of the Arab Spring (Egypt, Libya, Syria, Tunisia, and Yemen). This test

necessary measures' to protect civilians, NATO established a no-fly zone. With military assistance from the West and several Arab states, rebel forces took Tripoli in August 2011. In July 2012, the National Transitional Council (NTC) organised elections for an interim parliament, in which liberal, secular and independent candidates beat the Muslim Brotherhood-aligned Justice and Construction Party. A useful overview is given by Emanuela Paoletti, 'Libya: Roots of a Civil Conflict', *Mediterranean Politics*, 16/2: 313-319 (2011).

25 After three decades in power, mass protests forced Hosni Mubarak to resign in February 2011. Following his resignation, the Supreme Council of the Armed Forces (SCAF) assumed presidential powers. In June 2012, the Muslim Brotherhood's Mohammed Morsi was elected president. Only one year later however, he was deposed by the military after millions of protesters took to the streets supposedly against too much Islamic influence in politics and society. A new constitution was drafted in December 2013 and General al-Sisi was elected president in May 2014. On the political turmoil between 2011 and 2013 see Jeffrey T. Kenney, 'Movement Activism: The Society of Muslim Brothers After Egypt's Arab Spring', *Nova Religio*, 16/3: 95–104 (2013).

26 Facing mass protests against his 33-year rule in January 2011, Yemen's President Ali Abdullah Saleh ordered security forces against the demonstrators. After refusing to withdraw from office, the Hashid tribal federation and several army commanders decided to back the opposition. Against the backdrop of violent protests and clashes with security forces, Saleh resigned in November 2011 and his deputy, Abdrabbuh Mansour Hadi, was sworn in for a two-year term as president in February 2012. On Arab Spring in Yemen see April Longley Alley, 'Assessing (In)security after the Arab Spring: The Case of Yemen', *Political Science and Politics*, 46/4: 721–726 (2013).

27 After the self-immolation of street vendor Mohamed Bouazizi in December 2010, discontent at economic hardship, decades of autocratic rule and corruption erupted into mass protest against President Ben Ali. He resigned and fled to exile in Saudi Arabia in January 2011 and was later sentenced to life in prison in absentia. In October 2011, first democratic parliamentary elections were held and the moderate Islamist Ennahda party won more than 41% of the vote in the constituent assembly. Veteran dissident Moncef Marzouki was then elected president. The case of Tunisia is well covered by Sharon Erickson Nepstad, 'Nonviolent Resistance in the Arab Spring: The Critical Role of Military-Opposition Alliances', *Swiss Political Science Review*, 17/4: 485–491 (2011).

is meant to reveal to what extent these early warning tools were capable of anticipating the different outcomes or not. These five countries are selected because of two criteria. First, violent clashes between opposition and state forces led to a significant number of people killed in the process. Second, despite similar trigger events, mostly violent state repression, the uprisings followed very different paths. The table above illustrates these differences.

Causal Models: Greed vs. Grievance and Horizontal Inequalities

The Anglo-American based peace and conflict research is dominated by quantitative studies. This macro design approach allows scholars to identify structural or background causes of violent conflict and/or state failure. There is a variety of explanatory models that compete with each other in the discipline. The most prominent are the greed versus grievance debate and the horizontal inequalities model:[28]

The basic assumption underlying the grievance approach is that contradictions within a society lead to conflicts when parts of that society become aware of inequalities. It is argued that people take up arms against each other over identity issues such as social class, religion, ethnicity, or socioeconomic inequalities.[29] The approach draws on the causal relationship between relative deprivation, polarisation and inequality. Gurr argues that the discontent arising from the perception of deprivation is the primary and most agitating motivation for collective violence.[30] While Gurr's grievance argument is based on the poverty-deprivation nexus, the related 'horizontal inequality'-concept assumes that inequality between rich and poor alone is not sufficient to cause the outbreak of violent conflict. Østby argues that '[civil] wars are group conflicts – not confrontations between individuals randomly fighting each other. (...) Inequalities that coincide with ethnic cleavages may enhance both grievances and group cohesion among the relatively deprived and thus facilitate mobilization for conflict.'[31] Social polarisation and horizontal social inequality are positively associated with civil war outbreak.[32] Often described as a

28 Wulf and Debiel, *Conflict Warning and Response Mechanisms*, p. 7.

29 S. Mansoob Murshed and Mohammad Zulfan Tadjoeddin, 'Revisiting the Greed and Grievance Explanations for Violent Internal Conflict', *Journal of International Development*, 21/1: 87–111 (2009), pp. 96–98.

30 Ted Robert Gurr, *Why Men Rebel* (Princeton: Princeton University Press, 1970), pp. 39–45.

31 Gudrun Østby, 'Polarization, Horizontal Inequalities and Violent Civil Conflict', *Journal of Peace Research*, 45/2: 143–162 (2008), p. 144.

32 S. Mansoob Murshed and Mohammad Zulfan Tadjoeddin, 'Revisiting the Greed and Grievance Explanations for Violent Internal Conflict', pp. 96–99.

'justice-seeking' motivation for rebellion, the grievance approach and its sub-theories such as horizontal inequality, relative deprivation, and polarisation are not only useful because of the linear and plausible logic. Moreover, there is a variety of proxies to measure grievances. Murshed and Tadjoeddin convincingly demonstrate this variety:

> For instance, a simple starting point in measuring relative deprivation is to calculate the simple difference between two competing groups on particular socio-economic indicators, and examine their evolution over time. A worsening ratio for one group means an improving ratio for the other which may be perceived by the deprived group as unjust. (…) But for a variety of purposes, including cross-national comparisons, a single index number type measure of horizontal inequality is required, similar to the GINI coefficient for vertical inequality. We also need to be clear as to which groups we wish to apply this idea to: linguistic, tribal, religious and so on, as there may be some overlap across these categorisations. For example, in diverse countries such as India or Indonesia, horizontal inequalities across linguistic lines will be different from those along a confessional basis.[33]

The grievance-approach has been rivalled by 'greed' – the economic variant of the mobilisation argument. The basic assumption goes that civil war is driven by self-interested greed rather than grievances.[34] It is argued that the decision to take up arms is rational and based on calculations of economic gains.[35] Grievances are therefore rejected as sole explanatory factor. Regan and Norton argue:

> (…) [The] popular conception of rebellion as a result of severe deprivation is misleading and generally reflects a view of extant conditions used by the rebel leadership to generate support of potential rebel soldiers. (…) Those rebel organizations that are able to mobilize troops and sustain a war effort are those that are and remain economically viable. Without resources, even the most extreme grievances will be insufficient to generate civil unrest.[36]

33 Ibid., pp. 99–100.

34 S. Mansoob Murshed, *Explaining Civil War. A Rational Choice Approach*, (Cheltenham: Edward Elgar, 2010).

35 Paul Collier, 'Rebellion as Quasi-Criminal Activity', *Journal of Conflict Resolution*, 44/6: 839–853 (2000), p. 840.

36 Patrick M. Regan and Daniel Norton, 'Greed, Grievance, and Mobilization in Civil Wars', *Journal of Conflict Resolution*, 49/3: 319–336 (2005), p. 322.

Greed as motive for rebellion has been discussed against the backdrop of natural resource endowments. Scholars found that the abundance of diamonds, oil, or coca increases the risk of civil war as groups might wage war over control rights.[37] Influential and controversial research by Collier and Hoeffler suggests that countries dependent on the exportation of primary product commodities are prone to civil war outbreak for two reasons: First, rebels might loot these commodities in pursuit of financing their fighting. Second, these resources could further provide motivation for secessionist conflicts.[38]

To test the explanatory power of the greed/grievance debate, the most common proxies (e.g. GDP per capita, Human Development Index) will be discussed on the basis of Egypt, Libya, Syria, Tunisia, and Yemen.[39] According to Collier, '[the] countries most prone to the [conflict] trap are the marginalized low-income countries.'[40] Altogether, '[countries] with all three high-risk economic characteristics – low income, low growth, and dependence upon natural resources – are (…) playing Russian roulette'.[41] Collier specified his famous Russian roulette analogy by finding that countries providing less than 750 US$ GDP per capita would be particularly conflict-prone.[42]

Figure 1 shows that none of the depicted cases came close to the 750 US$ threshold – except for Yemen in the early 2000s. Other proxies such as the Human Development Index (HDI) are in line with these trends.[43] Libya and Tunisia belong to upper middle income countries, while Egypt, Syria, and far

37 Richard Snyder and Ravi Bhavnani, 'Diamonds, Blood, and Taxes. A Revenue-Centered Framework for Explaining Political Order', *Journal of Conflict Resolution*, 49/4: 563–597 (2005), pp. 563–564.

38 Macartan Humphreys, 'Natural Resources, Conflict, and Conflict Resolution: Uncovering the Mechanisms', *Journal of Conflict Resolution*, 49/4: 508–537 (2005), p. 510.

39 The Gini Index poses yet another proxy that is often applied in contemporary peace and conflict studies. However, due to lack of longitudinal data for these five countries the Gini Index is not made use of in the present article. An excellent introduction is provided by Joan Esteban and Debraj Ray, 'Linking Conflict to Inequality and Polarization', The American Economic Review, 101/4: 1345–1374 (2011).

40 Paul Collier, Lani Elliot, Håvard Hegre, Anke Hoeffler, Marta Reynal-Querol, and Nicholas Sambanis, *Breaking the Conflict Trap. Civil War and Development Policy. World Bank Policy Research Report*, (Washington D.C.: World Bank, 2003), p. 108.

41 Paul Collier, *Development and Conflict* (Oxford: Oxford University, 2004), p. 4.

42 Collier et al., *Breaking the Conflict Trap*, p. 108.

43 While Libya (64th) and Tunisia (94th) average as highly developed countries between 1980 and 2012, Egypt (112th) and Syria (116th) share a medium human development rank, while low human development is found in Yemen with its 160th rank. See United Nations Human Development Report, 'Inequality-adjusted Human Development Index (IHDI)', http://hdr.undp.org/en/statistics/ihdi, accessed 7 June 2014.

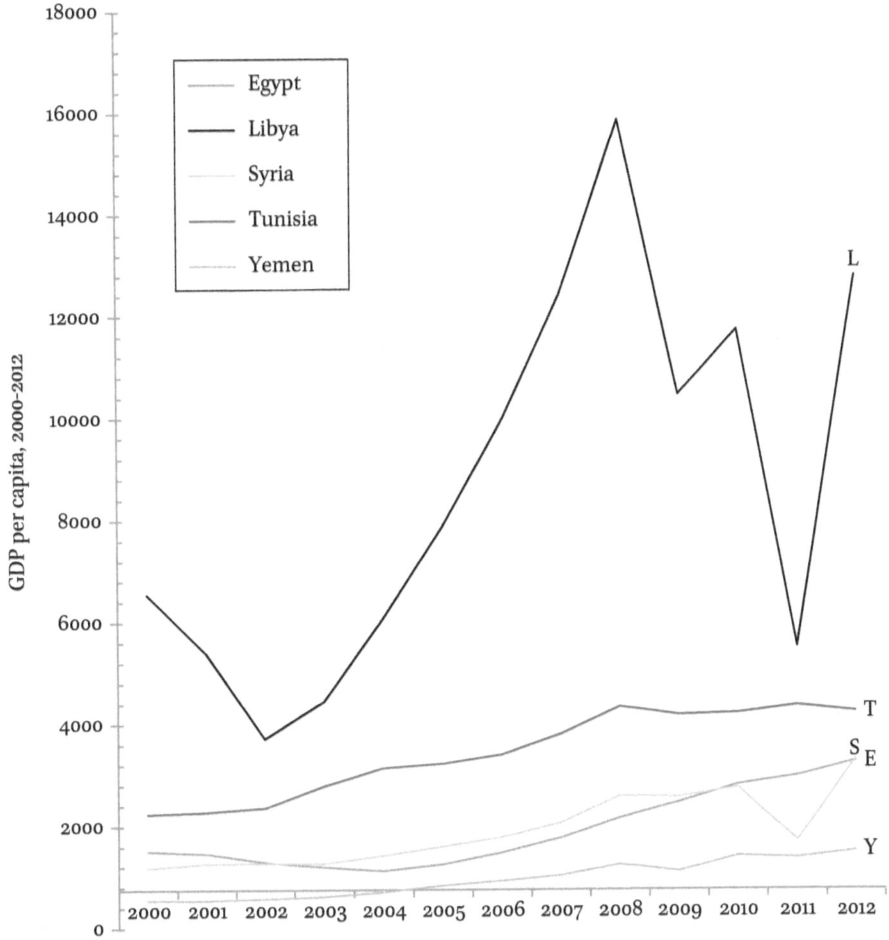

FIGURE 1 *GDP per capita (current US$ as of 2013), 2000–2012*[44]

behind Yemen are classified as lower middle income economies.[45] The Republic of Yemen experienced different violent episodes during the last two decades such as civil war in 1994.[46] However, compared to the cases of Syria and Libya, Yemen's Arab Spring uprising resulted in no more than 2000 people

44 World Bank, 'GDP per capita (current US$)', http://data.worldbank.org/indicator/NY.GDP.PCAP.CD, accessed 7 June 2014.

45 World Bank, 'Lower middle income', http://data.worldbank.org/income-level/LMC, accessed 27 February 2014.

46 Ayman Hamidi, 'Inscriptions of Violence in Northern Yemen: Haunting Histories, Unstable Moral Spaces', *Middle Eastern Studies*, 45/2: 165–187 (2009), pp. 166–167.

killed between 2011 and 2012. Taking Collier's Russian roulette analogy for granted, one would have expected the opposite. The comparison between 'rich' Libya and 'poor' Yemen is particularly striking in this regard. The claim for causality also seems to be built on sand when it comes to natural resources. Out of the mentioned cases, only the highly dependent net oil exporter Libya can be applied to the greed hypothesis. Before civil war outbreak in 2011, the majority of scholars explained political stability by large-scale distribution. This myth of the 'Rentier Peace' was built upon the assumption that potential rebels would not wage war against the state because they were bought off by the regime.[47] Apparently, the 2011 uprising in Benghazi was based on motivations that were beyond the issue of oil revenues. In sum, neither socioeconomic grievances nor the abundance of natural resources alone can explain why people suddenly took to the streets in early 2011 and would pursue such different paths.

Forecasting Model: PITF's Polity IV

According to the majority of scholars in the discipline, one of the best developed forecasting models is provided by PITF's Polity IV.[48] The much corroborated assumption is that fully established democracies and fully established autocracies are less prone to conflict than states that experience a transition process.[49] Vreeland explains the argument:

> Under pure dictatorship, opportunities to organize are too limited and the probability of successful collective action low. Pure democracy presents the possibility for peaceful collective action. Semidemocracies or "anocracies" are caught in the middle: they allow dissidents to organize, but nonviolent collective action may be too restricted to be effective. In this context, violence is more likely to be seen as the most effective recourse for dissidents, and the state reacts with violence accordingly.[50]

47 Matthias Basedau and Jann Lay, 'Resource Curse or Rentier Peace? The Ambiguous Effects of Oil Wealth and Oil Dependence on Violent Conflict', *Journal of Peace Research* 46/6: 757–776 (2009), p. 773.

48 Nicolas Rost, 'Will it happen again? On the possibility of forecasting the risk of genocide', *Journal of Genocide Research*, 15/1: 41–67 (2013); Michael D. Ward, Nils W. Metternich, Cassy L. Dorff, Max Gallop, Florian M. Hollenbach, Anna Schultz, and Simon Weschle, 'Learning from the Past and Stepping into the Future: Toward a New Generation of Conflict Prediction', *International Studies Review*, 15/4: 473–490 (2013).

49 Goldstone et al., 'A Global Forecasting Model of Political Instability', p. 197.

50 James Raymond Vreeland, 'The Effect of Political Regime on Civil War. Unpacking Anocracy', *Journal of Conflict Resolution*, 52/3: 401–425 (2008), pp. 401–402.

For a long time, the belief in the stabilising power of autocratic regimes was not questioned. Against this backdrop, the irony is that the recent upheavals in the Arab World have fundamentally challenged this dogma. Prior to 2011, an overwhelming majority of scholars and area studies had exemplified the hypothesis on the basis of autocratic regimes such as Egypt.[51] It therefore does not come as surprise that there are only some academics who explicitly admit the deficits of this causal relationship.[52] Figure 2 illustrates to what extent the

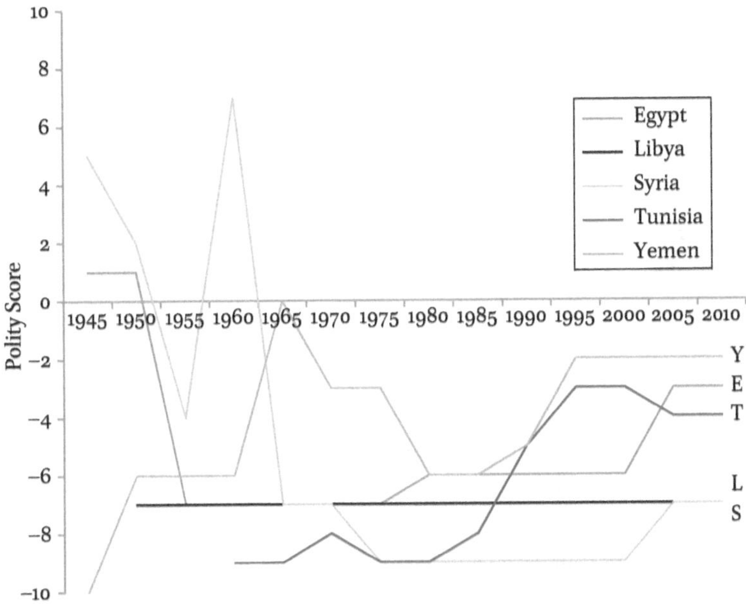

FIGURE 2 *PITF Polity IV Authority Trends, 1945–2010*[53]

51 Jason Brownlee, *Authoritarianism in an Age of Democratization*, (Cambridge: Cambridge University Press, 2007); Ellen Lust-Okar, *Structuring Conflict in the Arab World. Incumbents, Opponents, and Institutions*, (Cambridge: Cambridge University Press, 2005); Lisa Blaydes, *Elections and Distributive Politics in Mubarak's Egypt*, (New York: Cambridge University Press, 2011); Oliver Schlumberger, *Debating Arab authoritarianism. Dynamics and durability in nondemocratic regimes*, (Stanford California: Stanford University Press, 2007); Jason Brownlee, 'Executive Elections in the Arab World: When and How Do They Matter?', *Comparative Political Studies*, 44/7: 807–828; Kevin Köhler, 'Authoritarian Elections in Egypt: Formal Institutions and Informal Mechanisms of Rule', *Democratization*, 15/5: 974–990 (2008).

52 Gregory Gause III, 'Why Middle East Studies Missed the Arab Spring', p. 81.

53 The Polity IV project assesses a state's level of democracy based on the evaluation of elections for competitiveness, openness and level of participation. For each year and

cases of Egypt, Libya, Syria, Tunisia, and Yemen can be considered autocratic according to PITF and Polity IV.

The comparison between these five countries demonstrates the incapability of PITF to anticipate why people would suddenly take up arms against the ruling power. As Figure 2 shows, all five countries were built upon an authoritarian legacy at the latest since the early 1960s. If the relationship between authoritarian regime and political stability were actually true each of the five cases would have had experienced a similar impact by the mass protests in early 2011. However, particularly civil wars in Libya (around 30.000 battle-related deaths) and Syria (around 160.000 battle-related deaths until May 2014) foil this assumption. In other words, the long-time dogma of domestic stability by autocratic ruling perhaps retains explanatory power in some situations; however, it does not apply to the Arab Spring.

Risk and Performance Model: Failed States Index

The publication of the first Failed States Index (FSI) in 2005 led to a rise of research devoted to mostly quantitatively designed indices assessing state capacities. The FSI quickly became the primary reference project to scholars, policymakers, and media alike.[54] Established by the Foreign Policy Magazine and the Fund for Peace, it is based on twelve indicators. The major objective is to assess the changes of risk to state collapse of 178 countries.[55] The indicators are divided into three dimensions: social (e.g. refugees, demographics), economic (e.g. poverty, public services), political and military (e.g. state legitimacy, rule of law). For instance, in the 2013 Index, Somalia ranked number one for the 6th consecutive year, scoring a near 10/10 in almost all categories. In contrast to PITF's forecasting model, the FSI is not based on own data. The Index makes use of around 150 national and international media sources. The FSI does not explicitly claim predictive power over state failure or imminent armed conflicts. However, it claims to assess state vulnerability:

> Fault lines emerge between identity groups, defined by language, religion, race, ethnicity, nationality, class, caste, clan or area of origin.

---

country, a polity score is determined. It ranges from -10 to +10, with -10 to -6 corresponding to autocracies, -5 to 5 corresponding to anocracies, and 6 to 10 to democracies. See Polity IV, 'Country Reports 2010', http://www.systemicpeace.org/polity/polity06.htm, accessed 7 June 2014.

54 Wulf and Debiel, *Conflict Warning and Response Mechanisms*, p. 9.

55 Fund for Peace, 'The Methodology Behind the Index', http://ffp.statesindex.org/methodology, accessed 7 June 2014.

> Tensions can deteriorate into conflict through a variety of circumstances, such as competition over resources, predatory or fractured leadership, corruption, or unresolved group grievances. The reasons for state weakness and failure are complex but not unpredictable. (...) The Fragile States Index (FSI) (...) is a critical tool in highlighting not only the normal pressures that all states experience, but also in identifying when those pressures are pushing a state towards the brink of failure. (...) The strength of the FSI is its ability to distill millions of pieces of information into a form that is relevant as well as easily digestible and informative.[56]

Figure 3 below will shed light on the question of to what extent this holds true for the assessment of the Arab Spring.

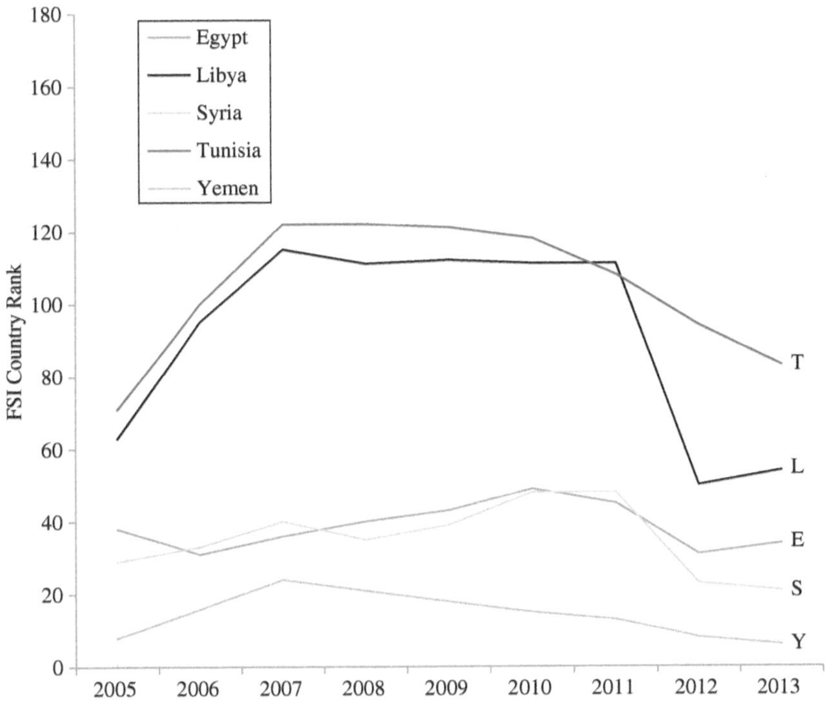

FIGURE 3 *Failed States Index, 2005–2013*[57]

56 Fund for Peace, 'The Methodology Behind the Index', http://ffp.statesindex.org/methodology, accessed 7 June 2014.

57 Fund for Peace, 'Failed States Index 2013', http://ffp.statesindex.org/rankings-2013-sortable, accessed 7 June 2014.

This figure illustrates the incapability of FSI to assess escalation potential on ex ante basis. Particularly the case of Libya demonstrates the shortcomings: First, before the eruption of civil war in 2011, it ranked among the relatively stable countries in the region. This was primarily because of the scholarly (and political) belief in the stabilising power of Libya's oil sector.[58] Second, after Gaddafi's fall and ending of civil war in October 2011 the country started climbing up the ranks again. Although short-term, this trend implies a linear path back to normalcy before civil war outbreak in 2011. However, this can lead to biased conclusions as the security vacuum beyond Tripoli is not indicated in the ranking. As a matter of fact, transitional state authorities keep struggling with militias in cities such as Bani Walid, Misrata, or Benghazi.[59] This critique holds true for the cases of Syria and Egypt that were supposedly on track of improving stability basically since 2005. However, the year 2011 meant a simultaneous setback in this respect. Apparently, neither the devastating drought in Syria between 2007 and 2010 leading to massive rural exodus nor the contested parliamentary elections in Egypt in November 2010 seemed to play a role in the respective FSI trend.[60] Despite its multidimensional framework, the FSI struggles to assess the vulnerability of states at risk on ex ante basis. This is problematic as the index character implies something else entirely. To be specific, the FSI claims to indicate trends. For instance, based on a five-year trend analysis (2008–2013), countries such as Ukraine or Lebanon have been labelled as 'improved' states in 2013.[61] This is inconsistent with the situations on the ground. While Ukraine is struggling with growing separatist violence in eastern parts of the country (foremost in Donetsk and Luhansk), Lebanon recently surpassed the number of one million refugees who have fled Syria.[62] According to the United Nations High Commissioner for Refugees (UNHCR), Lebanon now has the highest per capita concentration of refugees worldwide – one quarter of the local population.[63] In light of this, the current and upcoming

58 Basedau and Lay, 'Resource Curse or Rentier Peace?', p. 769.

59 Florence Gaub, 'A Libyan Recipe for Disaster', *Survival: Global Politics and Strategy*, 56/1: 101–120 (2014), pp. 101–102.

60 Christopher Phillips, *After the Arab Spring: power shift in the Middle East? Syria's bloody Arab Spring*, (London: London School of Economics and Political Science, 2012), p. 38.

61 Fund for Peace, 'Failed States Index 2013: Five-Year Trends, 2008–2013', http://ffp.statesindex.org/fsi-trends-2013, accessed 7 June 2014.

62 C.J. Shivers and David M. Herszenhorn, 'Separatists Defy Kiev and Putin on Referendum', *New York Times*, 8 May 2014; Ben Hubbard, 'Lebanon Hosts Over a Million Who Fled Syria, U.N. Reports', *New York Times*, 3 April 2014.

63 Norimitsu Onishi, 'Lebanon Worries That Housing Will Make Syrian Refugees Stay', *New York Times*, 11 December 2013.

existential challenges to Kiev and Beirut are inconsistent with the five-year trend as illustrated by the FSI. Particularly, Lebanon's critical refugee situation seems to have been forgotten by FSI analysts as thousands of people had begun to leave Syria already in 2011.[64]

Intelligence and Investigative Research: International Crisis Group

Unlike the aforementioned early warning tools, the ICG findings are based on qualitative data. Most of the (confidential) information that is used in reports and briefings is provided by field research. As the international think tank was able to establish access to influential non-governmental agents as well as high level policymakers right from the start in 1995, the direct exchange of knowledge has become its key asset.[65] The analytical focus is on peace negotiations and treaties in over 50 conflict contexts. All ICG reports present a list of policy recommendations directed at the former conflict parties and external actors.[66] ICG knowledge is used by policymakers and administration, scholars, as well as practitioners. Funded by governments and foundations and supported by top level figures from politics and economy (e.g. Javier Solana, Kofi Annan, George Soros), ICG prevailed as the only early warning think tank of its kind – while many others did not.[67] The ICG access to inside information on the ground is a constant balancing act: on the one hand, there is the supposed impartiality of a research institution, while on the other there is the systematic use of lobbying strategies.[68] Regardless of the ethical implications (see section below), a brief content analysis of ICG reports will test in the following to what extent the think tank was able to anticipate the timing and agency of uprisings prior to 2011.

In June 2008, the last ICG report was published on Egypt.[69] This and previous pieces either dealt with the Sinai situation or the Muslim Brotherhood and their gradual rise as influential stakeholder on political stage.[70] In terms of

---

64 Lorraine Charles and Kate Denman, 'Syrian and Palestinian Syrian Refugees in Lebanon: the Plight of Women and Children', *Journal of International Women's Studies*, 14/5: 96–111 (2013).

65 Wulf and Debiel, *Conflict Warning and Response Mechanisms*, p. 11.

66 Susanne Schmeidl, 'Early Warning at the Grass-Roots Level: Fine-tuning Early Warning to Context and User-Needs', paper presented at the Annual Convention of the International Studies Association, San Francisco, 26 March 2008, p. 7.

67 Wulf and Debiel, *Conflict Warning and Response Mechanisms*, p. 11.

68 Schmeidl, 'Early Warning at the Grass-Roots Level', pp. 7–8.

69 International Crisis Group, 'Egypt's Muslim Brothers: Confrontation or Integration?', Middle East/North Africa Report No. 76, 18 June 2008.

70 Ibid., p. ii.

early warning, the Cairo analysts stressed the need to better integrate the Brotherhood in the long term as the state's confrontation strategy led to growing tensions between Muslim and non-Muslim segments of society.[71] It is striking that only after the popular uprisings had started in early 2011 would ICG launch another report in February of the same year.[72] The way the case of Egypt was covered by ICG revealed two things. First, the Muslim Brotherhood was identified as only opposition force capable of organising some form of collective mass protest against the regime in power. Second, major proximate events such as the controversial 2010 parliamentary elections were not considered escalatory until the eruption of violence in early 2011. Similar to the aforementioned early warning systems, civil war in Libya was not anticipated at all by ICG. In fact, all reports that can be retrieved online are dated after the armed conflict erupted in March 2011.[73] A similar pattern is found when looking into the CrisisWatch Database that covers national and international media. Prior to March 2011, there was only sporadic coverage of violent incidents in Libya. The year 2004 is covered on monthly basis. The years 2005, 2009, and 2010 are not listed at all. The years 2006 to 2008 are covered once.[74] Although it remains difficult to say whether this lack of data might be due to lack of resources and access on the ground, the oil wealth argument is probably most convincing: ICG too had not seen civil war coming in Libya because analysts kept believing in the myth that rebels would not wage war against the state because they were bought off by the regime. The Syrian case is different in terms of coverage and focus. Prior to 2011, ICG focus was on foreign policy issues related to US and Israel.[75] Little attention was given to domestic questions of social dissent. Most striking, in December 2009 ICG pointed to some Islamist militant movements that might challenge the secular state architecture.[76] However, this very last report before Arab Spring blossomed in Damascus in early 2011 did not foresee any large-scale social unrest. Tunisia went entirely under the radar until 2011. There was no ICG report published before. The CrisisWatch Database lists two

71 Ibid.

72 International Crisis Group, Popular Protest in North Africa and the Middle East (I): Egypt Victorious? Middle East/North Africa Report No. 101, 24 February 2011.

73 International Crisis Group, 'Libya', http://www.crisisgroup.org/en/regions/middle-east-north-africa/north-africa/libya.aspx, accessed 22 February 2014.

74 International Crisis Group, 'CrisisWatch Database Libya', http://www.crisisgroup.org/en/publication-type/crisiswatch/crisiswatch-database.aspx?CountryIDs={28685262-BE79-473E-B18E-ED22761A0F17}, accessed 22 February 2014.

75 International Crisis Group, 'Reshuffling the Cards (I)? Syria's Evolving Strategy, Middle East Report No. 92', 14 December 2009.

76 Ibid., pp. 19–22.

violent Islamist attacks in January and February 2007. The list goes on in January 2011 giving a monthly-based overview of the revolution.[77] The irony of this little coverage of the Tunisian case is that President Ben Ali's ousting has been identified as crucial domino triggering mass protests elsewhere in the region.[78] Despite the little attention by scholars and media, the Republic of Yemen has been dealt with by ICG. Two reports were published before 2011. The first (2003) stressed the danger of terrorism and state failure while the second (2009) pointed to the secessionist violence in the northern governorate Saada since 2004.[79] Despite a more thorough CrisisWatch Database media coverage however, the ICG did not anticipate any social revolts in urban areas of the capital Sanaa in early 2011.[80] In sum, the brief overview of ICG data shows that despite the inside knowledge the think tank failed to assess domestic turmoil on ex ante basis either.

Critique

In more than twenty years after the end of the Cold War a number of explanatory approaches and early warning systems have been established that policymakers make use of. However, successful conflict prevention is still an exception. This is not only because of policymakers failing to implement the respective prevention tools. It is also because of the deficits in prevention research. The following overview will summarize the major critiques.

Diffuse Terminology

The scholarly debate is characterised by diffuse terminology. A huge number of different agents, ranging from think tanks to political decision-makers in ministries, bureaucracies, and organisations, apply different definitions and understandings of conflict prevention. These differences determine strategies

77 International Crisis Group, 'CrisisWatch Database Tunisia', http://www.crisisgroup.org/en/publication-type/crisiswatch/crisiswatch-database.aspx?CountryIDs={684E8DDD-7048-41F2-A1D0-8D34F565C336}#results, accessed 22 February 2014.

78 Mohammad Al-Momani, 'The Arab "Youth Quake": Implications on Democratization and Stability', *Middle East Law and Governance*, 3/1-2: 159–170 (2011), p. 160.

79 International Crisis Group, 'Yemen: Coping with Terrorism and Violence in a Fragile State', Middle East Report No. 8, 8 January 2003; International Crisis Group, Yemen: Defusing the Saada Time Bomb, Middle East Report No. 86, 27 May 2009.

80 International Crisis Group, 'CrisisWatch Database Yemen', http://www.crisisgroup.org/en/publication-type/crisiswatch/crisiswatch-database.aspx?CountryIDs={9D2149C0-C350-40FC-BE12-7693FB454AEE}, accessed 23 February 2014.

and thus can undermine prevention research and practice.[81] In broadening the term along the structural prevention approach (i.e. economy programs, land reforms etc.), there is the risk that the core argument of prevention is hollowed out and eventually falls behind: this is the prevention of violent confrontations between adversaries.[82]

Neglect of Structural Prevention

However at the same time, the focus of the early warning literature on the operational understanding of prevention is problematic. As it is explicitly including the postconflict phase (i.e. tertiary prevention), this focus is antagonistic with the genuine objective of avoiding conflict escalation in the first place. More than twenty years of experience have shown that the international community is particularly engaged during the postconflict consolidation phase. International stakeholders are strikingly reluctant when it comes to imminent conflict risks that require quick responses. This is a paradox given that the rebuilding phase is by far more cost-intensive.[83]

Ignoring the Local

The local environment is crucial to any prevention measures that are expected to improve people's lives in crisis situations. However, the local context is neglected by researchers in four ways. First, the majority of studies focus on the preventive role of external actors. In particular, states, intergovernmental organisations and NGOs are dealt with in this respect.[84] Second, most studies rely on quantitative longitudinal analysis. This design is likely to leave out issues of local relevance such as the genesis of civil society, participation, or mediation.[85] Third, the early warning industry is a domain of researchers, consultants, and policymakers from the Global North. 'Northerners' sometimes draw conclusions over local issues and the conflictivity of societies although they themselves lack local knowledge and sensitivity. This can lead to highly biased findings that are nonetheless communicated to the respective authorities.[86] Fourth, early warning tools that rely on investigative research are

81 Volker Matthies, *Krisenprävention. Vorbeugen ist besser als Heilen*, (Opladen: Leske + Budrich, 2000), pp. 29–30.

82 Ibid., p. 32.

83 Volker Matthies, 'Eine Welt voller neuer Kriege? Der vernachlässigte Blick auf den Frieden', *Der Bürger im Staat*, 54/4: 185–190 (2004), p. 188.

84 David Roberts, 'Post-Conflict Peacebuilding, Liberal Irrelevance and the Locus of Legitimacy', *International Peacekeeping*, 18/4: 410–424 (2011), pp. 410–411.

85 Wulf and Debiel, *Conflict Warning and Response Mechanisms*, p. 25.

86 Roberts, 'Post-Conflict Peacebuilding', p. 410.

criticised for their ambivalent role as think tank on the one hand and de facto lobbying organisation on the other. For instance, given that authors and many sources are often not transparent in the much corroborated ICG reports, the reservations do not come as surprise. It is against this backdrop that scholars discuss to what extent some authors of reports (including influential policy recommendations) are part of the political establishment before and after the peace negotiations.[87]

Early Warning ≠ Early Action

There is one major challenge in any prevention strategy. This is the difficulty to address the relevant agents that are capable of setting measures in motion. Empirics show that there is a striking gap between the communicated early warning on the one hand and the (missing) preventive action.[88] Two explanations are brought forward that shed light on the gap between early warning and early action. First, early warning advocates are criticised for underestimating the general conditions political decision-makers operate in. This lack of inside intuition leads to less politically adequate policy recommendations. Second, the lack of political will on behalf of the international community is criticised as governments too often take decisions on the basis of national (power) interests only.[89]

Large-n Dominance

Regardless of the limited predictive capability of early warning systems, peace and conflict studies face one major methodological problem: the dominance of quantitative research that is based on a huge time horizon and a huge case number. Short and middle term processes (e.g. politicization of ethnicity) are difficult to capture by large-n designs. Indeed, causal, forecasting, and performance models well assess the vulnerability of conflictive societies and states. However, in most cases these models are not capable of identifying when exactly, how, and by whom escalation processes were triggered. In light of this, the academic community needs to reconsider a complementary approach that adds a specific qualitative component to the research framework. For instance, this would make necessary a more systematic analysis of catalytic events (e.g. impact of self-immolations) and actor constellations on the ground

87 Berit Bliesemann de Guevara and Florian P. Kühn, 'The International Community Needs to Act': Loose Use and Empty Signalling of a Hackneyed Concept', *International Peacekeeping*, 18/2: 135–151 (2011), p. 135.

88 Matthies, *Krisenprävention. Vorbeugen ist besser als Heilen*, p. 57.

89 Ibid., p. 59.

(e.g. post-conflict integration of militias).[90] The same holds true for the spatial impact of conflict. So far, space has been dealt with merely as physical variable that determines rebels' retreat area (e.g. mountainous terrain).[91] In contrast, the role of social or cultural space (e.g. urban middle classes) rather went under the radar.[92] In addition to the imbalanced methodological practice in favour of large-n studies, conflict prevention is constrained by a variety of different and often competing explanatory approaches that coexist side by side. For instance, ethnic diversity is still highly contested as causal factor of civil war onset despite a huge number of studies.

Neglect of Negative Cases

Scholars, policymakers, and media disregard conflicts of little violence intensity. This one-directional focus on causes of war is in line with the dominant role of quantitative research in peace and conflict studies. The focus on war causes can be explained by the researchers' positivist desire for feasible facts on the one hand and the fear of counterfactual argumentation on the other. Tracing so-called peace causes proves a much more difficult task given that the threshold to large-scale violence is not crossed. In other words, if there is no smoking gun to be found what is the empirical analysis then based on? However, by leaving out the question of 'why not' escalation processes are not captured in their entirety.[93] Many deficits could be tackled if more attention was given to factors that inhibit the outbreak of large-scale violence. However, with little attention of 'non-bloody' conflicts or negative cases, the likelihood of research grants devoted to peace causes will remain low.[94]

---

90 Mariya Y. Omelicheva, 'Natural Disasters: Triggers of Political Instability?', *International Interactions: Empirical and Theoretical Research in International Relations*, 37/4: 441–465 (2011); George Joffé, 'The End of Autocracy? The Seeds of Libya's Civil War', *The rusi Journal*, 156/3: 12–19 (2011).

91 Halvard Buhaug and Scott Gates, 'The Geography of Civil War', *Journal of Peace Research*, 39/4: 417–433 (2002); Halvard Buhaug, Scott Gates, and Päivi Lujala, 'Geography, Rebel Capability, and the Duration of Civil Conflict', *Journal of Conflict Resolution*, 53/4: 544–569 (2009). Halvard Buhaug and Päivi Lujala, 'Accounting for scale: Measuring geography in quantitative studies of civil war', *Political Geography*, 24/4: 399–418 (2005).

92 Greg Martin, 'Conceptualizing Cultural Politics in Subcultural and Social Movement Studies', *Social Movement Studies: Journal of Social, Cultural, and Political Protest*, 1/1: 73–88 (2002).

93 Stephen McLoughlin and Deborah Mayersen, 'Risk and Resilience to Mass Atrocities in Africa: A Comparison of Rwanda and Botswana', *Journal of Genocide Research*, 13/3: 247–269 (2011), p. 248.

94 Matthies, 'Eine Welt voller neuer Kriege? Der vernachlässigte Blick auf den Frieden', p. 188.

Standing Aside?

In light of these challenges, the question is whether conflict prevention can be implemented at all. While idealists prefer a collective-altruistic prevention regime, realists are sceptic. The latter argue that no prevention is motivated by altruism alone. Rather all measures are at least indirectly driven by interests of states and international organisations.[95] Recent empirical reality affirms this assumption. For instance, the NATO intervention in Libya in 2011 was based on a broad coalition of states willing to support the opposition forces in Benghazi.[96] However, systematic violation of human rights in Darfur in 2003 and 2004 or more recently in Syria did not entail similar actions by the international community.[97] Despite all the critique against the lack of political will, the other side of the coin deserves at least the same (controversial) attention in the debate: do external actors always have to intervene each time there are signs of violent conflict escalation? Many realists refer to the accomplishments of the French Revolution as argument against an intervention reflex by the international community.[98] Imagine external actors such as allied monarchies would have sided with the French Royal Family and put down people's revolts on the ground at that time. What impact would this intervention have had with respect to the continuation of the feudal-absolutist system on the one hand and the deferral of the Enlightenment on the other? What principles would the Declaration of Independence have been based on by the North-American colonists? Provided it would have existed at all. In the end, the intervention issue is up to perspective. The meanwhile fragmented Syrian opposition has been asking for more external engagement for long. In the third year of civil war however, it is all about survival first. Far behind, the implementation of political reforms comes second.[99]

---

95 Andreas Heinemann-Grüder, 'Konfliktprävention – Alternative zu Militäreinsätzen?', In Bruno Schoch, Andreas Heinemann-Grüder, Jochen Hippler, Markus Weingardt, and Reinhard Mutz (eds.), *Friedensgutachten*, (Münster: LIT-Verlag, 2007), p. 128.

96 Jon Western and Joshua S. Goldstein, 'Humanitarian Intervention Comes of Age: Lessons from Somalia to Libya', *Foreign Affairs*, 90/6: 48–59 (2011), p. 49.

97 Nsongurua J. Udombana, 'When Neutrality is a Sin: The Darfur Crisis and the Crisis of Humanitarian Intervention in Sudan', *Human Rights Quarterly* 27/4: 1149–1199 (2005); Christopher S. Chivvis, 'Libya and the Future of Liberal Intervention', *Survival: Global Politics and Strategy*, 54/6: 69–92 (2012).

98 Matthies, *Krisenprävention. Vorbeugen ist besser als Heilen*, p. 23; Michael S. Lund, 'Underrating Preventive Diplomacy', *Foreign Affairs*, July/August 1995.

99 Philippe Droz-Vincent, '"State of Barbary" (Take Two): From the Arab Spring to the Return of Violence in Syria', *The Middle East Journal*, 68/1: 33–58 (2014), p. 33.

Conclusion

After more than two decades, the debate over proactive action on the one hand and reactive-curative support on the other lingers on. The emphasis on the latter understanding of prevention is a result of 9/11 and the focus of national strategies on security issues.[100] There have been positive developments during the last twenty years that deserve mentioning. For instance, in the aftermath of genocides in the early 1990s, more sensibilised political elites have advanced national and international norm setting.[101] Establishing early warning systems such as PITF, FSI, or ICG have also helped to professionalise staff both on the ground and at ministry headquarters.[102] Woocher finds that 'there is evidence that conflict prevention practitioners of all kinds have become more professional over time, learning lessons from experience and fine-tuning their techniques'.[103] Apparently, the use of 'do no harm' and other related conflict analysis and impact assessment methods have become fairly routine which well illustrates the successful efforts to mainstream conflict prevention.[104] Also the development of a variety of different non-governmental actors that are engaged with peaceful conflict management speaks volumes of the advancements.[105] In sum however, policymakers as well as scholars need to refine their respective capacities. The major problem in preventing collective violence is the lack of political will on the one hand and the lack of conceptual and operational capabilities on the other. This is not only because of the little attention de-escalatory measures are given by the public in contrast to violent (and bloody) conflicts. Rather the prevention paradigm and its agents fail in convincing political decision-makers to provide more resources for the sake of a more coordinated and coherent working together of ministries and agencies. This particularly refers to including local actors in terms of real ownership. As such, the sustainability of the prevention regime will be decided on the question whether the agents are willing to transform the public-related rhetoric into effective actions. The prevention concept will move from theory to politics only when the gap between a precise warning on the one hand and proactive action on the other is closed.

100 Gelijn Molier, 'Humanitarian Intervention and The Responsibility to Protect after 9/11', *Netherlands International Law Review*, 53/1: 37–62 (2006).

101 Andreas Heinemann-Grüder, 'Konfliktprävention – Alternative zu Militäreinsätzen?', pp. 128–129; Lawrence Woocher, *Preventing Violent Conflict. Assessing Progress, Meeting Challenges*, (Washington D.C.: United States Institute of Peace, 2009), pp. 6–7.

102 Ibid., pp. 9–10.

103 Ibid., p. 13.

104 Ibid., p. 10.

105 Ibid., pp. 8–9; Heinemann-Grüder, 'Konfliktprävention – Alternative zu Militäreinsätzen?', p. 132.

Critique is addressed to policymakers as it is to scholars. By demystifying famous early warning literature, this article did not attempt to play off Polity IV against the ICG or any other mentioned tool. Each has its own assets as well as problems. The specific critique against the prevention debate and political practice gave impetus for further thinking and discourse on ways of how to improve the existing early warning architecture. As the analysis of 'fixing' the process of knowledge production, transfer, and implementation goes beyond the scope of this article, at least two suggestions shall be mentioned here: First, the academic community needs to critically question whether the belief in the (quantitative) predictability of escalation processes is consistent with the contextual and local nature of any single conflict onset. Not least the Arab Spring has revealed that formerly unshakable truths such as the political stability in authoritarian regimes have a date of expiry. It is against this backdrop to show more scepticism towards the universalistic doctrine of variable-oriented research. At the same time, a complementary (qualitative) look into local dynamics would help to alleviate many deficits of prevention research. In particular, a differentiated look into agency, timing, and space is called for. Second, the academic community needs to generally question the genesis of scholarly expertise and the potential bias it reproduces. This raises a broader question of ethics and social science. Most social scientists measure and evaluate social phenomena by European criteria and proxies. The world and its parts are explained by theories based on European experiences and history. By looking to the US and Western Europe only ('the west and the rest'), other world regions are ignored.[106] This ignorance makes it difficult to capture and understand local dynamics – particularly in the Global South. In the worst case, important empirical data gets lost. In light of this, prevalent research paradigms need to be critically revised and complemented by ontologies and methodologies from the South. For instance, Russia's Crimea annexation and measures of international crisis prevention is most likely evaluated differently by social scientists in Beijing, New Delhi, or Riyadh than by analysts in Washington, London, or Sydney. Beyond all its implied normativity, opening up to perspectives that go beyond traditional western world views in social sciences would also improve analytical lenses.[107] This does not necessarily mean to leave one's own Anglo-American based IR ivory tower; though a first look out of the window would be a good start.

---

106 Andreas Mehler, 'Sozialwissenschaft und Globalisierung. Der Westen hat ausgedient', *Tagesspiegel*, 8 May 2014.

107 For instance, Ben Reilly has been working on innovative ways to improve the design of institutions for new democracies, particularly those facing deep ethnic or cultural cleavages. See Ben Reilly, 'Institutional Designs for Diverse Democracies: Consociationalism, Centripetalism and Communalism Compared', *European Political Science*, 11: 259–270 (2012).

CHAPTER 2

Who Is the Subject of Atrocities Prevention?

Bridget Conley-Zilkic
Tufts University
bridget.conley@tufts.edu

Abstract

This essay poses the question, who is the subject of atrocities prevention? Borrowing a rhetorical and argumentative model from Jacques Ranciere's work on the subject of human of rights, the essay explores the conceptual frameworks for the subjects of atrocities and queries their relevance to the specific context of prevention. The concepts that dominate work on mass atrocities were articulated in relation to atrocities that were underway or had concluded; they are a poor fit for prevention. New work on prevention, like that on 'factors of restraint' or resilience,' suggest revisions to the concepts and cases that currently dominate study of mass atrocities. Crucial amongst these concepts that require adjustment are how we address the subject of atrocities prevention.

Keywords

mass atrocities – prevention – subjects

Introduction

In 2004, political philosopher Jacques Rancière asked: 'Who is the subject of the Rights of Man?'[1] A question at least as old as the French Revolution, it is implicitly posed in the title of that period's central document, the '*Declarations des Droits de l'Homme et du Citoyen*'(1789), 'Declaration of the Rights of Man and Citizen'. Provocatively, the subject of rights is addressed as both 'man *and*

1 Jacques Rancière, 'Who is the Subject of the Rights of Man?' *South Atlantic Quarterly*, 103/2–3: 297–310 (2004).

 | DOI 10.1163/9789004299870_003

citizen,' with ample space for theoretical query about the status of the conjunction. Does it connect or separate the two potential subjects of rights? Nativity, the mere of fact of existing, is implied as the foundation of rights in 'man' or more appropriately 'human',[2] while inscription in a political community forms the basis of 'citizen' as subject.

However, neither 'human' nor 'citizen' provides a satisfying answer. If rights only belong to 'citizens', they appear as a tautology: political rights belonging to those who have that status of rights-holder within a political community. However, if rights belong to 'human' based on mere existence, as Hannah Arendt argued in the wake of the Holocaust and the post-World War II refugee crisis, they are revealed as rights that cannot be claimed. In Arendt's words:

> The conception of human rights based upon the assumed existence of a human being as such, broke down the very moment when those who professed to believe in it were for the first time confronted with people who had indeed lost all other qualities and specific relationships–except that they were still human.[3]

In short, human rights are meaningless. Italian philosopher Giorgio Agamben develops this position further, positing that these 'human' populations exist as 'bare life',[4] that is, life without political meaning, deemed outside the law, and thereby outside all protections. And so the question of the subject arrives at a dead-end: rights are either a tautology or void.

Unless, Rancière continues, we have asked the wrong question. The critical work is not to define the *subject*, but to understand the *work* of claiming rights. The political subject, named 'man', 'human' or 'citizen', does not describe a finalized condition, but rather forms the grounds of contestation, what he calls 'dissensus':

---

2 Rancière is acutely attuned to the exclusion enacted by the term "man" as a substitute for "human." The example he develops in his article is of a woman, Olympe de Gouges, rallying for women's rights during the French Revolution and demanding equal treatment as a political subject. De Gouge, as she mounted the guillotine, proclaimed that if a woman could be publicly killed for her political actions then she deserved the full rights of citizenship as well. The state had already acknowledged her as a political being with punishment; logic dictated that political life be acknowledged in its positive manifestations as well.

3 Hannah Arendt, *The Origins of Totalitarianism* (New York: The World Publishing Co., 1951), p. 299.

4 Giorgio Agamben, *Homo Sacer: Sovereign Power and Bare Life*, tr. Daniel Heller-Roazen (Stanford, CA: Stanford University Press, 1998).

> Political subjects [...] put to test the power of political names, their extension and comprehension. They not only confront the inscriptions of rights to situations of denial; they put together the world where those rights are valid and the world where they are not. They put together a relation of inclusion and a relation of exclusion.[5]

The identity of a rights-seeking individual, named man, citizen, or other, fails to help us understand how rights claims destabilize the status quo. It is not a subject we should seek in an attempt to stabilize the discourse of rights, but rather dynamic contexts of how and when rights are asserted. Rights claims do not restore a proper state of existence by reifying the position of citizen or human, but rather disrupt the given order. This disruption is political contestation. It marks the uncertain space of the conjunction, the 'man *and* citizen', as an opening into which political subjects:

> ...put to test the power of political names, their extension and comprehension. They not only confront the inscriptions of rights to situations of denial; they put together the world where those rights are valid and the world where they are not.[6]

This tale of how asking the wrong question lands one in seemingly impossible quandaries also applies to how we theorize the subject of mass atrocities, particularly in terms of prevention. The primary conceptual frameworks for the 'subject' of mass atrocities include terms that describe a person or group relative to acts of violence, as in victim or perpetrator; terms that attempt to characterize the group of people targeted for violence, as in ethnic, racial, religious or national group; or more broadly conceived and open ended terms like 'population' or 'civilian'. The first category is least relevant to a prevention framework because its most accurate and helpful deployment situates subjects in relation to a specific act of violence—in a preventive context this act has not occurred and ideally will not occur. The second category, which I will shorthand as 'groupness', can be helpful to the extent that it addresses social and political stratification that renders some people more vulnerable than others. The challenge, however, is that these terms tend to naturalize and homogenize groups, while crafting a static picture of power relations that fluctuate significantly. The third subjects, defined as 'population' (as developed in relation to a

5 Rancière, "Who is the Subject of the Rights of Man?", p. 305.

6 Rancière, "Who is the Subject of the Rights of Man?", p. 304.

'Responsibility to Protect') or 'civilian', simultaneously benefit from and are limited by the broad, unspecified nature of the terms.

So within the current vocabularies, we, too, arrive at a dead-end. The subject of atrocities prevention cannot be defined by acts that have not occurred. It must prove analytically relevant to disaggregated analysis of risk and vulnerability, but not substitute description of groups as wholesale identifiers of stable, fixed and unitary actors. It must have a broad enough lens to scan the social horizon for unexpected vulnerability, and yet retain enough analytical specificity to be relevant to the work of prevention. The challenge of defining the subject of atrocities prevention thereby arrives at an impasse: the conceptual frameworks for prevention alternatively veer too far into a discourse of inevitability or describe such general conditions as to be meaningless to a specific *atrocities* prevention agenda. Overdetermined or ill-specified—is there a way out of this impasse?

Here, as with rights, the impasse may be the result of asking the wrong question. The work of prevention cannot be adequately conceived as simply pushing a conceptual framework upstream, as it were. Even the basic vocabularies to describe on-going violence may be ill-suited for contexts where violence has not occurred. Worse yet, these vocabularies may obscure the very relationships and social structures that are best suited to protection. Some of the most compelling work on atrocities prevention today begins precisely at this impasse by challenging the assumptions of what factors are relevant to the work of prevention, adding new concepts to the analytical framework, and diversifying the cases that inform the work of atrocity prevention. Foremost among these efforts are the work of Scott Straus on 'factors of restraint' and Deborah Mayerson and Stephen McLoughlin's adaptation of 'resilience' to atrocities prevention. I argue that in parallel to these efforts, we must re-examine our 'subjects' of atrocity prevention. The 'subject' is not merely one among many concepts that need to be revised, but is a crucial starting point for how prevention is conceptualized.

Like Rancière, I do not argue that there is a more appropriate subject who could power its way through the impasse. Nor do I think atrocities prevention is a lost cause. Rather, I suggest that we can learn from the existing vocabularies, from work on restraint and resilience, and from the discourse of rights—and Rancière's discussion is relevant not merely as a rhetorical device but in its substance as well—to devise new strategies for prevention.

Existing Vocabularies

Of the three major conceptual vocabularies deployed to describe the 'subject' of atrocities--archetypes of perpetrators and victims; ethnic, national, racial and religious groups; and populations and civilians--none is without benefit nor limitation. Our task here is to explore both the value and challenges of each vocabulary and query their applicability to a prevention agenda. Each of these terms emerges out of a distinct historical and disciplinary context, which mark their current usage.

Referencing the voice of victims, their preferences, rights and moral status has become the *sine qua non* of work on violence. A 'victim' defined in relation to a specific experience of harm is a necessary term; the same holds true for 'perpetrator'. Problematic, however, is when either identity is abstracted and called upon to serve as legitimization for a range of other projects that have little do with the direct experiences of individual harm. For this reason, archetypes of victim or perpetrator are of very little relevance to prevention.

A 'victim' can be readily defined in relation to discrete harms suffered. This does not mean that the relationship between the individual and a wider group is necessarily elided, but that the articulation of the subject as 'victim' is defined in relation to a specific harm. See, for instance, the United Nation's *Basic Principles and Guidelines on the Right to a Remedy and Reparation for Victims of Gross Violations of International Human Rights Law and Serious Violations of International Humanitarian Law:*

> Victims are persons who individually or collectively suffered harm, including physical or mental injury, emotional suffering, economic loss or substantial impairment of their fundamental rights, through acts or omissions that constitute gross violations of international human rights law, or serious violations of international humanitarian law. Where appropriate, and in accordance with domestic law, the term 'victim' also includes the immediate family or dependents of the direct victim and persons who have suffered harm in intervening to assist victims in distress or to prevent victimization.[7]

This definition of victim helpfully includes a wider circle around the person who directly experienced violence, what Finnoula NiAolain has termed 'communities of harm.' She argues that neither rights nor harms attach solely to autonomous individuals: 'only when we see persons as infinitely connected to their families and their communities can we begin to see how that connection gives one person a quantifiable interest in the maintenance of equilibrium for another'.[8]

---

7 A/RES/60/147, 16 December 2005, p. 5.

8 Fionnuala Ni Aolain, 'Sex-based Violence and the Holocaust—A Reevaluaion of Harms and Rights in International Law,' *Yale Journal of Law and Feminism*, 12/1: 43–84 (2000), p. 82.

Nonetheless, the use of the term 'victim' remains tied to an experience of harm and the same holds for 'perpetrator'.

This is not the case when these terms are deployed in ways that define a stabilized, abstracted group identity. Raoul Hilberg's path breaking work on the Holocaust[9] introduced into historical analysis of atrocity a set of subject positions borrowed from the language of criminal law—*perpetrator* and *victim*—augmented with a term to capture those whose actions and inaction elude juridical distinctions, *bystander*. These subjects along with *rescuer* and *survivor* form the characterology of atrocities as inherited from Holocaust and genocide studies. They operate as a set of archetypes that too often approach their objects of study as entirely separate groups or as static designators of a group's moral status. These labels do harm when they set expectations that attach to all representations of the violence, functioning to shape and edit the record according to a pre-established narrative. For instance, study of gender based violence during the Holocaust was for many years lampooned by even leading scholars who argued that it was pointless to make differentiations within a victim group—that all victims were equally victimized.[10] Lost therein were historical facts, as well as the kind of nuanced understanding of patterns of violence and differentiated vulnerability to specific types of harms.

The labels of 'victim' or 'perpetrator' are not merely descriptive; they apply value judgment on the actors. The normative function of these subject identifiers proves problematic even in relation to perpetration of discrete harms, when the perceived moral clarity of the identity proves a mismatch for the context. For instance, when a child soldier commits violence or when the victim is not sympathetic—has political views with which one might object, has themselves committed terrible wrongs, etc.—or when the perpetrator is sympathetic for any number of reasons. Further complicated is when these norm-laden labels are abstracted from the context of a harm.

Once the victim is abstracted into a free-floating idea, it can be attached to any number of agendas. Kieran McEvoy and Kirsten McConnachie assert that 'victims serve a key practical and symbolic role in the 'legitimation work' (Barker, 2001) of almost all those who work in the field of transitional justice'.[11]

9 Raoul Hilberg, *Perpetrators, Victims, Bystanders: The Jewish Catastrophe 1933–1945* (New York: HarperCollins, 1992).

10 Lawrence Langer, for instance, argued against applying any analytical frames that would differentiate victim experiences in 'Gendered Suffering? Women in Holocaust Testimonies' in *Women and the Holocaust*, ed. D Ofer and L.J. Weitzman (New Haven, CT: Yale University Press, 1998).

11 Kieran McEvoy and Kirsten McConnachie, 'Victim and Transitional Justice: Voice, Agency and Blame,' *Social and Legal Studies*, 22/4: 489 – 513 (2013), p. 504.

One could extend this field to include atrocities prevention and engagement as well. The authors support efforts to mobilize victims and 'maximize community ownership and participation', but argue that 'such a perspective does not require the suspension of critical faculties or overly romanticized notion of community or civil society'.[12] The reference to victims' rights and voices must be critically appraised in relation to the ideological and political agendas it is used to rationalize. Further, they point out complications that the 'voice' of victims is not an antidote to political wrangling or resolution to the challenges of establishing legitimacy for programs. Victims' rights are referenced to support often contradictory agendas, including increasing punitive measures against perpetrators, greater examination of the structural context in which crimes take place, social reconciliation, or delivery of services to victims.[13]

Perhaps most problematically—and here there is a clear linkage with prevention—the identification of 'victim' and 'perpetrator' as archetypes or group identities can feed a sentiment of self-righteous immunity within a 'victim group', even to the point of justifying new perpetration of violence. As Yugoslavia began to fall apart in the 1990s, a historically grounded yet selective narrative of past experiences of Serbian victimhood made crucial contributions to the rationalization of violence in the war in Croatia (1991) and Bosnia (1992–1995). As Katherine Verdery writes, 'rediscoveries of World War II dead helped to ignite warfare in 1991, which yielded still other bodies in mass graves, sources of recrimination that fueled the wars further'.[14] The saliency of a victim narrative, often based on real experiences of historical suffering, is not incidental. These myths, as Jacques Semelin argues, play a central role in genocidal logic: 'the need for security.... gives material form to the rise to power for any process of violence'.[15] Citing examples of Bosnia and Rwanda, he argues, 'the awakening of painful memories and still vivid traumas is an effective way of stoking fear and developing hatred. This hatred can then be projected into action, armed with a desire for revenge'.[16] Past experience of victimization should not, although it is often asked to, stand in for evaluation of the political claims being made in the present.

---

12 McEvoy and McConnachie, 'Victim and Transitional Justice,' p. 499.

13 McEvoy and McConnachie, 'Victim and Transitional Justice,' p. 492.

14 Katherine Verdery, *The Political Lives of Dead Bodies: Reburial and Postsocialist Change* (New York: Columbia University Press, 1999), p. 97.

15 Jacques Semelin, *Purify and Destroy: The Political Uses of Massacre and Genocide* trans. Cynthia Schoch (New York: Columbia University Press, 2007), p. 42.

16 Ibid., p. 43.

Identifying 'victims' and 'perpetrators' of violence is necessary; the challenges with this term as a subject of atrocities arise when the label of 'victim' (let alone that of perpetrator) is assumed to adhere equally across an entire group, gloss over variations in vulnerability, or function as an absolute, unchanging category. Further, actions undertaken in the name of an amorphous group of victims can be contradictory, politically unexamined or manipulated, or even abstracted into irrelevance to the very 'victims' used to justify action. These limitations to the term are amplified in a context of prevention, when the harm that might otherwise ground a concept of 'victim' is anticipated rather than experienced. A 'would-be victim' or 'would-be perpetrator' cannot be the foundation of preventative work. Anticipatory victimization or perpetration can easily play into dynamics that escalate risks of violence.

Prevention cannot start from the position of perpetrator and victim in relation to a harm that has not occurred. Nor, I argue, is it beneficial to abstract these terms to cover entire groups. But this does not deny the fact that violence is often intended and experienced as an assault against entire groups because of their identity. Positing the group as the subject is the innovation of 'genocide,' which emerged in response to events of World War II,[17] and defines the 'subject' of concern as an ethnical, national, racial or religious group. For instance, during the Holocaust, there were multiple front-page stories about Nazi atrocities against civilians. However, most either failed entirely to note the selective targeting of Europe's Jewish population or were oblivious to the cumulative impact of measures targeting this specific group across the continent.[18] Further, as Raphael Lemkin, who coined the term 'genocide' in 1944,[19] notes, too few Allied leaders appreciated the way that the Nazis developed punitive measures against groups to match the Nazi imagination of a racial hierarchy. Blurring together all the victims of Nazi warfare, the Allied approach to World War II largely ignored the specific fates assigned to entire groups, notably the death sentence issued to the Jews. Not all civilians are equally

17 Raphael Lemkin's work on legal protections for groups predates his introduction of the term 'genocide' in 1944 and his later work significantly expanded the number and diversity of cases he thought were relevant to 'genocide.' His understanding that the problem of large-scale assaults against groups could not be limited to the context of World War II is what drove him to see the term transformed into international law. Our concern here, however, is how the prevailing imagination of groupness influenced his work.

18 Laurel Leff, *Buried by the Times: The Holocaust and America's Most Important Newspaper* (New York: Cambridge University Press, 2005).

19 Raphael Lemkin, *Axis Rule in Occupied Europe* (Washington, D.C.: Carnegie Endowment for International Peace, 1944),

vulnerable during times of violence and some forms of violence pose exceptional risk for entire groups of people.

Lemkin introduced the term 'genocide' precisely in order to focus attention on the vulnerabilities of entire national groups under Nazi occupation. He wrote: 'Genocide is directed against the national group as an entity, and the actions involved are directed against individuals, not in their individual capacity, but as members of the national group'.[20] Of considerable debate over the years is which groups should be included in 'genocide',[21] however, Lemkin makes it clear that his intellectual context is one of romantic nationalism, that is, a belief that the fruits of human civilization were the products of contributions of distinct national cultures:

> The world represents only so much culture and intellectual vigor as are created by its component national groups. Essentially the idea of a nation signifies constructive cooperation and original contributions, based upon genuine traditions, genuine culture and a well-developed national psychology.[22]

It was this understanding of humanity as much as the politics of the post-war period that influenced the selection of enumerated groups in the 1948 United Nations Convention on the Prevention and Punishment of the Crime of Genocide: ethnical, national, racial and religious groups. While the political manipulations of the colonial powers and Soviet-aligned nations influenced which groups were included in the law of genocide for Lemkin's contemporaries, it was common to view certain groups as natural and, therefore, having more historical meaning than other groups. Today, it is not merely the terms 'ethnical' or 'racial' that sound oddly out of step with our articulation of group identity, but also the proposed naturalization of groupness itself.

Increasingly influential are constructivist theories, which contribute ways of thinking about international relations and identity formation in terms of the impact of social and historical contingencies. This is reflected in disciplines that directly relate to atrocities. For instance, in applying the law of genocide, judges have struggled to arrive at delineations of 'groupness' that accurately

---

20 Ibid., p. 79.

21 See, for example, the discussion of debates over groups in William Schabas, 'Groups Protected by the Genocide Convention: Conflicting Interpretations from the International Criminal Tribunal for Rwanda,' *ILSA Journal of International and Comparative Law*, 6/1: 375–388 (1999).

22 Lemkin, *Axis Rule in Occupied Europe*, p. 91.

reflect the dynamics of cases they are hearing. In the first conviction for genocide after a trial, the Jean-Paul Akayesu case, judges at the International Criminal Tribunal for Rwanda described Hutu and Tutsi in relation to their social meaning, rather than any inherent, objective differences between groups. This approach has since become the norm, as legal scholar Antonio Cassese notes, proving objective group composition or difference is irrelevant. Instead, the law now hinges on how group identity functions within a particular context: 'it is sufficient that the perpetrator believes that the victim is a member of a group that he or she seeks to destroy'.[23]

Denaturalizing the bonds of groupness has also opened new way of thinking about the relationship between identity and violence. As Rogers Brubaker and David Laitin assert, urging caution about how much explanatory power resides in terms to describe 'groupness': '*That* political violence can be ethnic is well-established, indeed too well established; *how* it is ethnic remains obscure'.[24] New research on ethnic violence emerged since the 1990s (and influencing a parallel increase in studies of 'sectarian' or religious violence in response to violence in the Middle East in new millennium) has taken this warning to heart and explored the differing impacts of ethnicity on armed conflict,[25] the history and politics of how group differences come to matter,[26] and, among other issues, how intra-group power struggles can be just as lethal as inter-group conflicts.[27]

And, on the level of the individual, as Lee Ann Fujii points out in her work on the Rwandan genocide, ethnicity does not dictate actions, but is better understood as a script. She writes:

> If ethnicity operates as a script, then we would expect actors' performances to vary. We would expect performances to vary between actors

23 Antonio Cassese, *Cassese's International Criminal Law*, Third Edition (Oxford: Oxford University Press, 2013), p.121.

24 Rogers Brubaker and David Laitin, "Ethnic and Nationalist Violence" Annual Review of Sociology 24/1: 423–452 (1998), p. 427.

25 See, for instance, Nicholas Sambanis and Moses Shayo, 'Social Identification and Ethnic Conflict,' *American Political Science Review*, 107:2, 294–325 (2013).

26 See, for example, Mahmood Mamdani, *When Victims Become Killers: Colonialism, Nativism, and Genocide in Rwanda* (Princeton: Princeton University Press, 2001); Ivan Lovrenovic, *Bosnia: A Cultural History* (New York: New York University Press, 2001); Elissa Helms, *Innocence and Victimhood: Gender, Nation and Women's Activism in Postwar Bosnia-Herzegovina* (Madison, WI: University of Wisconsin Press, 2013).

27 Kathleen Gallagher Cunningham and Nils B. Weidman, 'Shared Space: Ethnic Groups, State Accommodation, and Localized Conflict,' *International Studies Quarterly*, 54/4: 1035–1954, (2010).

> such that some actors would adhere to the text more faithfully than others. We would also expect performances to vary by individual, such that the same actor's performances might be more convincing in some instances than in others. We would also expect actors to know the difference between the world of the play and the world outside the play.[28]

In short, in posing 'groupness' (even if one were to expand it to cultural, gender and political groups) as the subject of atrocities it is too easy to fall into the traps of naturalizing, simplifying, homogenizing, and assuming too much based on group identity. Any prevention agenda that would aim to deploy categories of 'groupness' would have to retain conceptual flexibility in order to avoid reifying the very group identities that are often manipulated into cause for violence in fragile situations. Instead, prevention must seek to define subjects in relation to cross-group and intra-group variations, even while problematizing the nature of the 'group' itself.

At the far end of the spectrum from 'groupness,' are the terms 'civilian' and 'population'—concepts whose contribution is their unspecified nature. Legal protections for civilians in international humanitarian law were crafted in 1949 and 1977, and assert: 'civilians and all persons not taking part in combat may under no circumstances be the object of attack and must be spared and protected'.[29] Defined in opposition to combatants, those who take up arms, the civilian is a negative concept; someone who is, in theory, not a rightful target of armed combat. The enemy during war is thereby differentiated into those who may and may not be killed. As Hugo Slim writes:

> ...this modern version of a timeless moral sense gives rise to what we might call the civilian ethic in war—a certain morality now enshrined in international law which spells out how this special group must be cared for and protected.[30]

The starting point for a concept of 'civilians' as the subject of atrocities is the equality of all who are not legitimately targets of violence, based on their own actions. Defined in reference to the context of armed conflict, the 'civilian'

28 Lee Ann Fujii, *Killing Neighbors: Webs of Violence In Rwanda* (Ithaca: Cornell University Press, 2009), p. 13.

29 The legal categories related to 'mass atrocity' that address crimes against 'civilian populations' include genocide, crimes against humanity, and war crimes.

30 Hugo Slim, *Killing Civilians: Method, Madness and Morality in War* (New York: Columbia University Press, 2008), p. 1.

universalizes the promise of protection. There is benefit to this broad conceptualization, particularly when it is deployed specifically to take advantage of its unspecified nature.

For example, *The Global Burden of Armed Violence*[31] takes an exceptionally broad view of the affects of lethal violence and returns insights that challenge central assumptions of the field of mass atrocities in terms of which situations require address, the mutability of forms of violence, and the policies that might be best applied to specific cases. They note, for instance, that globally civilians increasingly are threatened from violence in scenarios that do not adhere to the examples of genocide from history that describe overwhelming force from one side against another within the context of armed conflict. Considerably more civilians are at risk from situations that are endemic, involve a multitude of non-state actors, and blur the lines between political and criminal violence. These hybrid forms of violence are increasing even as mass atrocities are globally decreasing.[32]

So while study of armed violence makes conceptual divisions between organized and interpersonal violence, conflict and criminal contexts, state-sponsored and non-state actors, systematic versus incidental, and so forth, such distinctions are confounded by actual cases. Different forms of violence can exist at the same time: 'armed violence can have multiple and overlapping motives; different political, economic, identity-based, ideological, and other motives…'.[33] Even if one form of violence dominates at a certain point, it often evolves over time. Labels must be understood as time- and context-specific.

However, 'civilian' does not solve our problem. It does not lend itself well to analysis of the ways that risks of violence can be differentiated by group, gender, class or other markers. The contribution of equalizing protection also can overlook how harms during crises are related to pre-existing power hierarchies—in other words, vulnerability before, during and after mass atrocities or armed conflict is situated within power relations that are never equal. It also fails to capture and perhaps even obscures the extent of harm that is inflicted on noncombatants as part of the larger consequences of war: displacement, malnutrition, disease, impoverishment, and non-lethal violence. In irregular conflicts, differentiations between civilian and military forces and targets can

---

31 Geneva Declaration, *The Global Burden of Armed Violence* (Cambridge: Cambridge University Press, 2011).

32 Birger Heldt, 'Mass Atrocity Early Warning Systems: Data Gathering, Data Verification and Other Challenges,' 2012, http://papers.ssrn.com/sol3/papers.cfm?abstract_id=2028534, accessed 18 March 2014.

33 Geneva Declaration, *The Global Burden of Armed Violence*, p. 15.

at times be difficult to discern. Further, those who work on mass atrocities or genocide often note that while there is a high correlation between armed conflict and systematic targeting of unarmed people, nonetheless, such violence can occur outside of wars.

Sharing some of conceptual benefits and limitations with 'civilians' is the idea of 'populations' as articulated in the core documents related to the principle of a Responsibility to Protect (R2P). The use of 'population' within R2P stems from the original conceptualization of sovereignty as responsibility, articulated by Francis Deng in his capacity as the Special Rapporteur on Internally Displaced Persons (IDPs) for the United Nations Secretary General. A 'population' is foremost defined by a people's existence on a shared geography—hence its relationship to sovereignty as the parallel concept of a political authority over a territory.

Three poles anchor the concept of population: political authority, groups of people and a defined geographic area. Hence, its logic within the principle of R2P which attempts to disrupt the prerogatives of political authority in a given territory when a group of people is deemed to be at risk of violence. In this manner, R2P is less concerned with the nature of the 'subject of atrocities' and concentrates on how political authority and geography intersect in regard to the population. In fact, more than with any of the other terms discussed herein, 'populations' are *objects* of concern that can be studied, abstracted, queried, and deemed someone's responsibility, but they are not primarily *subjects*. As such, the language obscures internal variations of a 'population' and elides analysis of the actions members of a population might themselves take.

These seemingly theoretical distinctions prove their relevance when the concepts cannot withstand application. For example, in the aftermath of the NATO-led international intervention in Libya (2011), which was justified in terms of R2P principles, judgment on the intervention's success or failure hinged, to some extent, on whether one thought the intervention was justified to protect 'civilians' at immediate risk or 'populations,' including those armed portions of the population who aimed to overthrow the Gaddafi government. In the early days of unrest, the casualties were clearly civilian, unarmed protestors. But over the days and weeks that followed, some amongst the protesters took up arms and organized to overthrow the government. While the Gaddafi government clearly exceeded the bounds international humanitarian law in how it targeted its defense against these armed groups, if 'civilians' is locus of concern then the fact that they armed and organized themselves is highly relevant. If our concern, however, is 'populations', the situation is less clear.

This distinction cannot encompass the full range of issues involved in assessing the Libya intervention. My point here is that the competing conceptual language to define the subject of atrocities does not help clarify the political debate, rather, sloppy conceptualization diminishes the possibility of even having a coherent debate. Post-facto assessments of the Libyan war diverged sharply: was it a successful example of the international community acting with speed and focus to protect civilians whose government was preparing to massacre them?[34] Or, was it an opportunistic international alliance to militarily defeat a nasty rogue government with minimal western casualties, rationalized in the name of protecting a Libyan population (including its armed elements)?[35] Regardless of one's position in this debate, post-Libya, the idea of civilian protection—and the centrality of the 'civilian' within its model--needed protection itself. Addressing the Libya intervention, UN Secretary General Ban Ki Moon stated on May 22, 2012:

> However, the extent to which its implementation [UNSC Res 1973 authorizing military force in Libya] was perceived to go beyond the protection of civilians raised concerns among some Member States that continue to colour the Council's discussions on the protection of civilians and related issues in other situations. It may also have had the unintended effect of undermining the protection of civilians agenda, including as a framework for action in future crises. In the future, in addition to complying scrupulously with international humanitarian law and human rights law, the implementation of such decisions must be limited to promoting and ensuring the protection of civilians.[36]

---

34 Jon Western and Joshua S. Goldstein, 'Humanitarian Intervention Comes of Age: Lessons from Somalia to Libya,' *Foreign Affairs*, November/December 2011, http://www.foreignaffairs.com/articles/136502/jon-western-and-joshua-s-goldstein/humanitarian-intervention-comes-of-age?page=show accessed 10 March 2014.

35 Hugh Roberts, 'Who Said Gaddafi Had to Go?' *London Review of Books*, 33/22: 8 – 18 (17 November 2011).

36 'Report of the Secretary General on the protection of civilians in armed conflict,' S/2012/376, 22 May 2012, (Paragraph 19). The Brazilian ambassador to the UN went further, by pointedly asserting that that there is a responsibility 'while protecting' that imposes limitations to the coercive approach. In a letter to the UN General Assembly, Ambassador Antonio de Aguiar Patriota, Minister of External Relations of Brazil, wrote: 'There is a growing perception that the concept of the responsibility to protect might be misused for purposes other than protecting civilians, such as regime change. This perception may make it even more difficult to attain the protection objectives pursued by the international community.' See, 'Letter dated 9 November 2011 from the Permanent Representative of Brazil to the United Nations addressed to the Secretary-General,' /A/66/551; paragraph 10.

R2P deploys the term 'population' as part of its inheritance from practices related to IDPs and as an intentional address to state and international authority. It describes a political-geographic grouping of humans. Inherently, it also speaks to 'civilians' through its reference to legal categories (like 'crimes against humanity' which does address the subject as civilian), but rejects the option to frame its principle within this language. While to some extent, this rejection may be due to concern about the limitation of a context of armed conflict, it also relates to R2P's lack of concern with the agency of at-risk groups. In R2P, the *subjects* are states and the international community, who deliver services, protect or harm populations. This lack of interest in the agency of the 'population' may correctly characterize the immediate context of extreme vulnerability, but it glosses over and even obscures significant differences from the associated term, 'civilians', as well as the historical and social grounding embedded in 'groupness' categories. And it also demonstrates a limitation when the context changes. For better or worse, frameworks that erase the agency of individuals or groups in the name of any agenda—even protection—risk being incapable of anticipating, weighing and engaging that agency at earlier or later points. For this reason, 'population' is a poor term for understanding the subjects of atrocities, and it is even less relevant for prevention.

On the other hand, 'civilian' offers analytical and practical benefits because of its wide embrace of individuals categorized by their actions. What this suggests for a prevention agenda is that there are distinct advantages to using terms that do not assert assumptions about a vulnerable group but which deploy the widest perspective possible, both in terms of the types of vulnerabilities that exist, the fluidity of contexts where subject positions may be best defined by choices the individual makes, and the research and policy approaches that might most effectively be applied. However, this benefit is only realized when it is consciously engaged as a tool to paint a broad picture of vulnerability. Otherwise, it can stand in for a failure to make important distinctions.

In the above section I have tried to illustrate some of the difficulties of the given vocabulary of atrocities and indicate how these difficulties compound when applied to prevention. However, it is very easy to get lost in the kind of caveats and conundrums of applying a vocabulary from one context to another; instead, we need to further explore what makes the context of prevention distinct and how does that re-write the parameters for our 'subject of prevention'?

Specifying a Prevention Agenda

Study of genocide and mass atrocities has long staked a claim to prevention as an ethical and practical goal, often expressed as simply as 'never again', a phrase whose appeal is matched by its lack of specificity.[37] In terms of research or policy designed to focus exclusively, and with a strong evidence base, on how to prevent genocide or mass atrocities, the field is in its infancy. Being young, it is marked by certain fundamental challenges.

Perhaps most crucial is the lack of consistency in defining the term 'mass atrocity.' Among the variables at play in establishing parameters for the phenomenon and structuring studies to analyze engagement, are whether it includes killing, increased mortality or other harms like sexual assault or destruction of livelihoods; varying thresholds, which, even in approaches that are tied exclusively to killing, can vary from several hundred, to 1,000, to tens of thousands in historical studies; whether the focus is only on state-sponsored violence or if it includes the actions of non-state actors; and, as will be explored in greater depth below, the description of the people at risk.

Another point of contention is precisely what is meant by 'prevention'. Engagement with mass atrocities or threats thereof is generally grouped into three phases. First, is address of root causes or structural risk factors that render certain states more prone to mass violence, known as risk assessment. This is not early warning of impending violence, but rather an assessment of the core conditions understood to correlate with a potential risk of atrocities. Second is proximal or direct prevention, which addresses factors that might trigger mass violence and attempts to articulate anti-escalatory actions--early warning. The goal of activities under this heading is to target a place hovering on the brink of or already experiencing violence and to de-escalate the crisis. Third, is response to on-going widespread and systematic violence against people (however defined). Actions during any of these phases can be described as 'prevention.' See, for instance, a report from the UN Secretary General of 25 July 2012, which states: 'Some may consider that prevention and response are at opposite ends of the spectrum. In practice, however, the two often merge'.[38] My intervention is directed at structural risk assessment, which is clearly a point at which one can describe engagement as 'prevention', although some of the observations may be relevant to other phases as well.

The work on risk assessment for atrocities has grown considerably over recent years, but remains imprecise. A key contribution of work in this area has been to debunk or at least challenge some of the assumptions that the field of atrocities prevention inherited from genocide studies about the conditions ripe for systematic violence. For instance, while early work on genocide learned

37 Thomas Cushman, 'Is Genocide Preventable? Some Theoretical Considerations', *Journal of Genocide Research*, 5/4: 523–542.

38 A/66/874, 25 July 2012, p. 4.

much from the examples of fascism and communism to emphasize strong states with well-articulated ideologies, later work has noted that atrocities today often occur in 'anocracies' –that is states whose governance model exists somewhere between autocracy and democracy.[39] State-sponsored exclusionary ideologies remain an important factor, but the nature of the ideology and how it maps unto other social schisms is significant.[40] Hate, often identified with genocide, has proven less salient an explanation as work on perpetrators reveals a much broader mix of motivations.[41]

Nonetheless, those who work on atrocity prevention recognize that advances in research have not yet translated into finely honed and specific systems for preventing atrocities. Much of what is known about atrocities prevention emerges from the field of conflict prevention, even though these two related phenomenon are not the same.[42] Further specifying the distinct *atrocities* prevention agenda remains a goal of the field. Currently, there are a number of strategies being pursued, among them: moving away from root causes and structural risk towards a model borrowed from criminology focused on identifying perpetrators, victims and permissive environments; amalgamating multiple risk assessment systems and combining them with expert analysis; and trying to change the path of information so that it gets to the people immediately at risk rather than solely to international authorities.[43] These and other approaches to improving atrocities prevention will certainly contribute to furthering the knowledge base of the field and informing policy; but they are limited to a triage approach—that is, finding the location of greatest threats and suppressing those threats or drivers of violence.

---

39 Jay Ulfelder and Benjamin Valentino, 'Assessing Risks of State-Sponsored Mass Killing', February 2008. Available at http://ssrn.com/abstract=17033426. Retrieved 23 October 2013.

40 Scott Straus, 'Retreating from the Brink: Theorizing Mass Violence and the Dynamics of Restraint,' *Perspectives on Politics*, 10:02, (2012), 343–362.

41 See, for example, James Waller *Becoming Evil: How Ordinary People Commit Genocide.* (New York: Oxford University Press, 2002); Stathis Kalyvas, *The Logic of Violence in Civil War* (New York: Cambridge University Press, 2006); and Lee Ann Fujii, *Killing Neighbors: Webs of Violence in Rwanda* (Ithaca: Cornell University Press, 2009).

42 Rubin Reike, Serena Sharma and Jennifer Welsh, 'A Strategic Framework for Mass Atrocity Prevention', March 2013, http://acmc.gov.au/wp-content/uploads/2013/11/3–2013-A-Strategic-Framework-for-Mass-Atrocity-Prevention.pdf, accessed 12 February 2014.

43 See for instance, the approach suggested by Rubin Reike, Serena Sharma and Jennifer Welsh, 'A Strategic Framework for Mass Atrocity Prevention', March 2013; the early warning project led by Jay Ulfelder for the U.S. Holocaust Memorial Museum, an early warning project led by Alex Bellamy, Sara Davies and Stephen McLoughlin at Griffith University, and the work of the Sentinel Project.

A different approach will be needed to inform productive policies; that is, the knowledge base and engagement parameters for contributing positively to societies' capacities to develop in ways that minimize the chance of atrocities. There are a few traits of this approach that strongly differentiate it from the above prevention efforts: 1) it explores the negative cases in greater depth asking why places with comparable risk profiles do not manifest atrocities; 2) it tends towards qualitative analysis to explore the gaps in what current quantitative work can explain; 3) it emphasizes local agency and capacities; and 4) suggests a potential framework for critical engagement with current international practices, versus the tendency within dominant atrocities prevention paradigms to emphasize creation of new programs and functions.[44] Amongst the most compelling work taking this approach are Scott Straus' discussion of 'factors of restraint' and Deborah Mayersen and Stephen McLoughlin's adoption of 'resilience' to analysis of prevention.[45]

If we are to understand why atrocities occur in some places and not others, and to gain greater insight into the processes of escalation, Scott Straus asserts, researchers need not only to explore factors that increase risk for atrocities, but also those that restrain violence. The interaction of escalating and restraining forces can help explain where, when and why violence occurs, and offer new insights into where, when, and why such violence does *not* occur. From these latter insights, new approaches to prevention are possible.

Straus emphasizes the restraining factors that exist at the national (macro) level as being the most potent when social, economic and political conditions deteriorate and open the door for violence. He downplays the impact of meso-level organizations like religious centers, trade unions, or other non-governmental organizations, and individual (micro) sources of restraint, like personal moral or religious beliefs, or self-interested factors, in a context where the state has determined to pursue a policy of atrocities, noting that these factors may be more influential on a longer time-horizon. Among the national-level sources of resilience are economic, demographic, political, military and ideological factors—some of these can also be found in risk assessment systems, but Straus offers new layers of nuance about how the various contributors of risk and restraint factors operate together.

---

44 As an example of this, see Genocide Prevention Task Force, 'Preventing Genocide: A Blueprint for U.S. Policymakers,' 2008, http://media.usip.org/reports/genocide_taskforce_report.pdf, accessed May 30, 2014.

45 Straus, 'Retreating from the Brink' and Deborah Mayersen and Stephen McLoughlin, 'Risk and Resilience to Mass Atrocities in Africa: A Comparison of Rwanda and Botswana', *Journal of Genocide Research* 13:3 (2011) 247–269.

He details several economic factors, which boil down to the fact that widespread violence disrupts economies by inhibiting taxation, tourism, agriculture, and other industries that require skilled labor or well-developed infrastructure. If these factors are crucial for a state's ability to raise funds, they can operate as restraints on use of mass violence. Opposed to this, for example, are extractive industries, where a regime can rely on relatively small labor base, and key resources are located at geographically isolatable (and therefore secure-able) sites, and which produce large revenues streams directly to governments tend not to act as restraints on violence. He continues to note that countries with a significant middle class or commercial elites, whose livelihoods rely on a functioning and integrated economy can be forces that resist deployment of violence.

Democratic institutions also function as restraints. While study of exclusionary ideologies is a trademark of genocide and atrocities studies, Straus draws attention to the fact that the inverse may also hold true: inclusive ideologies may inhibit violence. As an example, Straus compares Rwanda with Côte d'Ivoire. Rwanda entered into independence with deeply politicized ideas about ethnicity. In Côte d'Ivoire, there was an ideology of inclusion, present since independence of the country and instilled in the young nation by its first leader, Felix Houphouet-Boigny. Straus writes:

> In short, unity, dialogue, economic growth, and peace represent core national values that Houphouet promoted...He [Houphouet-Boigny] sought multi-ethnic representation in his cabinets, he encouraged ethnic/religious mobility rather than exclusion and rigidity, and, under him, there was widespread intermarriage.[46]

Straus argues that Houphouet-Boigny spoke repeatedly about the values of solidarity, peace, and tolerance and a 'spirit of permanent dialogue',[47] and that this served as a 'reservoir of moderation' even years later when the distinction between long-resident citizens and immigrants (designated as foreigners) became politically salient and produced violence following contested elections in 2010. While building on established risk assessment and early warning work, Straus' articulation of risk and restraint offers new ways to think about why and where violence does not happen, may improve forecasting accuracy, and supports the policy assumption that 'external investments in peace can make a difference'.[48] It also implies that the external investments that would

46 Straus, 'Retreating from the Brink', p. 355.

47 Ibid.

48 Ibid., p.356.

most meaningfully make a difference for prevention will be those that simultaneously recognize sources of escalation while augmenting existing sources of restraint.

Like Straus, Mayersen and McLoughlin are concerned with what goes right in some countries in order to 'glean insights useful for the prevention of mass atrocities in the future'.[49] Also like Straus, they use a comparison with Rwanda, this time with Botswana, to understand what they term 'resilience,' social characteristics that resist use of mass violence. Their comparison looks at politics and ethnicity during the decolonization process, post-independence approach to ethnicity, indigenous conflict-resolution capacities, governance, economic development, economic and environmental challenges, and centralization of power, among other factors. Throughout, they find resilience in social, political and economic factors that provide continuity, transparency, accountability, and dynamism. Both historically contingent factors as well as structural ones contribute to resilience. Importantly in their analysis, no single factor rises above all the others, but rather the preponderance of resiliency is reinforced and strengthened across the social fabric in Botswana--while it is worn thin in Rwanda.

They offer many examples. For instance, in Rwanda, ethnicity was politicized and inserted into government policies and ideology throughout the post-independence era. In Botswana, the rising leadership opted for a model of inclusive democratic rule, and envisioned the decolonization process as one of partnership with the former powers, rather than a radical break. Further cementing a process of continuity, traditional leaders were given a role in the upper house, a House of Chiefs, alongside the elected parliament. This created a system of concentration of wealth and power, but has favorably inhibited violence. It also meant that traditional conflict-resolution mechanisms survived the transition into independence and continued to function effectively in Botswana, whereas they were disrupted in Rwanda. Botswana also offers an example of a country with ethnic fragmentation—that is, many ethnic groups, versus Rwanda which is highly polarized, having two main groups with one as the overwhelming majority. While some policies in Botswana clearly favored the traditional elites, who were of the Tswana tribe, other practices demonstrated greater equality, such as merit-based employment in the public sector. In Rwanda, ethnic quotas and favoritism marked all state practices. In a point that provides an interesting parallel with Straus' comments on the place of ideology, McLoughlin and Mayersen note that, despite inequalities, there was

49 Mayersen and McLoughlin, 'Risk and Resilience to Mass Atrocities in Africa: A Comparison of Rwanda and Botswana', p. 248.

never a question in Botswana that its minorities belonged to the country, whereas in Rwanda, the so-called Hamitic myth postulated that Tutsi were foreigners, not as genuinely 'Rwandan' as Hutu.

The key contribution of Mayersen and McLoughlin's analytic framework is a sense of how these factors interrelate to contribute to systemic resilience that endures over time. This element of interconnectedness and historical perspective are important as they suggest comparable systemic and long-term engagement would be necessary to bolster domestic sources of resilience in places where risk is high. Their conclusion, echoed in Straus' work, is that: 'levels of risk and resilience are a result of a complex and dynamic interplay between risk and mitigating factors across time'.[50]

In using the term 'resilience', Mayersen and McLoughlin are picking up on a broader trend that favors this term across wide range of disciplines and contexts. As one advocate of 'resilience' recently wrote, the term 'is currently used to describe anything that resists time and decay from firms which withstand stock-market volatility to the survival of man in nature to the child's or adult's resistance in a context of precariousness, abuse or violence'.[51] The fields of development and crisis management, both of which closely relate to atrocities prevention and response, also use the term. While the diversity of fields can magnify discrepancies in how a concept is deployed, it also opens a window for sharing insights across areas of knowledge and practice. This may be particularly important in the case of 'resilience'. As Mayersen and McLoughlin note in their discussion and as is the case with how the term is used in most other contexts, 'resilience' describes a capacity to resist change that is enabled by the congruence of multiple factors. To that end, the fact that the term is used across multiple disciplines as an organizing concept may prove highly valuable for bringing together the diversity of perspectives, evidence and theories to try to capture this congruence.

Needless to say, as an organizing concept it has generated its own set of debates. Summarizing these debates, Adam Pain and Simon Levine[52] note that the term can be used to describe the ability of a community or individual to

50 Ibid., p. 265.

51 Margot Phaneuf, 'Resilience: Abstract Concept of Survival Skill' 2007. http://www.infiressources.ca/fer/Depotdocument_anglais/Resilience_abstract_concept_or_survival_skill.pdf, accessed 30 May 2014.

52 Adam Pain and Simon Levine, 'A conceptual analysis of livelihoods and resilience: addressing the 'insecurity of agency' Humanitarian Policy Working Group, HPG Working Paper, November 2012, http://www.odi.org.uk/publications/6976-resilience-livelihoods-agency-socio-economic-security, accessed 30 May 2014.

alternatively avoid collapse, recover, or adapt. It is sometimes treated as a given characteristic of societies or individuals *per se*, or, alternatively, to their capacities when faced with crises. Other times, it is used as a mere opposite to 'vulnerability' or to capture the fact that some places even when faced with severe crises do not develop into catastrophic situations. While in practice this might mean that a people barely survives, the term tends to be deployed as a positive descriptor. The normative meaning might prove problematic if it treats mere survival as a lauded goal, or in certain contexts where a given social, economic or political system is highly resilient—in that its basic form persists despite threats—but is also deeply inequitable or violent.

However, and here we return to core question of this paper, Pain and Levine argue that gaining stronger coherency in the conceptual insights offered by 'resilience' will require 'focus on reducing people's vulnerability and enhancing their agency'.[53] This cannot be done via a singular concentration on subjects, however, but must position vulnerability and agency in the context of 'constraints to choice and action that might exist because of power inequalities and exclusion within the community'.[54] In such analysis we can also better understand how the questions that inform atrocities prevention can contribute to the wider array of disciplines engaging with resilience: an atrocities prevention lens[55] necessarily is concerned with the differentiated dynamics of vulnerability and resilience within communities, as well as the politics that animate those dynamics.

Thereby we begin to arrive at stronger parameters for placing individuals and groups into dynamic contexts such as ought to inform prevention of atrocities. The key question for prevention should not be who is most vulnerable and how to protect those individuals or groups alone? Rather, one must ask: how is a society structured to inhibit or promote agency? What 'givens' pre-set the stage unto which actors may find themselves increasingly vulnerable or empowered? Asking these questions in a prevention context better enable exposure of the relationships, historical narratives, economic ties and political manipulations that cause risk to fluctuate. They also better identify the sources of moderation that be bolstered in productive policies.

53 Ibid., p. 3.

54 Ibid., p. 10.

55 I borrow this phrase from Alex Bellamy, 'Mass Atrocities and Armed Conflict: Links, Distinctions, and Implications for the Responsibility to Protect', February 2011, http://www.stanleyfoundation.org/publications/pab/BellamyPAB22011.pdf, accessed 30 May 2014.

Conclusion: Subjects, Agency and Prevention

We do not have vocabularies to describe the subjects of mass atrocities that adequately capture the fact that vulnerability to violence and agency are differentiated across and within various ways of grouping people and over long duration. These variations are dynamic and situational, even as they emerge out of historically constructed social and political hierarchies. In order for a unique atrocities prevention agenda to develop, it will require revising the terms of engagement, not only identifying a positive framework for policies and points of interaction, but also for conceptual frameworks of the key subjects. For preventative engagement to work, it must eschew attempts to finalize the status of the actors it aims to engage—it must be conceived differently from post-violence analytical frameworks as the worst has not yet happened and might be avoided. It must ask different questions.

The knowledge and practices of existing paradigms for atrocities that include international humanitarian benchmarks or quantitative analysis of risk can inform this work, but it is of a different nature. In seeking a subject of prevention, we depart from the today's dominant prevention model in two ways. First, for atrocities prevention to realize its potential impact, it must depart from the triage model that presupposes emergency international engagement measures to ward off overwhelming evil. That is a moral model of international relations in which 'subjects of atrocity' are defined apolitically, as subjects with agency only in relation to acts of horror that define and fix them within an ethical hierarchy. This approach is, as Rancière likewise described the 'vicious circle of a theory' regarding the subject of rights, based on a strategy of depoliticization. Atrocities prevention, like democratic practice, is inherently political, long-term, and grounded in the unique resources within a given society. Second, there is no subject, per se, but rather a stage that has been pre-set. Understanding how risk and resilience (or moderation) function alongside vulnerability and escalation on this stage requires that one not fix the actors into normative categories, but rather query the parameters of the stage and what roles are open to which actors.

CHAPTER 3

Rethinking the Structural Prevention of Mass Atrocities

Stephen McLoughlin
Griffith University
s.mcloughlin@griffith.edu.au

Abstract

Interest amongst scholars and policy decision-makers in the prevention of genocide and other mass atrocities has grown in recent years. Despite this, many have overlooked problems inherent in the commonly accepted notion of prevention. Crystalized in the Carnegie Commission's 1997 report, 'Preventing Deadly Conflict', prevention has typically been understood in two parts, one addressing impending cases of violence (direct prevention) and the other focusing on the underlying causes of violence (structural prevention). The concept of structural prevention is especially problematic. Commonly defined as the identification and addressing of 'root causes', this conceptualisation contains at least two limitations: first, there is an implicit assumption that root causes lead inevitably to violence, and second, there has been a tendency for international actors to decide, in general and global terms, what counts as root causes and how to ameliorate them, downplaying the role of local contexts and overlooking the preventive work of local and national actors. This article argues that the concept of structural prevention needs broadening to incorporate an understanding of the dynamic interaction between the risk that root causes pose, and locally-based mitigation factors that foster resilience. Effective long-term prevention should be based – not only on identifying and ameliorating negative characteristics in countries at risk – but also on contributing to the complex management of diversity. While this makes intuitive sense – and may in fact reflect the reality of how much preventive work is done – such an approach has not hitherto been reflected in conceptual understandings of prevention adopted by the United Nations, as well as academic researchers.

Keywords

prevention – genocide – mass atrocities – Responsibility to Protect (R2P) – resilience

 | DOI 10.1163/9789004299870_005

Introduction

Over the last decade, there has been a growing interest amongst scholars and policy-makers – particularly in the UN – in the prevention of genocide and other mass atrocities. In 2004, the Office of the Special Adviser for the Prevention of Genocide (OSAPG) was established within the UN Secretariat.[1] In 2005, international consensus was reached on the recognition of the primary responsibility of states to protect their populations from such violence.[2] Declaring mass atrocities to be an issue of national security, President Obama established an Atrocities Prevention Board in 2012.[3] The increased capacity of the UN Department of Political Affairs as well as greater support for UN-led political missions in a number of vulnerable countries and regions is another indication of the strengthening and diversification of international efforts to prevent mass atrocities.

Despite this growing commitment, researchers and policy decision-makers have largely overlooked problems inherent in the commonly accepted notion of prevention. Crystalized by the Carnegie Commission in its 1997 report, *Preventing Deadly Conflict*, prevention has typically been understood in two parts, one addressing impending cases of violence (direct prevention) and the other focusing on the long term causes of violence (structural prevention). The concept of structural prevention, in particular, is problematic. Using prevention in public health as a model, the report defined it as the identification and addressing of 'root causes'.[4] This conceptualisation contained at least two limitations: first, there was an implicit assumption that root causes would lead inevitably to violence, and second, there has been a tendency for international actors to decide, in general and global terms, what counts as root causes and how to ameliorate them, downplaying the role of local contexts and overlooking the preventive work of local and national actors.[5]

1 S/2004/567, 13 July 2004.

2 '2005 World Summit Outcome', UNGA Res. 60/1, 16 September 2005.

3 The White House, 'Fact Sheet: A Comprehensive Strategy and New Tools to Prevent and Respond to Atrocities'. 23 April 2012, (http://www.whitehouse.gov/the-press-office/2012/04/23/fact-sheet-comprehensive-strategy-and-new-tools-prevent-and-respond-atro), accessed 12 December 2012.

4 David Hamburg, and Cyrus R Vance, *Preventing Deadly Conflict – Final Report*. (Washington DC: Carnegie Commission on Preventing Deadly Conflict, 1997). For further discussion of the medical dimension of prevention, see Jacques Semelin, *Purify and Destroy: The Political Uses of Massacre and Genocide* (London: C. Hurst & Co, 2007), p. 368.

5 See, for example, Ban Ki-moon, *Report of the Secretary-General on the Implementation of Security Council Resolution 1625 (2005), on Conflict Prevention, Particularly in Africa*, S/2008/18,

Indeed, this notion of structural prevention does not cast a lens over domestic sources of resilience. Certainly, the identification of root causes is crucial for understanding risk, but prevention in practice (particularly by local and national actors) often entails a range of complex and contextually specific processes that do not have as their goal (or their outcome) the amelioration of root causes, but rather the ongoing management of diversity. Even in public health, this approach to prevention is a contentious one, with some peer-reviewed studies claiming that it has the tendency to lead to over-diagnosis and unnecessary medical interventions.[6] Perhaps it is no surprise that the idea of resilience – where 'people are given time to let their normal coping and support mechanisms to come into play'[7] – is emerging as a valued dimension in some areas of medical therapy.[8] Likewise, in the prevention of mass atrocities, approaches which are premised on an understanding of how resilience is fostered in the face of risk, have the potential to yield fresh insights into the myriad ways that local and national actors develop their own 'coping and support mechanisms', as well as build social, political and economic stability.

In this paper, I argue that what is needed is a broadening of the concept of structural prevention so that it incorporates not only an account of root causes, but also an understanding of the dynamic interaction between the risk that root causes pose – and locally-based mitigation factors that foster resilience to risk. This two-step approach allows for long term preventive strategies – particularly those involving external actors – to facilitate local and national processes that already work. Effective long-term prevention is based on identifying

---

14 January 2008; Rasheed Draman, 'Conflict Prevention in Africa: Establishing Conditions and Institutions conducive to durable Peace' in David Carment and Albrecht Schabel (eds.), *Conflict Prevention: Path to Peace or Grand Illusion?* (Tokyo: United Nations University Press, 2003), p. 234; Peter Wallensteen, 'Reassessing Recent Conflicts: Direct vs Structural Prevention' in Fen Osler Hampson and David M Malone (eds.), *From Reaction to Conflict Prevention: Opportunities for the UN System* (Boulder CO: Lynne Rienner Publishers, 2003), p. 214.

6 See, for example, Gilbert H. Welch and William C Black, 'Overdiagnosis in Cancer', *Journal of the National Cancer Institute* 10, pp. 605–613 (2010); Gilbert H. Welch, *Overdiagnosed: Making People Sick in the Pursuit of Health* (Boston: Beacon Press, 2011).

7 Pat O'Malley, 'Resilient Subjects: Uncertainty, Warfare and Liberalism', *Economy and Society* 39/4: 488–509 (2010), p. 99.

8 See, for example, J. Murphy, and A Cohn, 'Mental Health Innovations with the Australian Defence Force', *Journal of Occupational Health and Safety in Australia and New Zealand*, 24/6 (2008); O'Malley, 'Resilient Subjects'; S. Southwick, M Vyhiligan and D Charney, 'The Psychobiology of Depression and Resilience to Stress: Implications for Prevention and Treatment', *Annual Reviews of Clinical Psychology* 1: 255–291 (2005).

and ameliorating negative characteristics in countries at risk, but also on contributing to the complex management of diversity. While this makes intuitive sense – and may in fact reflect the reality of how much preventive work is done – such an approach has not hitherto been reflected in conceptual understandings of prevention adopted by the United Nations, as well as academic researchers.

This article is organised in three parts. In the first section I will present an overview of the concept of structural prevention, particularly the way it has evolved since the end of the Cold War. The second section highlights two major limitations in the way that structural prevention has been conceptualised by researchers and by the UN – the assumption that the existence of root causes makes violence inevitable, and a tendency towards external diagnosis and prognosis. In the third section I propose a framework which broadens the concept of structural prevention in relation to mass atrocities to incorporate an understanding of the relationship between risk and resilience.

The Concept of Structural Prevention

The concept of long-term prevention took shape following the end of the Cold War. The OSCE was the first organisation to broaden the focus of prevention beyond preventive diplomacy and early warning, to incorporate strategies that addressed the root causes of potential conflict. The UN also embraced this approach – in *An Agenda for Peace*, Boutros Boutros-Ghali declared the importance of addressing the underlying causes of conflict in addition to preventive diplomacy,[9] thus challenging policy makers to broaden the lens of prevention within the UN system. In 1997, the Carnegie Commission consolidated these two approaches in its report, *Preventing Deadly Conflict*, where it established a two-pronged definition of prevention. Direct prevention was defined as addressing escalating tensions when conflict and violence appeared imminent, and structural prevention was framed as 'strategies to address the root causes of deadly conflict'.[10] In this conceptualisation of prevention, the authors of the report likened conflict prevention to 'primary prevention in public health'[11] – addressing symptoms of ill health before they manifest into disease.

9 Boutros Boutros-Ghali, *An Agenda for Peace: Preventive Diplomacy, Peacemaking and Peace-keeping*, A/47/277, 31 January 1992.

10 Hamburg and Vance, *Preventing Deadly Conflict*, p. 69.

11 Ibid, p. xviii.

This two-part definition subsequently underpinned the approach adopted by the UN. Secretary-General Kofi Annan, in his calls for the UN system to adopt a culture of prevention, released three reports on conflict prevention, all embracing the notions of direct and structural prevention, and all reinforcing the idea that structural prevention entailed identifying and addressing root causes.[12] This was further consolidated by the Security Council, whose resolution on conflict prevention equated the creation of the 'conditions for durable peace and sustainable development' with the addressing of root causes.[13] Ban Ki-moon's 2008 report on conflict prevention added support to this notion, and declared the neglect to do so would warrant negative outcomes: 'If we do not deal with the root causes of conflict – and offer sustainable solutions – we will be left with humanitarian emergencies and peacekeeping operations without end'.[14] What unfolded in these reports was an intimate connection between root causes and violent outcomes, and an obligation for international actors to 'deal' with them.

Premising structural prevention on the addressing of root causes is also apparent in specific relation to mass atrocities. The Carnegie Commission's two-tiered definition was adopted by the International Commission on Intervention and State Sovereignty (ICISS), in its development of the principle of the Responsibility to Protect (R2P). In its 2001 report, *The Responsibility to Protect*, the Commission emphasised this approach: 'Encouraging more serious and sustained efforts to address the root cause of the problems that put populations at risk, as well as more effective use of direct prevention measures, is a key objective of the Commission's efforts'.[15] When member states endorsed the principle of R2P at the 2005 World Summit, they acknowledged the role that both direct and structural prevention played in ensuring the protection of populations from the crimes of genocide, war crimes, ethnic cleansing and crimes against humanity. In emphasising the role of individual states in carrying out their responsibility, the document stressed, 'this responsibility entails

12 Kofi Annan, *Prevention of Armed Conflict: Report of the Secretary-General*, A/55/985, 7 June 2001; Kofi Annan, *Interim Report of the Secretary-General on the Prevention of Armed Conflict*, A/58/365, 12 September 2003; Kofi Annan, *Progress Report on the Prevention of Armed Conflict: Report of the Secretary-General*, A/60/891, 18 July 2006. The 2006 report also added 'systemic prevention' as a complement to structural and operational prevention. Systemic prevention involved strategies that address transnational systemic factors that facilitate conflict, such as the illicit arms and drugs trade.

13 S/RES/1366, 30 August 2001.

14 S/2008/18, p. 14.

15 International Commission on Intervention and State Sovereignty (ICISS). *The Responsibility to Protect* (Ottawa: IDRC, 2001), p. 20.

the prevention of such crimes, including their incitement'.[16] Subsequent to the World Summit, structural prevention of the four included has continued to be articulated along similar lines. UN Secretary General Ban Ki-moon's 2009 report, *Implementing the Responsibility to Protect*, for example, emphasised the need to address the 'underlying fissures in the social and political fabric particularly in states and regions where ethnic tensions run high and deep inequalities among groups persist'.[17]

The Office of the Special Adviser for the Prevention of Genocide (OSAPG) has used the same definition of structural prevention in relation to its long-term strategies. According to the Special Adviser, 'To prevent genocide and genocidal conflicts, it is critically important to understand their root causes', which 'revolve around inequalities between identity groups'.[18] Once these root causes in any given place are identified, the Special Adviser advocates their eradication: 'In terms of prevention, the critical step is to identify the factors (discriminatory practices) in a given situation that lead to/account for acute disparities in the administration of a diverse population, and to seek ways to diminish and eventually eradicate these possible causes of genocidal violence'.[19]

This notion of long-term prevention has also resonated widely in the academic literature. Prior to the coining of the terms 'direct' and 'structural' prevention, Stedman articulated the difference between these approaches as 'preventive diplomacy' and 'conflict prevention', with the latter addressing 'the supposed roots of such conflicts: poverty, environmental degradation, overpopulation, resource competition, and lack of legitimate political institutions'.[20] Following the Carnegie Commission's 1997 report, a number of publications used this distinction to formulate long term and proximate approaches to potential conflict and atrocities based on an understanding of root causes and escalating factors, and corresponding options for ameliorating

16 '2005 World Summit Outcome', para. 38.

17 Ban Ki-moon, *Implementing the Responsibility to Protect: Report of the Secretary-General*, A/63/677,12 January 2009, p. 19.

18 United Nations Office of the United Nations Special Adviser on the Prevention of Genocide, 'Preventing Genocide, Crimes Against Humanity, Ethnic Cleansing and War Crimes', 2012, http://www.un.org/en/preventgenocide/adviser/un_role.shtml, accessed 5 January 2013.

19 United Nations Office of the United Nations Special Adviser on the Prevention of Genocide, 'Preventing Genocide', 2012, http://www.un.org/en/preventgenocide/adviser/genocide_prevention.shtml, accessed 5 January 2013.

20 Stephen John Stedman, 'Alchemy for a new world order: overselling "preventive diplomacy"', *Foreign Affairs* 74/3: 14–20 (1995), p. 18.

them. In broad terms, key publications exploring prevention followed similar lines of investigation: an exploration of the concept of prevention; a discussion of the causes of conflict and/or mass atrocities; a presentation of key preventive strategies to address these causes; and finally an exploration of the key preventive actors with the capacity to adopt such strategies.[21]

In the conceptual explorations of structural prevention found in these and other publications, one common feature is that structural prevention is premised on removing root causes. Jentleson, for example, adopts the Carnegie Commission's definition of prevention, acknowledging that addressing the root causes of conflict lies at the heart of structural prevention.[22] Carment and Schnabel point out that having knowledge of the root causes of conflict is crucial in order for practitioners to devise strategies based on sound analysis.[23] A similar long term approach to prevention is also emphasised by Cockell: 'if the nature of the problem is viewed as the perpetuation of structural conditions of human insecurity, more proactive measures may be planned to begin to address the various sources of that structural violence'.[24] Wallensteen also adopts this notion of structural prevention, stressing that this long-term approach to prevention involves adopting measures such as 'the promotion of democracy, ethnic integration, international regional cooperation, arms control, and disarmament'.[25] Promoting such measures, as the Carnegie Report points out, is akin to ameliorating root causes.[26] In their exploration of

21 See, for example, David Carment and Albrecht Schnabel (eds.), *Conflict Prevention: From Rhetoric to Reality* (Lanham: Lexington Books, 2003); Fen Osler Hampson and David M. Malone (eds.), *From Reaction to Conflict Prevention: Opportunities for the UN System* (Boulder: Lynne Rienner, 2003); Chandra Likha Sriram and Karin Wermester (eds.), *From Promise to Practice: Strenghtening UN Capacities for the Prevention of Violent Conflict* (Boulder CO: Lynne Rienner, 2003); David A Hamburg, *Preventing Genocide: Practical Steps Toward Early Detection and Effective Prevention* (Boulder: Paradigm, 2008).

22 Bruce W. Jentleson, 'Preventive Diplomacy: a conceptual and analytic framework', in Bruce W Jentleson (ed.), *Opportunities Missed, Opportunities Seized: Preventive Diplomacy in the Post-Cold War World* (Lanham MD: Rowman & Littlefield, 2000), p. 10.

23 David Carment and Albrecht Schnabel, 'Conflict Prevention – Taking Stock', in David Carment and Albrecht Schnabel (eds.), *Conflict Prevention: Path to Peace or Grand Illusion?*, p. 15.

24 John G. Cockell, 'Early Warning Analysis and Policy Planning in UN Preventive Action', in David Carment and Albrecht Schnabel (eds.), *Conflict Prevention: Path to Peace or Grand Illusion?*, p. 186.

25 Peter Wallensteen, 'Reassessing Recent Conflicts: Direct vs Structural Prevention', in Fen Osler Hampson and David M Malone (eds.), *From Reaction to Conflict Prevention: Opportunities for the UN System* (Boulder CO: Lynne Rienner, 2004), p. 214.

26 Hamburg and Vance, *Preventing Deadly Conflict*, p. 69.

preventive actors within the UN, Sriram and Wermester premise the efficacy of such actors in terms of their capacity to address root causes.[27]

In relation specifically to the crime of genocide, Hamburg uses the public health analogy to illustrate the root cause approach. Prevention, he argues,

> involves identifying an ailing nation's specific problem(s) and employing evidence-based responses toward resolving them. Some measures, such as early, skilful, and respectful preventive diplomacy, can quickly show beneficial results, just as expert care of a sprained ankle results in rapid healing and prevents an injury from getting equitable, socioeconomic infrastructure, take longer to apply and even longer to show results, but the effects are likely to be lasting and pervasive, just as promoting a healthy lifestyle and environment can achieve much better health for a society that is accustomed to health-damaging habits such as cigarette smoking.[28]

What this quote illustrates is that structural prevention not only entails identifying and addressing the root causes of genocide, but that the responsibility for identifying such problems as well as prescribing action to remedy them lies with actors external to the places of concern. Much like the relationship between a doctor and a patient, conceptual approaches to structural prevention demonstrate distinctions between prevention actors and prevention recipients.

Since the end of the Cold War there has clearly been a growing interest in the prevention of intrastate conflict and mass atrocities. In that time the concept of prevention evolved and took shape by distinguishing two main approaches – direct prevention and structural prevention. The concept of structural prevention is premised on the identification and amelioration of the root causes of potential deadly violence. Understanding these underlying causes is clearly a crucial dimension in efforts to prevent violent conflict and mass atrocities of which such root causes are antecedents. Moreover, the growing capacity of regional and international actors in implementing preventive strategies has indeed resulted in successful cases of conflict/violence aversion.[29] Despite

---

27 Chandra Likha Sriram and Karin Wermester 'Preventive Action at the United Nations: From Promise to Practice?' in Fen Osler Hampson and David M Malone (eds.), *From Reaction to Conflict Prevention* (Boulder CO: Lynne Rienner, 2003), p. 288.

28 Hamburg, *Preventing Genocide*, p. 5.

29 Two examples are the OSCE's (formerly CSCE) mediation in Latvia in 1992, and the UN's preventive deployment in Macedonia between 1995 and 1999.

this, the concept of structural prevention is limited in its neglect to consider and incorporate domestic sources of resilience that hold valuable insights into the process of the management of diversity and the mitigation of risk.

The Limitations of Structural Prevention

By framing structural prevention as the identification and addressing of root causes, researchers and policy makers are faced with two major limitations. First, this notion of prevention assumes that the existence of root causes will necessarily result in a violent outcome if not dealt with, suggesting a linear connection between cause and outcome. Second, the public health model approach to long term prevention has encouraged a tendency towards external diagnosis and prognosis, prioritising the role of international actors in determining what the root causes of potential conflict are, as well as determining the correct strategies to deal with them. These limitations exclude a consideration of the local and national capacities for building resilience to the risk that such root causes pose, and as a consequence overlook the role that domestic actors play in the prevention of mass atrocities. Such an oversight leads to the possibility of not only wasting limited resources on expensive, externally-driven strategies, but it also risks undermining local capacities that already exist. These limitations will be explored in greater detail below.

Assuming Linear Inevitability

Premising prevention on the identification and removal of root causes assumes a linear relationship between cause and outcome – that such violence will inevitably occur if the root causes are not dealt with. It suggests that the existence of conditions that amount to root causes necessitates their removal, and that doing so will result in the prevention of mass atrocities. Often the linear relationship between cause and violent outcome is suggested through the positioning of root causes as the first of a number of stages, or phases, eventually culminating in violence. The stages of conflict typically progress from 'pre-violence', or 'potential violence' – representing the existence of root causes – then usually passes through periods of 'gestation' and 'escalation'.[30] While there are

30 Rasheed Draman, 'Conflict Prevention in Africa: Establishing Conditions and Institutions conducive to durable Peace', in: David Carment and Albrecht Schabel (eds.), *Conflict Prevention: Path to Peace or Grand Illusion?* (Tokyo: United Nations University Press, 2003), p. 234; Donald Rothchild, 'Third-party incentives and the phases of conflict prevention',

caveats,[31] the assumption of a linear relationship between cause and outcome nonetheless remains. Framing structural prevention within a 'conflict continuum'[32] or a 'temporal continuum'[33] invites a certain policy logic – that not only is it better to tackle these problems earlier rather than later, but that not tackling such problems at an early stage will inevitably result in the need to deal with more complex challenges later on. Dress and Rosemblum-Kumar advocate the need to 'develop interventions aimed at poverty alleviation, social empowerment, and reducing horizontal inequality'.[34] Draman regards such early stage prevention by international actors (particularly the UN) as 'morally imperative', and crucial to ensuring the genie does not escape the bottle.[35] Once such root causes are known to exist, there is a need to act, lest these causes are allowed to progress from the stage of pre-violence to one of gestation.

However, just as some contend that preventive approaches in public health have the tendency to lead to over-diagnosis, there is a similar risk that approaches to conflict and mass atrocities prevention may conclude wrongly that violent outcomes are inevitable without action. Indeed this assumption holds little currency in the research by scholars of genocide and mass atrocities – here there is general consensus on the argument that long-term structural preconditions to such violence (otherwise referred to as root causes) have at best a tenuous causal link with mass violence. While they create the conditions that are conducive to atrocities, these preconditions are not sufficient in and of

---

in: Chandra Lekha Sriram and Karin Wermester (eds.), *From Promise to Practice: Strengthening UN Capacities for the Prevention of Violent Conflict* (Boulder, London: Lynne Rienner, 2003), pp. 44–56; Gregory H. Stanton, Gregory, *The 8 Stages of Genocide*, 1996, http://www.genocidewatch.org/images/8StagesBriefingpaper.pdf, accessed 23 November 2012.

31 For example, the articulation of phases is not meant to be a restrictive guide (See, for example, Sriram and Wermester, *From Promise to Practice*, 20–29), and each episode of conflict or mass violence has its own unique contextually-specific set of drivers.

32 Tobi P. Dress, and Gay Rosenblum-Kumar, 'Deconstructing Prevention: A Systems Approach to Mitigating Violent Conflict', in Fen Osler Hampson and David M. Malone (eds.), *From Reaction to Conflict Prevention: Opportunities for the UN System* (Boulder: Lynne Rienner, 2003), p. 241.

33 Andrea Kathryn Talentino, 'Evaluating Success and Failure: Conflict Prevention in Cambodia and Bosnia', in David Carment and Albrecht Schnabel (eds.), *Conflict Prevention: Path to Peace or Grand Illusion?* (Tokyo: United Nations University Press, 2003), p. 71.

34 Dress and Rosenblum-Kumar, 'Deconstructing Prevention', p. 241.

35 Ibid. See also Jan Eliasson, 'Establishing Trust in the Healer: Preventive Diplomacy and the Future of the United Nations', in Kevin Cahill (ed.), *Stopping Wars Before they Start: Preventive Diplomacy* (New York: Basic Books, 1996) p. 318.

themselves to directly cause such episodes of violence.[36] In fact, the perpetration of mass atrocities is rare – the exception rather than the norm, as Bartoli, Ogata and Stanton state: 'Most states do not commit genocide most of the time. State interest normally does not coincide with genocidal intent, and the predisposition of governments is generally non-genocidal'.[37] According to Genocide Watch's survey of countries that experienced significant risk of genocidal violence between 1945 and 2008,[38] for every country that reached stage seven (genocidal, as well as non-genocidal massacres), there were two that did not.[39] Chirot and McCauley point out that genocide, a crime that occurs predominantly during violent conflict, is 'far less common than warfare itself'.[40] Therefore, it is clear that risk often exists without inevitably resulting in the perpetration of mass atrocities. There is a gap between the assumptions embedded in the concept of structural prevention, and the findings of the research conducted on the causes of mass atrocities.

To suggest that it is necessary to ameliorate such root causes once they have been identified, indeed runs counter to what is known about the long term causes of mass atrocities. If, as the scholarship on comparative genocide studies suggests, the existence of root causes does not indicate an inevitable violent outcome, what other outcomes are common? In countries that contain these root causes, the local dynamics and processes that steer them away from violent outcomes are clearly worthy of investigation, and are potentially a valuable insight into national sources of resilience that deter violent outcomes. As the Secretary-General pointed out in the 2009 report on R2P, how states develop their own capacity to prevent genocide and mass atrocities, needs to be better understood.[41]

36 See, for example, Helen Fein, *Accounting for Genocide* (New York: The Free Press, 1979); Barbara Harff, 'No Lessons Learned from the Holocaust? Assessing the Risks of Genocide and Political Mass Murder since 1955' *The American Political Science Review* 97/1: 57–73 (2003); Leo Kuper, *Genocide: Its Political Use in the 20th Century* (New Haven: Yale University Press, 1981); Jacques Semelin, *Purify and Destroy*.

37 Andrea Bartoli, Tetsushi Ogata and Gregory H. Stanton, 'Emerging Paradigms in Genocide Prevention', *Genocide Prevention* (Bern: Federal Department of Foreign Affairs, Confederation of Switzerland, 2009), p. 21.

38 Stage four or above, according to Stanton's 'Eight Stages of Genocide'.

39 Genocide Prevention Advisory Network, 'Genocides, Politicides, and Other Mass Murder Since 1945 With Stages in 2008', 2009, www.gpanet.org/content/genocides-politicides-and-other-mass-murder-1945-stages-2008, accessed 24 November 2012.

40 Daniel Chirot and Clark McCauley *Why Not Kill Them All?* (Princeton: Princeton University Press, 2006), p. 95.

41 A/63/677, p. 13.

In fact, such positive dynamics are also largely overlooked in comparative genocide studies. Despite the consensus on the fact high risk prevalence is not sufficient for the perpetration of mass violence, very little research has been conducted into the reasons why many states that contain these root causes have *not* resulted in violent outcomes. Such scholarship itself has a tendency to focus on 'what goes wrong'. Methodologically, the approach amongst most comparative genocide scholars is to select a number of cases of past genocides and to examine their contributing factors – those factors that are common across cases then form the theoretical bases found in comparative genocide studies.[42] While such research has yielded valuable knowledge on the antecedents of past genocides, very little knowledge has been gained on why the risk posed by these antecedents does not lead to mass atrocities in many cases. Such knowledge is clearly valuable for the long-term prevention of genocide and other mass atrocities.

Emphasis on International Actors

The oversight of understanding regarding the positive processes that build resilience is also apparent in the way that research and preventive strategies have been shepherded principally by international actors, a tendency that – in public health parlance – is characterised by external diagnosis and prognosis. In fact, research and policy-making on conflict/atrocities prevention is almost entirely focussed on the role of international actors, consequently neglecting what states and communities already do themselves to manage diversity and mitigate risk. Principal proponents of prevention include the United Nations, regional organisations, international NGOs and wealthy nations acting as

42 See, for example, Helen Fein, *Accounting for Genocide* (New York: The Free Press, 1979); Ben Kiernan, *Blood and Soil: A World History of Genocide and Extermination from Sparta to Darfur* (Melbourne: Melbourne University Press, 2005); Robert Melson, *Revolution and Genocide: On the Origins of the Armenian Genocide and the Holocaust* (Chicago: University of Chicago Press, 1992); and Semelin, *Purify and Destroy*. While negative cases (non-genocidal cases) are sometimes referred to, they are never included as one of the principal analytical subjects. For a discussion on the methodological limitations of such approaches, see Stephen McLoughlin and Deborah Mayersen, 'Reconsidering Root Causes: A New Framework for the Prevention of Genocide and Mass Atrocities' in Bert Ingelaere, Stephan Parmentier, Jacques Haers and Barbara Segaert (eds.), *Genocide, Risk and Resilience: An Interdisciplinary Approach* (Basingstoke: Palgrave, 2013); and Scott Strauss, 'Retreating from the Brink: Theorizing Mass Violence and the Dynamics of Restraint,' *Perspectives on Politics* 10/2: 343–362 (2012).

donors. It is rare in the literature on structural prevention to consider the role of local and national actors. This does not mean that international actors do not make valuable and often crucial contributions in terms of structural prevention. Rather, the role of such actors is discussed without considering what local and national actors might already be doing to mitigate the risk of mass violence. Consequently, the role international actors play in prevention is not discussed in terms of how they may support processes of risk mitigation.

In the literature on structural prevention, key prevention actors are almost always external to the places deemed to be at risk. Indeed, some definitions of prevention explicitly exclude local and national actors in places of concern.[43] Other sources, in discussing prevention actors, typically identify the United Nations, regional organisations, international NGOs and western liberal-democratic states as the key players. Local communities and national governments in places where preventive strategies are directed are mentioned largely in passing, if at all.[44] This is reflected in the key (mostly edited) publications on prevention that have appeared over the last decade – in chapters devoted to the role of preventive actors, international and regional organisations are featured prominently, as are (albeit to a lesser extent) national external actors and international NGOs.[45] There are a few exceptions to this. For example, Dress

43 See, for example, Emma J. Stewart, *The European Union and Conflict Prevention: Policy Evolution and Outcome* (New Brunswick USA: Transaction, 2005), p. 13; Wallensteen, 'Reassessing Recent Conflicts', p. 214.

44 See, for example, Carment and Schnabel, 'Conflict Prevention – Taking Stock', pp. 18–20; Fen Osler Hampson, Fen Osler, Karin Wermester & David M. Malone,'Introduction: Making Conflict Prevention a Priority', in Fen Osler Hampson and David M. Malone (eds.), *From Reaction to Conflict Prevention: Opportunities for the UN System* (Boulder: Lynne Rienner, 2003), pp. 8–10; Michael S. Lund, 'From Lessons to Action', in Fen Osler Hampson and David Malone (eds.), *From Reaction to Conflict Prevention: Opportunities for the UN System* (Boulder: Lynne Rienner, 2003), pp. 159–163; Mukesh Kapila and Karin Wermester, 'Development and Conflict: New Approaches in the United Kingdom', in Fen Osler Hampson and David M. Malone (eds.), *From Reaction to Conflict Prevention: Opportunities for the un System* (Boulder: Lynne Rienner, 2003), p. 299; Sriram and Wermester, 'Preventive Action at the United Nations', p. 393; Hamburg, *Preventing Genocide*, pp. 5–6.

45 David Carment and Albrecht Schnabel (eds.), *Conflict Prevention: From Rhetoric to Reality* (Lanham: Lexington Books, 2003); Fen Osler Hampson and David M Malone (eds.), *From Reaction to Conflict Prevention: Opportunities for the UN System* (Boulder: Lynne Rienner, 2003); Chandra Likha Sriram, and Karin Wermester (eds.), *From Promise to Practice: Strenghtening UN Capacities for the Prevention of Violent Conflict* (Boulder CO: Lynne Rienner, 2003); Hamburg, *Preventing Genocide.*

and Rosenblum-Kumar stress there is a need to consider the way that a *broad* spectrum of preventive actors – from local to international – can improve the capacity for such action. Chirot and McCauley go further by examining a range of state policies aimed at managing tension between identity groups in countries, such as India, Switzerland and Canada, where ethnic and religious diversity exist.[46] Despite these exceptions, there is a tendency in the academic literature to regard the business of identifying and addressing root causes as the concern principally of external actors. Consequently, overlooking domestic examples of success in the effective management of risk and diversity accentuates the culture of external diagnosis and trouble-shooting, and gives preventive action a paternal character, particularly when it is rare for such research to consider what is already happening in such places to prevent conflict and mass atrocities.

Even when the parlance of prevention shifts to incorporate greater state responsibility, there remains much ambiguity about what state responsibility actually looks like, particularly in states where numerous risk factors are present. State responsibility is repeatedly stressed in numerous UN reports on prevention. Kofi Annan's first report on prevention stated, 'the primary responsibility for conflict prevention rests with national governments, with civil society playing an important role'.[47] Subsequent reports by both Annan and Ban Ki-moon echoed this.[48] However, there is almost no guidance in the literature on prevention about how to observe successful cases of responsibility being carried out. Much is known about the absence of responsibility, but little about its presence. The three-pillar strategy of the principle, arising from the 2005 World Summit Outcome document, clearly identified state responsibility as having primary importance when it comes to prevention. This was an endorsement of a principle for the prevention of mass atrocities that does not assume third party diagnosis and prognosis as the starting point. Yet it is surprising that there is very little research that investigates what states do to effectively carry out this responsibility, and little attention paid to the limited research that already exists, despite Ban Ki-moon's call for such an approach: 'More research and analysis is needed on why one society plunges into mass violence while its neighbours remain relatively stable…'[49]

46 Chirot and McCauley, *Why Not Kill Them All?* p. 155.

47 A/55/985, p. 2.

48 A/60/891, p. 1; S/2008/18, p. 2; A/63/677, p. 8.

49 A/63/677, p. 10.

Developing a Framework for Understanding the Prevention of Mass Atrocities

I argue the concept of prevention needs to be broadened to incorporate not only an understanding of root causes, but also an understanding of sources of resilience. The purpose of this is to provide an analytical model that provides a lens not only on root causes, but the dynamics and processes within states and communities that already have some measure of success at mitigating the risk inherent in such root causes. An approach to prevention that incorporates resilience starts with the idea that in states that display risk of mass atrocities, local and national actors have the capacity to develop strategies to manage this risk. Although there may be cases where external support is needed with structural prevention, such support is best utilized when investing in processes of risk mitigation that have been initiated by domestic actors. In this sense, understanding the extent that domestic sources of resilience are able to mitigate the risk of mass atrocities becomes a valuable dimension of structural prevention.[50] In order to incorporate resilience into a framework for long-term prevention, I draw on three questions:

1. What coping and support mechanisms exist – at a local and national level – to manage the risk of mass atrocities in societies?
2. How do political and social institutions absorb crises?
3. How do these institutions and communities adapt and improve their management of diversity and mitigation of risk over time so that stability is enhanced?

The underlying logic of these questions flows from the observation that no country is entirely resistant to risk.[51] Given this, long term prevention needs to be premised on an understanding of what local and national actors do to build resilience and mitigate the risk that is present. As Ban Ki-moon has stated in his 2013 report on R2P, building resilience in order to deal with the particular configurations of risk unique to each country helps to enable domestic actors to 'navigate periods of stress.'[52] How states navigate through stresses is the

50 Alex J. Bellamy, 'Mass Atrocities and Armed Conflict: Links, Distinctions and Implications for the Responsibility to Prevent', *The Stanley Foundation: Policy Analysis Brief* (2011), p. 11; Ban Ki-moon, *State Responsibility and Prevention*, p. 8.

51 Ban Ki-moon, *Responsibility to Protect: State Responsibility and Prevention*, A/67/929-S/2013/399, 9 July 2013, p. 6.

52 Ibid, p. 7.

focus of the first question; the incorporation and understanding of internal coping and support mechanisms is a logical starting point in understanding what states at risk already do to mitigate the risk of mass atrocities. The UN also draws on resilience in its approaches to disaster reduction. International Strategy for Disaster Reduction defines resilience as 'the ability of a system, community or society exposed to hazards to resist, absorb, accommodate and to recover from the effects of a hazard in a timely and efficient manner'.[53] The second question is premised on the fact that the turning point in the causal path to the perpetration of mass atrocities is upheaval, or crisis. Given this, one test of a country's resilience is its ability to respond during acutely challenging circumstances. Similar questions are asked in ecological systems thinking, where resilience is defined by one source as 'the capacity of a system to absorb shocks and disturbance and still maintain function'.[54] One important dimension of resilient societies is how effectively they (where such instances have occurred) have absorbed the 'shock and disturbance' of upheavals including economic crises, natural disasters, military coups and revolutions. The long term resilience of states is not only premised on how well they are able to absorb the shocks of upheaval, but also the extent to which they are able to adapt and build stability in a regional and global environment subject to constant change. Thus the third question seeks to understand how local and national actors adapt to challenge over long periods of time, in regional and international contexts that are subject to constant change. These questions are designed to underscore the various ways that sources of resilience in states mitigate the risk of mass atrocities; and the framework below represents a synthesis of the research conducted on the key structural risk factors (or root causes) on the one hand, and key mitigating factors on the other.

These questions can be addressed using a two-tiered framework that identifies both long-term risk factors and sources of resilience. Such a framework extends the root cause paradigm through its second tier, which casts a lens over domestic processes of risk mitigation. The first tier synthesizes research conducted into the causes of genocide and other mass atrocities. Scholarship in the field of comparative genocide studies as well as on the early warning and long term risk of genocide and genocide-like violence commonly identify a range of

53 The United Nations Office for Disaster Risk Reduction, 'Terminology', http://www.unisdr.org/we/inform/terminology#letter-r, (2013), accessed 4 March 2013.

54 Fikret Berkes and Carl Folke, 'Linking Social and Ecological Systems for Resilience and Sustainability', in Fikret Berkes and Carl Folk (eds.), *Linking Social and Ecological Systems. Management Practices and Social Mechanisms for Building Resilience* (Cambridge: Cambridge University Press, 1998), p. 12.

root causes (or risk factors) of social, political and economic dimensions. These include identity-based division;[55] state-based discrimination;[56] past atrocities;[57] issues of governance, including widespread human rights violations, limited rule of law, absence of or weak democracy;[58] and finally, low integration into the world economy,[59] and inequality of wealth and opportunity.[60]

The second tier contains a broad set of risk mitigation factors, initiated by local and national actors. Due to the smaller pool of research, such factors are necessarily illustrative of the processes of risk mitigation that exist. Nevertheless, they offer an adequate starting point for observing the complex and contextually specific relationship between risk and resilience. For instance, implementing policies that ensure social cohesion and promote the benefits of diversity can create a base from which a memory of stability rather than a memory of violence is formed. Indeed, religious or ethnic diversity in a society is not a problem in itself – problems arising from diversity stem from largely from government policies that discriminate along social lines.[61]

A strong civil society can also foster social cohesion. The extent of activity, and the influence that civil society groups have are indications of the level of inclusion at a grass roots level.[62] Organisations as varied as unions, human

55 Stanton, *The Eight Stages*; Kuper, *Genocide*, pp. 57–58; Semelin, *Purify and Destroy*, pp. 22–30.

56 Barbara Harff, 'Assessing Global Risks of Genocide and Politicide', in Joseph J. Hewitt, Jonathan Wilkenfeld, and Ted Robert Gurr (eds.), *Peace and Conflict 2012* (Boulder, CA: Paradigm, 2012), p. 54; Raul Hilberg, *The Destruction of the European Jews* (New York: Holmes and Meier Publishers, 1985), p. 83; Adam Jones, *Genocide: A Comprehensive Introduction* (Oxon: Routledge, 2006), p. 391.

57 Harff, 'No Lessons Learnt', p. 63, Jones, *Genocide*, p. 389.

58 Jack A. Goldstone, Robert H. Bates, Ted Robert Gurr, Michael Lustik, Monty G Marshall, Jay Ulfelder & Mark Woodward, 'A Global Forecasting Model of Political Instability', *American Journal of Political Science* 54/1:190–208 (2010); Matthew Krain, 'Democracy, Internal War, and State-Sponsored Mass Murder', *Human Rights Review*, 1/3: 1–24 (2000); R. J. Rummel, *Death By Government* (New Brunswick: Transaction Publishers, 1994).

59 Harff, 'No Lessons Learnt, p. 64.

60 Frances Stewart, 'Horizontal Inequalities and Conflict: An Introduction and some Hypotheses', in Frances Stewart (ed.), *Horizontal Inequalities and Conflict: Understanding Group Violence in Multiethnic Societies* (New York: Palgrave Macmillan, 2008).

61 Stanton, *The Eight Stages*; Jack A. Goldstone, Robert H. Bates, Ted Robert Gurr, Michael Lustik, Monty G Marshall, Jay Ulfelder & Mark Woodward, 'A Global Forecasting Model of Political Instability', *American Journal of Political Science* 54/1:190–208 (2010).

62 Albrecht Schnabel, 'Human Security and Conflict Prevention', in David Carment and Albrecht Schnabel (eds.), *Conflict Prevention from Rhetoric to Reality, Volume 2: Opportunities and Innovations* (Lanham: Lexington Books, 2004), p. 123.

rights groups, religious organisations and welfare groups all play a valuable role in campaigning against injustices and in favour of safety nets, and providing support to those who need it. In Zambia, for example, a coalition of civil society organisations formed the groundswell of a new political movement that challenged the authority of the longstanding authoritarian government, and became a leading player in the burgeoning era of multi-party democracy in the early 1990s.[63]

Good governance, including strong rule of law, a democratic system that avoids factionalism, and inclusive leadership all have a protective effect on the risk of mass atrocities. It is premised on the rule of law, defined as the accountability of all people and institutions (both public and private) to laws that are promoted with transparency, equitably applied and independently arbitrated.[64] Bearing in mind that no state is entirely free of discrimination, an independent judiciary gives citizens the chance to seek justice non-violently, and to redress any potential wrongs. A strong rule of law enables the provision of fair laws that do not disadvantage some groups over others, and discourages the need to look outside due process for justice.[65] Adherence to the rule of law provides accountability even in the face of discriminatory policies from governments, ensuring a safety net for minority groups. In addition, strong rule of law ensures that institutions of public service and protection are under the control of civilians, and are 'competent, honest and accountable'.[66] In fact, as Fine argues, there is very little that either local or international actors can do in relation to prevention, 'in the absence of a political, economic and civil environment that honours at least some major rules of law and practices the rudiments of public discourse'.[67] Rule of law is the foundation of stable and prosperous democratic states.

A transparent and functioning democratic system is arguably the strongest protective factor against mass atrocities, a claim that is shared by both large N and case-study-based qualitative research. A rise in the level of democracy

63 Miles Larmer, 'Zambia Since 1990: Paradoxes of Democratic Transition', in Abdul Raufu Mustapha and Lindsay Whitfield (eds,), *Turning Points in African Democracy* (Cumbria: James Currey, 2009), pp. 118–119.

64 United Nations, 'United Nations and the Rule of Law', 2014, http://www.un.org/en/ruleoflaw/, accessed 19 May, 2014.

65 A/67/929, p. 11.

66 *Preventing Deadly Conflict*, p. xxxiv.

67 Keitha Sapsin Fine, 'Fragile Stability and Change: Understanding Conflict during the Transitions in East Central Europe', in Abram Chayes and Antonia Handler Chayes (eds.), *Preventing Conflict in the Post-Communist World: Mobilizing International and Regional Organizations* (Washington DC: The Brookings Institution, 1996), p. 543.

lowers the risk of war and ensuing atrocities.[68] According to the PITF, democratic regimes possess the resilience needed to cope with the 'myriad social, demographic, economic and environmental forces that are often cited as causes of political instability'.[69] In a separate study on regime type, level of democracy and conflict, Hegre et al argue that civil peace is greater, more just and more durable in democratic societies.[70] When political competition is fair and open, when opposition parties are robust and active, then the resilience and stability of a state is much higher. Such competition is most resilient when it is absent of factionalism that may exacerbate any social difference that may be apparent. According to the UN Secretary-General, 'the diffusion and sharing of power can engender political pluralism, which promotes the peaceful coexistence of different interests'.[71] Such coexistence decreases the likelihood that dissenting groups and their interests will be marginalised, or will seek to fulfil their goals by taking up arms. A liberal democratic system has a positive effect on economic growth,[72] and economic growth in turn increases the political stability of a country.[73] In other words, the ability to adapt and improve is much stronger in states with multi-party democratic systems.

Inclusive leadership can also mitigate the risk of mass atrocities. Such leadership is characterized by inclusionary ideologies that transcend narrow identity-based divisions within countries. The promotion of an inclusive national identity, the equitable provision of public services and the inclusion of a broad representation of local and national elites are ways that inclusive leadership can promote the management of diversity. Such leadership is especially crucial in post-colonial states during the formative years of nation-building.[74]

Resilience also has an economic dimension, including trade openness, equality of economic opportunity and sustained economic growth. Evidence of trade openness as a protective factors stems from the work of Barbara Harff

68 Human Security Report Project, *Human Security Report*, p. 38.

69 Jack A. Goldstone, and Jay Ulfelder, 'How to Construct Stable Democracies', *The Washington Quarterly* 28/1: 9–20 (2004), p. 11.

70 Havard Hegre, Tanja Ellingsen, Scott Gates and Nils Petter Gleditsch, 'Toward a Democratic Civil Peace? Democracy, Political Change, and Civil War, 1816–1992', *The American Political Science Review* 95/1: 33–48 (2001), p. 44.

71 A/67/929, p. 9.

72 Yi Feng, 'Democracy, Political Stability and Economic Growth', *British Journal of Political Science* 27/39: 401–418 (1997), p. 413.

73 John B. Londregan and Keith T Poole, 'Poverty, the Coup Trap, and the Seizure of Executive Power' *World Politics* 42/2:151–183 (1990), p. 182.

74 See Stephen McLoughlin, *The Structural Prevention of Mass Atrocities: Understanding Risk and Resilience* (Oxon: Routledge, 2014), pp. 157–159.

and the PITF – they noted that the more interdependent a country is with others, the less likely it is that leaders from that country will commit genocide or politicide.[75] In addition equitable access to employment and the development of human skill and capacity promotes greater well-being, greater stability, and mitigates the risk of mass atrocities, by dampening the resentment that often arises from economic marginalisation.[76] Sustained economic growth also mitigates the risk of mass atrocities. The Human Security report concluded that conflict decrease as per capita income rises. Supporting this is the economic transformation that occurred in East Asia in the post-Vietnam War period from the late 1970s to the 1990s. In this time, average incomes increased by almost 100 per cent, while the number of conflicts decreased by nearly half.[77] Clearly there is a correlation between economic growth, primarily reflected in rising incomes, and the avoidance of civil war and atrocities, making it an important contributing factor to political stability and resilience.

The research used to develop these mitigating factors demonstrates that the key players in the effective long term prevention of mass atrocities are local and national actors. Instead of aiming to eradicate root causes, these actors use strategies that seek to manage the tensions inherent in such risk – a process which is dynamic and ongoing. Although the research cited here is not exhaustive, it provides a broad lens over the complex interplay between risk and mitigation, and in doing so, premises long term prevention in an understanding of what states at risk are already doing to build resilience. Preventive strategies which overlook such dynamics run the risk of undermining local and national sources of resilience, potentially impeding a country's ability to sustain long term prevention on its own terms. It also has the potential to increase a country's dependence on external actors and externally-driven strategies for its internal stability. Overlooking sources of resilience also devalues past cases of success in risk mitigation – cases which could provide insights for future preventive efforts. With the various findings represented in the research above, we can begin to build a general picture of

---

75 Harff, 'No Lessons Learnt', p. 65; Barbara Harff, 'Assessing Global Risks of Genocide and Politicide: A Global Watch List for 2012', in J Joseph Hewitt, Jonathan Wilkenfeld and Ted Robert Gurr (eds.), *Peace and Conflict 2012* (Boulder CA: Paradigm, 2012), p. 54; Goldstone et al., 'A Global Forecasting Model'.

76 Ban Ki-moon, *State Responsibility and Prevention*, p. 11; Hamburg and Vance, *Preventing Deadly Conflict*, p. 84; Arnim Langer, 'When do Horizontal Conflicts Lead to Conflict? Lessons from a Comparative Study of Ghana and Côte d'Ivoire', in Frances Stewart (ed.), *Horizontal Inequalities and Conflict: Understanding Group Violence in Multiethnic Societies* (Basingstoke: Palgrave, 2008), pp. 163–189.

77 Human Security Report Project, *Human Security Report* p. 52.

the various ways that diversity is managed, and the risk inherent in the presence of root causes is mitigated through strategies that foster social cohesion, good governance and relative economic strength. Of course, this framework is not without its limitations. Because it synthesises a very small pool of research, the list of factors is not exhaustive – inevitably there are gaps in our knowledge about the comprehensive ranges of factors which mitigate the risk of mass atrocities. As such, the framework is best utilised as a guide, rather than a restrictive lens. Nevertheless, the broadness of the categories allows for the examination of a diverse range of dynamics and processes that build stability and resilience over time.

Conclusion

This article challenges the commonly held notion of structural prevention, specifically in relation to mass atrocities. It argues that the way structural prevention is commonly conceptualised is limited – premising prevention solely on the identification and amelioration of root causes is problematic in two ways. It assumes that there is a linear inevitability between cause and violent outcome, and it prioritises the role of international actors in determining what the root causes are and how to deal with them. Research into the root causes of genocide and other mass atrocities does not support the idea of causal inevitability – root causes, or preconditions are necessary but not sufficient factors for such violent outcomes. Despite this, there is very little interest in why mass atrocities do not occur, especially in countries that are deemed at risk. This article argues that investigating why mass atrocities do not occur provides important insights into the prevention of mass atrocities that the concept does not currently incorporate. What is needed is a broader focus – one which adopts a lens seeking to understand not only what risk factors, or root causes are present, but also what the sources of resilience are, and how they mitigate risk. This is an approach which currently receives little attention, both by researchers of genocide and mass atrocities, and by key prevention actors. In response to this apparent oversight, an alternative framework is presented, which provides a lens to the complex relationship between risk and resilience in relation to mass atrocities. While it may be true that an ounce of prevention is worth a pound of cure,[78] when the key preventive actors are deemed to be external to the places where prevention is carried out, the costs involved can often be prohibitively high. For

78 See, for example *Preventing Deadly Conflict*, p. xlvi.

structural prevention strategies, the political will needed to mobilise investment in preventive strategies becomes challenging when a non-event at some non-determined time in the future is the outcome. There is little evidence that the will to finance such strategies will materialise.[79] When tensions escalate to the point where direct preventive strategies (such as preventive diplomacy and preventive deployments of peace keepers) are needed to avert a likely path to violence, such strategies remain controversial, and the international consensus needed to enact them is often absent.[80]

Broadening the conceptual lens of structural prevention overcomes these limitations in two key ways. It treats seemingly static structural features related to potential mass atrocities as context-specific, dynamic and indicative of not one narrow and inevitable outcome, but of a range of possibilities.[81] A greater understanding of the complexities of risk and resilience within communities and states then allows for the development of a repository of knowledge that then accounts for – with the help of this framework – the myriad strategies and practices that local and national actors adopt to manage risk, by strengthening coping and support mechanisms, absorbing upheaval, and developing strategies to adapt to unfolding challenges. A recent example illustrating how experience in managing diversity can translate into lessons for prevention is the work of the Tanzanian National Committee in conducting an inter-faith workshop in Dar-es-Salaam. Roughly equal numbers of Christian and Muslims in Tanzania are a potential faultline for social division and violence.[82] The country's demographic characteristics are similar to Nigeria's, where protracted religious-based violence continues to occur.[83] Tanzania's proactive provision of a forum for dialogue provides an opportunity for domestic religious leaders to engage

---

79 See, for example, Edward Luck 'Prevention, Theory and Practice, in Fen Osler Hampson and David M. Malone (eds.) *From Reaction to Conflict Prevention: Opportunities for the UN System* (Boulder, CA: Lynne Rienner Publishers, 2002), pp. 257–258; Alex J. Bellamy, *Responsibility to Protect: The Global Effort to End Mass Atrocities* (Cambridge: Polity, 2009), p. 99.

80 See, for example, Jennifer M. Welsh, 'Turning Words Into Deeds? The Implementation of the 'Responsibility to Protect'', *Global Responsibility to Protect* 2/1–2: 149154 (2010), p. 153.

81 For more on the tendency to treat structural risk as static, see Brett R. O'Bannon, 'Monitoring the Frog in Africa: Conflict Early Warning with Structural Data', *Global Responsibility to Protect* 4/4: 449–474 (2012).

82 Office of the Special Adviser on the Prevention of Genocide, 'Work of the Office', 2014, http://www.un.org/en/preventgenocide/adviser/engagement_partners.shtml, accessed 14 May 2014.

83 Lissi Rasmussen, *Christian-Muslim Relations in Africa: The Cases of Northern Nigeria and Tanzania Compared* (London: British Academic Press, 1993).

in dialogue to offset any possibility of tensions escalating. The country is also able to draw on fifty years of peaceful relations between its religious communities, to consolidate inter-faith harmony into the future.[84] Extensive knowledge and practice of this kind would certainly serve to increase the repertoire of options for prevention. In addition, premising prevention on an understanding of what processes already work enables international actors – where needed – to provide a facilitative, rather than prescriptive role. Managing risk and building resilience takes prevention beyond the conceptual limitations which regarded the best outcome as a non-event. Instead, building resilience has many tangible benefits that build social cohesion, enhance good governance and foster equitable economic benefits – outcomes which are beneficial in and of themselves.

84 See McLoughlin, *The Structural Prevention of Mass Atrocities*, pp. 134–136.

PART 2

Investigating the Non-Occurrence of Genocide and Other Mass Atrocities

CHAPTER 4

International Affinity and the Prevention of Genocide: Implications for R2P

Manus I. Midlarsky
Rutgers University, New Brunswick
midlarsk@rci.rutgers.edu

Abstract

The question of the absence of genocides where they might have been expected is an important one; answering this question successfully can help establish the empirical validity or instead, disconfirmation, of proposed explanations for genocide's occurrence. Affinity of populations or governments (ethnoreligiously similar or ideologically sympathetic) with the power and influence to actively intervene or to provoke intervention on behalf of the victims is understood to be a major genocide preventive. Cases examined include a contrast between Greek survival and genocide of the Armenians in the Ottoman Empire, the absence of the genocide of Jews in Poland at the time of the Partitions, absence of genocide of the Irish Catholics by the British after the First World War, and a contrast between the absence of the Holocaust in the early stages of the Nazi occupation of Europe, but its presence upon the German invasion of Russia in 1941. Protection of threatened populations in peacetime but their extreme vulnerability in time of war is a paradox of the affinity condition. Implications of affinity for R2P are developed in the international propagation of the R2P norm and the deft use of the diplomacy in the service of protecting threatened populations.

Keywords

genocide – affinity – Jews – Ottoman Greeks – Irish Catholics

Introduction

The intriguing question of genocides that did not occur where they might have been expected is an important one; answering this question successfully can

 | DOI 10.1163/9789004299870_006

help establish the empirical validity or instead, disconfirmation, of proposed explanations for genocide's occurrence. If only cases of genocide are examined, then we are left with partial validation of a theory that has not been adequately exposed to the possibility of invalidation.

In *The Killing Trap*,[1] I examined two broad categories of 'dogs that didn't bark'. In the first, European allies of Nazi Germany in the Second World War were found to consist of two distinct sets: countries that collaborated with Germany's request for deportation of their Jewish citizens and those that did not. Countries that collaborated with Germany were found to have experienced territorial losses prior to their cooperation in Jewish annihilation. These countries were Vichy France, Italy, and Romania. Countries that prevented deportation of their Jewish citizens included Bulgaria[2] and Finland, both of which actually experienced territorial *expansions* prior to the Nazi requests for deportation.

The importance of prior losses in yielding genocide suggested a second overall category of 'dogs that didn't bark': countries within the domain of losses (as were Vichy France, Italy, and Romania), but that did not actually commit genocide, or collaborate with it. An additional variable, the existence of affine or supporting governments and populations is suggested to distinguish between countries within the domain of losses that, on the one hand, proceeded to commit genocide and on the other, countries which did not. This finding has considerable significance for efforts to implement the Responsibility to Protect (R2P) threatened populations.

The affinity variable is important for the would-be perpetrators, because the targeted victim should not be in a position to react effectively or be able to call upon effective help from like-minded or ethnoreligiously similar populations. The existence of such potential allies, if deemed to be sufficiently powerful or at least influential in the international arena, could deter genocidal activity by a potential victimizer, even within the domain of losses. Essentially, victim

1 Manus I. Midlarsky, *The Killing Trap: Genocide in the Twentieth Century* (Cambridge: Cambridge University Press, 2005). See also Manus I. Midlarsky, *Origins of Political Extremism: Mass Violence in the Twentieth Century and Beyond* (Cambridge: Cambridge University Press, 2011).

2 Although Bulgaria did save virtually its entire indigenous Jewish community, earlier Bulgaria did respond positively to the German request for deportation of the Thracian and Macedonian Jewish communities. Bulgaria was administering these territories without conferring Bulgarian citizenship on their populations. See Tzvetan Todorov, *The Fragility of Goodness: Why Bulgaria's Jews Survived the Holocaust*, trans. Arthur Denner (Princeton, NJ: Princeton University Press, 2001), p.158; Frederick Chary, *The Bulgarian Jews and the Final Solution, 1940–1944* (Pittsburgh: University of Pittsburgh Press, 1972), p. 127.

vulnerability, a necessary condition for genocide, has been reduced by the affinity condition.

However strong the genocidal impulse in a potential victimizer, a prudent realpolitik demands avoidance of the extreme risk of offending a large affine population or powerful government that can come to the aid of the victim. Of course, the fog of war strongly increases the likelihood of an imprudent realpolitik that can be genocidal, as we shall see.

Interestingly, the Ottoman Empire itself demonstrates the presence and absence of affinity but with respect to two separate populations, the Ottoman Greeks (ultimately expelled in 1922 in an exchange of populations after the failed invasion of Turkey by Greece) and the Armenians. The Holocaust is complex enough so that we will find the disappearance of the affinity condition associated with the rapidly worsening treatment of the European Jewish population. In addition to experiencing loss, a requirement for the cases to be examined here is that potential perpetrators must have been keenly aware of the genocidal choice as a policy option, preferably in their own past experience.

These considerations lead to the examination of the Ottoman Empire in its very different treatment of Armenians and Greeks, and Nazi Germany before and after the invasion of the Soviet Union. Here the behavior of perpetrators differs over space (Ottoman Empire) and over time (Nazi Germany). To complete the analysis, two non-genocidal potential victimizers are chosen: late 18th century Poland, and the British in Ireland in 1916–21. Poland experienced extreme losses in the late 18th century, and clearly fulfills the remaining conditions for inclusion. As we shall see, the Poles recognized the availability of genocide, or at least widespread massacre as options. The British understood full well the possibility of genocide as a policy option. In addition to losses at the front in WWI, the British had the long, tortured history of Anglo-Irish relations, where the charge of genocidal behavior in Ireland was leveled against them during at least three historical moments.

Affinity and Genocide

To fix ideas, the absence of affinity is understood as the absence of any affine population or government (ethnoreligiously similar or ideologically sympathetic) with the power and influence to actively intervene or provoke intervention on behalf of the victims. Large neighboring kindred populations, especially if they appear to have political influence, can serve as protective umbrellas for threatened populations. The affinity does not have to be ethnoreligious, although in practice that is most frequently the case.

The actual presence of affinity can be signified in two ways. First, the *direct* protection of the potentially victimized population is available through the political influence of a neighboring affine population. Here the influence of highly placed Soviet Jews may have given pause to whatever German genocidal intent toward Jews may have existed prior to the June 1941 German invasion of the Soviet Union, as did an expanded and more powerful Greece protect ethnic Greeks in the Ottoman Empire. Second, an *indirect* two-tiered process may protect the potential victims. Here the threatened population is protected by a neighboring affine people or government, which *in itself* is protected by one or more great powers. Ethnic Greeks living in the Ottoman Empire were subject to both the direct and indirect varieties – the existence of 1) a larger (as of 1913) independent Greece, and 2) European great powers intent on its welfare -- thereby distinguishing Ottoman Greeks from the far more threatened Armenians without either protection.

Greeks in the Ottoman Empire

We begin with differential outcomes for Armenians and Greeks in the Ottoman Empire. Ethnic Greek communities had existed in Anatolia since ancient times. After the independence of Greece from the Ottomans in 1832,[3] these communities remained under Ottoman rule, numbering 1,792,206 Greeks out of a total of 18,520,016 Ottoman citizens in 1914, or nearly 10% of the total population.[4] Economically, of all ethnic groups including Turks, Arabs, Armenians, and Jews, the Greeks were predominant in 1912, controlling 43% of internal trade, 49% of industry and crafts and 44% of the professions.[5] Given this degree of prominence outweighing even the Armenians (roughly 1.3 million in number and averaging 25% economic dominance), and the obvious Ottoman preference for a religiously if not ethnically homogeneous society, why were the Greeks not targeted for extinction along with the Armenians, or even before them?

Beyond their size and economic importance, both communities were threatening to the Ottomans. While the Armenians established nationalist

3 Yorgos A. Kourvetaris and Betty A. Dobratz, *A Profile of Modern Greece in Search of Identity* (Oxford: Clarendon Press, 1987).

4 Stanford J. Shaw and Ezel Kural Shaw, *History of the Ottoman Empire and Modern Turkey, Volume II: Reform, Revolution, and Republic: The Rise of Modern Turkey, 1808–1975* (Cambridge: Cambridge University Press, 1977), p. 241.

5 Charles Issawi, *The Economic History of Turkey: 1800–1914* (Chicago: University of Chicago Press, 1980), p. 14.

groups and made separatist claims, the Greeks 'vastly expanded the activities of their *syllogues,* the political organizations they dubbed "literary and scientific" associations. With financial support from the Greek government and rich Greeks, ... the *syllogues* sprang up in all the major Ottoman localities inhabited by Greeks and added political momentum to the cultural awareness disseminated by the existing Greek educational institutions. In the Istanbul area alone the Greeks had over one hundred schools as early as 1878, and the number had nearly doubled by the end of the century.'[6]

While the Armenians were threatening in eastern Anatolia and to some extent in Constantinople, the Greeks were even more numerous in that city.[7] Perhaps most important, the Greek population was situated principally along the shores of the Black, Aegean and Mediterranean Seas, making it a prime target for subversion of the Ottomans by British and Russian naval emissaries. And the loyalties of Ottoman Greeks were highly suspect, even those of Greek deputies of the Ottoman Assembly who espoused widely held pan-Hellenic sympathies. In the widely quoted words of one of them, Boşo (Boussios) Efendi, 'I am as Ottoman as the [foreign dominated] Ottoman Bank.'[8] Armenians, Jews, and Maronite Catholics were far more welcome in the Ottoman administration than were Greeks.[9]

Threats of Ottoman Loss

The nineteenth century witnessed a virtually unmitigated series of disasters. Lost wars with Russia in 1829 and again in 1878 led to further shrinkage of the empire; this pattern of losses would continue into the early twentieth century. Between 1750 and 1914, the area of the empire had been almost halved, from 3,470,000 to 1,790,000 square miles.

Perhaps the greatest threat came from Greek adherence to the 'Great Idea' of incorporating all of the Mediterranean and Black Sea Greek communities into the Greek state. This was the overriding goal of Greek foreign policy from the inception of the state until the early 1920s. With Greek boundaries guaranteed by Great Britain, France and Russia in the three-power treaty of 1827,

6 Kemal H. Karpat, *The Politicization of Islam: Reconstructing Identity, State, Faith, and Community in the Late Ottoman State* (Oxford: Oxford University Press, 2001), pp. 324–25.

7 Shaw and Shaw, *History of the Ottoman Empire*, p. 242.

8 Quoted in Feroz Ahmad, 'The Late Ottoman Empire,' in Marian Kent, ed., *The Great Powers and the End of the Ottoman Empire* (London: George Allen and Unwin, 1984), p. 409.

9 Ilber Ortayli, 'Greeks in the Ottoman Administration During the Tanzimat Period,' in Dimitri Gondicas and Charles Issawi, eds., *Ottoman Greeks in the Age of Nationalism: Politics, Economy, and Society in the Nineteenth Century* (Princeton, NJ: Darwin Press, 1999), p. 165.

foreign policy concerns extended principally to the unincorporated Greek communities.[10]

Precisely because the Greek state initially incorporated only about 1/3 of ethnic Greeks in the greater Mediterranean region, the 'Great Idea' became the most pressing concern of Greek foreign policy. With a small nearby state agitating for incorporation of large numbers of Ottoman citizens, the Ottoman state must have perceived threats to its security that genocide could have averted.

There were two forms of threat to the integrity of the Ottoman state. The first threatened direct incorporation of territories inhabited principally by Greek communities. The classic expression of this form of threat (essentially the 'Great Idea') is that put forward in a speech by Ioannis Kolettis before the Constituent Assembly in Athens in 1844:

> The Kingdom of Greece is not Greece. [Greece] constitutes only one part, the smallest and poorest part. A Greek is not only a man who lives within this kingdom but also one who lives in Jannina, in Salonika, in Serres, in Adrianople, in Constantinople, in Smyrna, in Trebizond, in Crete, in Samos and in any land associated with Greek history or the Greek race. … There are two main centres of Hellenism: Athens, the capital of the Greek kingdom, [and] 'The City' [Istanbul], the dream and hope of all Greeks.[11]

The second possible strategy was less bellicose in its implications, but no less threatening to the social and religious coherence of the Ottoman state. Through the good offices of the Ottoman state, educational and cultural life of the Greek communities could expand at will, as we just saw in the near doubling of Greek schools between 1878 and the end of the 19th century in the Constantinople area alone. Paraphrasing the written views of Pavlos Karolidis, a Greek deputy in the Ottoman parliament of 1908 and a leading intellectual, Richard Clogg tells us that:

> From an economic point of view the Ottoman Empire already constituted a Greek state, since all economic life and many public works were carried out either by Greeks or by Greek capital. Greek and unbiased

10 Theodore A. Couloumbis, John A. Petropulos, and Harry J. Psomiades, *Foreign Interference in Greek Politics: A Historical Perspective* (New York: Pella Publishing Co., 1976), p. 22.

11 Quoted in Richard Clogg, 'The Greek *Millet* in the Ottoman Empire,' in Benhamin Braude and Bernard Lewis, eds., *Christians and Jews in the Ottoman Empire: The Functioning of a Plural Society*, Volume 1 (New York: Holmes and Meier, 1982), p. 193.

> foreign observers... deplored the hostile policy of Greece towards the Ottoman Empire, believing the Hellenization of the Ottoman state to be a simple matter of time. Although expressed with characteristic hyperbole such attitudes were by no means uncommon among both Greeks of the empire and Greeks of the kingdom.[12]

Thus, the Ottoman state itself would eventually fall into Greek hands by simply waiting for these socioeconomic processes to continue on their course.

Awareness of Genocidal Possibility

Given the massacres of Armenians in 1894–96 and again in 1909, leading to approximately 250,000 deaths, there was clear awareness of genocide as an option. That option, of course, was exercised in the deaths of over 1,000,000 Armenians during WWI.

Two Types of Affinity for the Greek Communities

Yet the Greek state prior to the First World War possessed another property that brings us to the first direct affinity condition protecting the Ottoman ethnic Greeks. The Greek state of 1914 was no longer the tiny truncated state of 1832, the year of its formation. As a result of the Balkan Wars, by 1913 Greece had acquired most of Macedonia, southern Epirus, many Aegean islands, and Crete, a major foreign policy goal for decades. Greece had increased its territory by 68% and its population from approximately 2.7 to 4.4 million. And 'for the first time since independence, Greece had expanded territorially as a result of its own efforts rather than through the good graces of the powers'.[13]

Thus, Greece had emerged as a significant Mediterranean power in its own right. If that power were to be activated, then the Ottomans would face another opponent in the context of the First World War and its grave uncertainties.

The second, the indirect form of the affinity condition, is that provided by great power(s) protection of the affine country. Even before the beginning of Greek statehood the great powers had been active in support of Greek independence. By the Treaty of London in 1827, Great Britain, France and Russia agreed to mediate the conflict between insurgent Greece and the Ottoman Empire. This policy led to the Battle of Navarino in October 1827 – the last major naval battle with opposing ships of sail – in which an allied fleet led by the British Admiral, Sir Edward Codrington, utterly destroyed a combined

12 Ibid, p. 197.

13 Couloumbis, Petropulos, and Psomiades, *Foreign Interference in Greek Politics*, p. 35.

Turco-Egyptian fleet.[14] The later treaty of May 1832 among the three European powers placed the new Greek state 'under their protection,' with Otto of Bavaria accepting the Greek throne.[15]

Throughout the 19th century, the European powers intervened in Greek affairs often to limit Greek interference in the Ottoman Empire that Britain, in particular, sought to preserve as a bulwark against Russian expansion. The British and French even occupied the port of Athens, Piraeus, in 1854 and 1857 in order to still the Greek efforts at generating turbulence in the Ottoman Empire.[16] Yet despite this and other limitations on Greek sovereignty (the treaty authorizing these interventions was ended only in 1923), the interests of Greece were protected and even advanced during this period. In 1864, the British ceded the Ionian islands to Greece, adding roughly a quarter of a million to the population.[17] In the aftermath of the Russo-Turkish War of 1877–78 and the ensuing Congress of Berlin, Greece was allowed to annex Thessaly and the Arta district of Epirus in 1881, adding a territory roughly 25% of pre-war Greece and a sizeable population.[18]

Although Britain was in the forefront of these activities, by 1913 France and Germany also sought to woo the expanding Greek state. For example, although the Greek government under pressure was prepared to yield one of the furthest of her conquests in the Second Balkan War, Kavala, both France and Germany supported its retention by Greece. Even Austria-Hungry represented by count Johann von Pallavicini in Constantinople, lectured the Turks on their 'foolish' persecution of the Greeks in Thrace.[19]

Culturally, all of the European powers felt indebted to the Greek heritage. Great Britain and France emphasized ancient Greek democracy, Germany, the archaeological and literary treasures of Greece, and Russia, its religious heritage of Orthodoxy. Given these political and cultural ties, wholesale attacks on the Ottoman Greeks would have profoundly angered not only the Entente powers, but Germany and Austria-Hungary as well, the allies upon whom the Ottomans were deeply dependent. Under these conditions genocide of the Ottoman Greeks simply was not a viable option.

---

14 Clogg, "The Greek *Millet* in the Ottoman Empire", p. 42.

15 Ibid, p. 47

16 Ibid, p. 57.

17 Ibid, p. 61.

18 Ibid, p. 73.

19 F.R. Bridge, 'The Habsburg Monarchy and the Ottoman Empire, 1900–18,' in Marian Kent, ed., *The Great Powers and the End of the Ottoman Empire* (London: George Allen and Unwin, 1984), p. 45.

Many Greeks, however, were massacred by the Turks, especially at Smyrna (today's Izmir) as the Greek army withdrew at the end of its headlong retreat from central Anatolia at the end of the Greco-Turkish War. Especially poorly treated were the Pontic Greeks in eastern Anatolia on the Black Sea. In 1920 and particularly in 1921 as the Greek army advanced, many Greeks were deported to the Mesopotamian desert as had the Armenians before them.[20]

Massacres most likely did take place at Amisos and other villages in the Pontus. Yet given the large numbers of surviving Greeks, especially relative to the small number of Armenian survivors, the massacres apparently were restricted to the Pontus, Smyrna, and selected other 'sensitive' regions. Despite having the recent experience of successfully killing most Anatolian Armenians, this experience did not extend into a similar policy for all Anatolian Greeks. At the end of the Greco-Turkish War, 1,500,000 Ottoman Greek refugees arrived in Greece.[21] When one adds to this total the Greeks of Constantinople who, by agreement, were not forced to flee, then the total number comes very close to the 1,792,000 Ottoman Greeks enumerated in 1914.

Jews in Eastern Europe

Having juxtaposed the radically different outcomes for two ethnic communities in the Ottoman Empire, we can now turn to a diachronic analysis of Jews in Eastern Europe before and after the German invasion of the Soviet Union in June 1941. According to Christopher Browning, 'the invasion of the Soviet Union would ultimately have an immensely radicalizing effect on Nazi Jewish policy, from which no Jews in the German empire – and those in Poland in particular – would be spared.'[22]

Threats of German Loss

Prior to mid-August 1941, the Nazis had not yet experienced the losses that would invoke their memory of the First World War and its domain of losses, which inspired their movement from the outset. The extraordinary difficulty of the invasion began to be manifested in mid-August, suggesting that the domain

20 Michael Llewellyn Smith, *Ionian Vision: Greece in Asia Minor, 1919–1922* (Ann Arbor: University of Michigan Press, 1998), p. 211.

21 Ibid, p. 319.

22 Christopher R. Browning, *The Origins of the Final Solution: The Evolution of Nazi Jewish Policy, September 1939-March 1942* (Jerusalem: Yad Vashem and Lincoln: University of Nebraska Press, 2004), p. 137.

of losses evoked at WWI's end would soon extend to the German armies in Russia.[23] Goebbels in his diaries reflects these deepening concerns about the future. On July 17, he noted 'the enemy's extraordinarily strong resistance on all fronts.' Within two days, he was describing the war as a war of survival between Bolshevism and Nazism. On July 26, Germany was described as fighting for her life.[24] On August 11, Franz Halder, chief of the German army's general staff, noted that 'the whole situation makes it increasingly plain that we have underestimated the Russian colossus.'[25] Thus, one would not expect a wholesale extermination policy to be implemented before August. Despite the great importance of these losses in later initiating the Holocaust, one can still see the impact of affinity in the relatively restrained (for the Nazis) early treatment of Jews in comparison with the brutality meted out to Poles immediately after the invasion of September 1939.[26]

Awareness of Genocidal Possibility

Clearly, Hitler was aware of the possibility of annihilating the Jews from at least two perspectives.[27] First, the vulnerability of Jewish communities was demonstrated emphatically by the pogroms of the Russian civil war, yielding in 1918–20 approximately 150,000 Jewish dead from direct murder and diseases induced by starvation.[28] Second, as Hitler on the eve of the 1939 invasion of Poland said to his Wehrmacht commanders justifying the killing of Polish civilians: 'Only thus shall we gain the living space [*Lebensraum*] which we need. Who after all, speaks today of the annihilation of the Armenians?'[29]

Perceived Jewish Affinity with the Soviets

Among those deeply influenced by the Bolshevik Revolution were Hitler and Himmler. With their firm belief in the veracity of the tsarist forgery *The Protocols of the Elders of Zion*, and the news from the East brought back by

23 Midlarsky, *The Killing Trap*, pp. 141–53.

24 Philippe Burrin, *Hitler and the Jews: The Genesis of the Holocaust*, trans. Patsy Southgate (London: Edward Arnold, 1994), pp.137–138.

25 Franz Halder, *The Halder Way Diary: 1939–1942* , Charles Burdick and Hans-Adolf Jacobson, eds. (Novalto, CA: Presidio, 1988) p. 506.

26 Midlarsky, *The Killing Trap*, p. 338.

27 Ibid, pp. 44–54.

28 Ibid, p. 45; N. Gergel, 'The Pogroms in the Ukraine in 1918–1921,' YIVO *Annual of Jewish Social Science* 6, pp. 237–52.

29 Quoted in Helen Fein, *Accounting for Genocide: National Responses and Jewish Victimization During the Holocaust* (New York: The Free Press, 1979), p. 21.

returning German soldiers after the First World War, the Jewish-Bolshevik connection became firmly rooted in the Nazi mind. Indeed, the infamous and influential 'stab in the back' accusation that Kaiser Wilhelm II made on his way out of Germany had its origin partly in the East. Walther von Kaiserlingk, the German admiralty's chief of operation visited Petrograd (St. Petersburg) in the winter of 1917–18. He saw the government as 'run by Jews in the interests of Jews; it was "insanity in power," and it presented a mortal threat not only to Germany but to the civilized world. Wilhelm agreed that the Russian people had been "turned over to the vengeance of the Jews, who are connected with all the Jews of the world."'[30]

Who were these Jews? First among them and initially second only to Lenin in power and authority was the leader of the Red Army, Leon Trotsky (née Bronstein). Grigori Zinoviev (Radomyslsky), a celebrated orator, was president of the Communist International and chairman of the Petrograd Soviet. Lev Kamenev (Rosenfeld) was a member of the party Central Committee, edited Pravada, the party newspaper, and chaired the Second Congress of Soviets. He also briefly was nominal head of state and chaired the Moscow Soviet. Other prominent Jews were Adolf Yoffe, chair of the Revolutionary Military Committee of the Petrograd Soviet, and who headed the Soviet delegation negotiating the Brest-Litovsk Treaty with Germany. Yakov Sverdlov was secretary and principal organizer of the Bolshevik Party in 1917 and 1918 and was head of state after Kamenev.

Most important, the Soviet secret police, the Cheka (by now the NKVD) had a significant number of Jews right up to the start of the Second World War. For example, in 1937 at least 10% of the 407 Cheka officials who had been decorated had obviously Jewish names.[31] High level Jews at that time were Lazar Kaganovich, a close associate of Stalin, the head of the secret police, Genrich Yagoda, and the diplomat Maxim Litvinov, who although dismissed as Foreign Minister prior to the Nazi-Soviet Pact of 1939, nevertheless continued in power until 1943, occupying the extremely important position of ambassador to the United States with its large Jewish community.

Of course so many other leaders such as Friedrich Engels, Vladimir Ilyich Lenin, August Bebel and Georgy Plekhanov were not Jewish, but even many of the non-Jews were so called 'Jewifiers' (in the parlance of anti-Semites) who valued the Jews even more than they valued their own nationalities. Lenin, for

30 Quoted in Albert S. Lindemann, *Esau's Tears: Modern Anti-Semitism and the Rise of the Jews* (New York: Cambridge University Press, 1997), p. 424.

31 Ibid, p. 454.

example, commented to Maxim Gorky that 'an intelligent Russian is almost always a Jew or someone with Jewish blood in his veins.'[32]

But even Lenin, the non-Jew, had a Jewish grandfather who had converted to Christianity in marrying his grandmother, who was herself of Christian German origin. Although culturally Great Russian, he was widely believed by anti-Semites to be Jewish. Mikhail Kalinin, the president of the Soviet Union was considered by Jewish Bolsheviks to be 'more Jewish than the Jews' possibly because of his open expression of emotion. For example, in a speech describing the pogroms of the Civil War, he broke down and cried, and was unable to complete the speech.[33] Felix Dzerzhinsky, head of the Cheka, was originally a member of the Polish gentry and learned to speak Yiddish in his youth in Vilna. He was friendly with many Jews and was married to one.

Deeply offending powerful Jews in the Soviet Union by killing Polish or other Jews based on 'racial' classification would not have been in the Nazi self-interest. The Soviets were allied with the Nazis after June 1939, an alliance that brought considerable benefit in the successful invasion of Poland, an outcome that would not have been possible without Soviet neutrality, even support.

The timing of the war with Russia might have been affected. Perhaps more than any other contemporaneous leader, Hitler understood the value of surprise in both war and politics. He also understood the value of careful preparations in anticipation of a major military action, especially one that entailed the extraordinary risks associated with an invasion of the Soviet Union. If leading Jews in the Soviet Union had been alarmed unduly by the onset of genocide, then early Soviet preparations for war might have forced Hitler's hand and the onset of a war for which Germany would not have been adequately prepared. By not engaging in excessively brutal behaviors toward Jews, at least not highly visible ones, Hitler could retain the initiative to be utilized at a time and place of his own choosing. Stalin's utter surprise and consequent misconduct of the war immediately after the Nazi invasion is a vindication of Hitler's early restraint.

Another fear of the Nazis, of course, was Jewish influence in America that could lead the United States into war against Germany. Genocide in Europe might have galvanized action in America leading to the two-front war so dreaded by the Nazis. Ever mindful of the international situation, especially in wartime, Hitler would exercise caution in attempting to avoid the major pitfall of simultaneous war with the Soviet Union and the United States.

---

32 Quoted in Ibid, p. 426.

33 Ibid, p. 433.

The non-exterminatory approach to the Jewish population at this time helps explain an apparent anomaly. During this period, in January 1940, the Germans allowed a Jewish welfare organization to be established named 'Jewish Social Self-Help' (ŻSS, the acronym in Polish) headed by a Michael Weichert. It was the only Jewish institution that was allowed to function in German occupied Poland. As Weichert commented, 'It simply wasn't logical. On the one hand they persecute Jews to the utmost, and on the other they discuss a central organization for social aid with them.'[34] In part, the answer resides in Nazi policy goals. American welfare organizations such as the Commission for Polish Relief and the American Red Cross were active in Poland at this time. Risking American intervention by engaging in war crimes at this early stage in the war was simply not on Hitler's agenda.

Poland at the Time of the Partitions

Now, instead of a diachronic comparison first between a period of restraint but later genocide in a single case, we now consider cases where genocide might have been expected to occur, but did not. The affinity condition will prove to be important, if not decisive.

Polish Losses

The Polish experience, because of its large concentration of Jews, becomes emblematic. The Jews of Poland found themselves at a critical juncture in late eighteenth century Poland. The Polish partition of 1772 had shorn the country of nearly 30% of its territory and 35% of its population. Austria received not only 83,000-sq. km. and 2,650,000 inhabitants but some of the most fertile and densely populated lands with valuable salt mines. Russia received the lion's share of territory – 92,000-sq. km. – but fewer inhabitants, 1,300.000 in all, and fewer fertile lands with no appreciable mineral assets. The Prussian share was the smallest at 36,000 sq. km of territory and 580,000 inhabitants.[35] This apparent inequity was strongly compensated by her presence now at the mouth of the Vistula River. As a consequence of this geopolitical coup as well as other holdings in Silesia and later Pomerania, the overwhelming proportion

34 Quoted in Yisrael Gutman, *The Jews of Warsaw, 1939–1943: Ghetto, Underground, Revolt*, trans. Ina Friedman (Bloomington: Indiana University Press, 1982), p. 41.

35 Aleksander Gieysztor, Stefan Kieniewicz, Emanuel Rostworowski, Janusz Tazbir, and Henryk Wereszycki, *History of Poland*, 2nd ed. (Warsaw: PWN-Polish Scientific Publishers, 1979), pp. 281–2.

of Polish trade had to pass through Prussian territory. Trade treaties, ratified in 1775, imposed heavy customs duties on goods leaving Poland, low duties on those entering Poland and exorbitant charges on Polish transit trade. There was a real danger that the new truncated Polish state could become a Prussian economic vassal.

These new economic debilities in many ways precipitated an economic crisis. 'Frederick's [Frederick II of Prussia] economic war crippled Poland' although it did not destroy it.[36] Poland had been in economic decline for more than a century; indicative of this decline is the increased dependence of royal revenues on the sale of alcohol. In 1564, in the heyday of Polish grain production, the manufacture of alcohol accounted for 0.3 percent of revenues from royal properties. By 1764 it accounted for an astonishing 37.6 percent and by 1789, over 40 percent. A reasonable interpretation of these statistics is that more than one third of the royal income depended on an inebriated mostly peasant population. And Jewish proprietors were at the heart of the so called *propinacja*, a specialized form of the *arendar* in which Jews were leaseholders of crown estates; in the instance of the *propinacja*, the lease entailed the manufacture and sale of alcoholic beverages. Jewish operated taverns dotted the Polish countryside. In the midst of an economic crisis, the nonproductive nature of this form of economic enterprise came to the attention of many reform-minded Poles. With the attempt to confront the new economic liabilities imposed by the first partition, the role of Jews in the Polish economy came under increasing, frequently hostile scrutiny.

In other areas of the Polish economy Jewish traders and business people of various types found themselves in competition with the Polish burghers who were approximately equal in number.[37] Here one sees the insecurities of an incipient Polish middle class in a growing state of conflict with its only domestic competition. The size of this burgher class, disproportionately small relative to the overall Polish population size, must have exacerbated its insecurities in comparison with an equally large counterpart among the Jews, despite the fact that Jews constituted only 10% of the population of Poland. In Cracow, for example, Christian merchants complained that 'Jews are expanding their commerce ever more. They have imported various commodities, including Christian and holy objects of need to Catholics. And Jews sell them

36 Jerzy Lukowski, *The Partitions of Poland 1772, 1793, 1795* (London: Longman, 1999), p. 110.

37 Daniel Stone, *Polish Politics and National Reform, 1775–1788* (Boulder, CO: East European Monographs, Distributed by Columbia University Press, 1976), p. 82.

openly – which is a disgrace for the Christians. They manufacture and sell all sorts of products.'[38]

Efforts at Reform and Jewish Exclusion

The four-year Sejm (Polish national legislature), lasting between 1788 and 1792, became a focus for burgher efforts to permanently exclude Jews from the towns. In this last ditch effort at Polish national renewal, all sectors of Polish society attempted to exert their respective influence on the Sejm. Hostility towards Jews by the burghers reached its height in 1790, as they were agitating for Jewish exclusion. On May 15, a riot erupted in which Jews were attacked and their wares stolen; the violence did not end until the army intervened. The immediate cause of the disturbances was a contract awarded to Jewish suppliers.[39] The outcome of this violence, along with other burgher efforts, led to the virtual exclusion of Jews from the towns, except when expressly permitted by the town authorities. Even more important was the exclusion of Jews as a group from public law. Although freedom of religious practice was guaranteed by the new constitution, the Jewish community, in contrast to others, was excluded from public law. This outcome not only was ominous for the future continued existence of this least assimilable Polish community, but stood in stark contrast to its traditional legal standing.

For two centuries, between the union of 1569 and the mid to late 18th century, Jewish autonomy was granted by royal charter. The *kehilla* (pl. *kehillot*) or community in Hebrew, was constituted as the legal representation of the local Jewish community. It was responsible for administering the religious and social affairs of this community and perhaps most important, for taxes collected, a substantial portion of which was rendered to the Polish authorities.[40] Jewish communities therefore came under royal protection, or where less applicable because of distance from the capital, under the protection of local magnates. The legal standing of the *kehillot* was undisputed; beginning in the 1580s they begun to function under a larger organization called the Council of Four Lands. 'This council, through its federated structures, sought to direct, regulate, and protect far-flung Jewish communities, otherwise subjected to

38 Quoted in Simon Dubnov, *History of the Jews: From the Congress of Vienna to the Emergence of Hitler*, Volume 5, trans. Moshe Spiegel (New York: Thomas Yoseloff, 1973), p. 360.

39 Hillel Levine, *Economic Origins of Antisemitism: Poland and Its Jews in the Early Modern Period* (New Haven, CT: Yale University Press, 1991), p. 213.

40 Norman Davies, *God's Playground: A History of Poland in Two Volumes, Volume 1: The Origins to 1795* (New York: Columbia University Press, 1982), p. 325.

different domains of authority and the conflicting interests of diverse segments of Polish society.'[41]

By the mid-18th century, however, the political and financial difficulties of the Polish commonwealth were evident. The Szlachta (Council of the Nobility) of 1764 resolved to abolish the Council of Four Lands that had been functioning successfully for nearly two centuries.[42] Tax collection would now be done directly by the Polish representatives, a move to economize by eliminating the prior tax-collecting agent, namely the Council of Four Lands. To be sure, a certain proportion of the funds was used for administrative purposes by the Council. But at the same time, Jewish communal administration, charities, religious organizations, burial societies, learned institutions and the like, could no longer be administered by a central Jewish organization. The individual *kehillot* were on their own.

Violence Against Jews and Genocidal Possibility

The gradual fragmentation of the Polish state had another consequence, namely the first major communal violence targeting Jewish communities since 1648 and the Chmielnicki pogrom, which was carried out by Ukrainians, not Poles. In the following century, the Russian Empress Catherine II, by now serving as 'protector' of the Polish state, also now sought to protect the rights of Eastern Orthodox Polish citizens. This action raised the question of the rights of others such as Protestants and even Jews, thereby precipitating a vigorous Roman Catholic reaction among the nobility. The Confederation of the Bar was formed under conservative Catholic leadership, which had the additional consequence of precipitating a peasant reaction to the Confederates mainly in the predominantly Orthodox areas of the Ukraine. Cossack forces rampaged throughout the Ukraine with the purpose of hanging from the same tree 'Pole, Jew and dog – all of the same faith.'[43] Estimates of the number of Jewish dead vary from conservative estimates of thousands,[44] to the 10–20,000 range,[45] and up to tens of thousands.[46] Clearly the visibility of the Jewish *arendar* (whether or not involved in the *propinacja*) as an agent of the Polish nobleman made him a handy target for the venting of violent rage, despite the immediate origins of the violence in issues of Catholic supremacy.

41 Levine, *Economic Origins of Antisemitism*, p. 35.

42 Dubnov, *History of the Jews*, p. 359.

43 Quoted in ibid, p. 364.

44 Gieysztor et al, *History of Poland*, p. 278.

45 Dubnov, *History of the Jews*, p 366.

46 Levine, *Economic Origins of Antisemitism*, p. 162.

Thus, the period of the first partition in 1772, especially the four-year Sejm, was immediately preceded by two extraordinary blows experienced by the Jewish community. Its overarching communal organization had been legislated out of existence and once again as in the preceding century, the threat of massive violence hung over its head. In this climate of threat and vulnerability, little could be expected by the Jews of the four-year Sejm despite their best efforts at influence and the high praise of the Sejm by observers such as Jean-Jacques Rousseau, among others.[47] Although the constitution resulting from this Sejm conformed to many liberal principles of the Enlightenment, it did little to respond to the Jewish predicament. If anything it worsened it considerably by not referring to the Jewish community. Exclusion from the public law of the time was the consequence. Ten percent of the population therefore was effectively excluded from this constitutive process. Interestingly, the book index for the most comprehensive recent treatment of this constitution, a book 562 pages in length, has not a single entry for the word 'Jew', 'Jewish', 'Judaism', or any other variant.[48] This exclusion stands in contrast to other countries in Central Europe where Jewish corporate existence continued to be recognized both in privilege and disability.[49]

In further contrast, the Law of the Towns explicitly recognized the rights of Christian burghers, including foreigners as well as the freedom of townspeople from feudal obligation. Burghers could now purchase estates, were granted rights to lower level judicial and administrative appointments; several hundreds were even elevated to the level of gentry.[50] Last minute efforts to introduce a draft resolution concerning Jewish corporate rights failed, consistent with the continued Jewish exclusion from the towns.

Jewish reactions to this new (non) status varied, but most perceived the dangers. Perhaps most perceptive are the comments of the British Lord George Gordon who later converted to Judaism. He wrote,

> There has been something not sincere in the Polish Revolution, a sort of false pretence in favour of Liberty, which is now too apparent, and they [the Poles] themselves are suffering the fatal consequences of the deception....The Assembly of France, you know, has prudently admitted the Nation to the equal rights of Citizens. The Jews in France were soon

47 Samuel Fiszman, ed., *Constitution and Reform in Eighteenth-Century Poland: The Constitution of 3 May 1791*, (Bloomington: Indiana University Press, 1997).

48 Ibid.

49 Levine, *Economic Origins of Antisemitism*, p. 229.

50 Ibid, p. 218.

> penetrated with admiration and respect, on beholding the multiplied acts of Justice, which proceeded from that Assembly; and they deposited in the midst of them the solemn testimony of their patriotism and devotedness: their solemn oath to sacrifice, in every instance, *their lives and fortunes* (sic) for the public good; for the glory of the nation and the king. One sole object rules and animates all their thoughts, the good of their country, and a desire of dedicating to it all their strength. In that respect they will not yield to any inhabitants of France; they will dispute the palm with all the citizens for zeal, courage and patriotism....But what encouragement does the present Diet hold out to the Polish Jews which they did not enjoy under the old Republican Government? None at all.[51]

In a much darker and perhaps prophetic tone, a poem was written in 1789 and published in 1790 saying that:

> How to correct this, here is a cure. Trees are in abundance, but gallows are sparse. So each year we must hang one hundred Jews. Crime will diminish... in this way turn bad into good.[52]

Yet even here we do not see a recommendation for wholesale massacre or genocide. However, I do identify this as a pre-genocidal condition. Moreover, Poles must have been keenly aware of the massacre of Jews in 1768, even more so as the result of the much more widespread massacres (approximately 100,000 dead) of the earlier Chmielnicki pogroms during the preceding century.

First, we have the corporate exclusion from public law. Although not nearly so severe as the racial laws of Nazi Germany, this exclusion nevertheless represents an abrupt departure from the explicit recognition of Jewish corporate rights in the preceding centuries. The earlier abolition in 1764 of the Council of Four Lands likely paved the way for this later exclusion.

Second, extensive violence against Jews leading to the probable deaths of at least 10–20,000 in eastern Poland in 1768, largely unpunished, suggests a commonality with the later massacres of 1918–20.

Third, Jewish and Christians refugees must have been a major concern during this period. The massacres of 1768 must have had the effect of dislocating many Jews, as did the later partition of 1772. Indeed, after the partition, the Prussian government simply forced the more poverty-stricken Jews from their

---

51 Quoted in Israel Solomons, 'Lord George Gordon's Conversion to Judaism,' paper read before the Jewish Historical Society of England, June 2, 1913, p. 257.

52 Quoted in Levine, *Economic Origins of Antisemitism*, p. 212.

homes and dumped them back onto Polish territory.[53] Within Poland itself, Jews were expelled from villages and towns where burghers were no longer forced by the gentry or the crown to coexist with them. A new class of 72,000 unemployed Jews and 9,000 paupers was thus generated, nearly 10% of the Jewish population and a much larger proportion of its adult male population.[54] In addition, approximately 200,000 Germans and 300,000 Russians migrated to Poland at this time, creating additional population pressures, although it is unclear how many of them were Jews.

Fourth, the First Partition must have generated an extreme state insecurity. After almost a century as virtually a Russian satellite, not terribly dissimilar to that of Poland during the post-Second World War era, nearly 30% of her territory and 35% of her population were lost to three much stronger powers. Obviously fears of another partition were rife and led to various efforts at national rejuvenation, including of course, the May 3, 1791 constitution. Clearly these efforts were not sufficient because in 1793 and 1795 the second and third partitions ended the sovereign existence of the Polish state. Under these conditions of an ever-expanding domain of losses one would expect a sharpening of antagonism toward those perceived as less centrally important members of the polity.

Fifth, ideational justifications for these antagonisms were increasing. The Blood Libel, a medieval calumny that claimed Jewish use of Christian blood in the celebration of Passover (directly contradicting a fundamental Jewish law forbidding the ingestion even of animal blood), was on the rise. Although various high Church officials, even several popes condemned the Blood Libel as an absurdity, nevertheless it persisted at the local parish or regional level as a rallying cry and justification for attacks on Jews, whether verbal or physical. And as Hillel Levine[55] indicates, from the mid-18th century, especially after one especially heinous case in Zhitomir in 1753, the Blood Libel was increasing in frequency and intensity. The rapid emergence of the Roman Catholic church as a defender of Poland against all 'schismatics' (Eastern Orthodox believers) and others such as the Jews, is characteristic of this period.[56]

Avoidance of Genocide

Given these conditions constituting a pre-genocidal syndrome, why in point of fact did a genocide of the Jews not occur? Here again several reasons

53 Levine, *Economic Origins of Antisemitism*, p. 167.

54 Raphael Mahler, *A History of Modern Jewry 1780–1815* (New York: Schocken Books, 1971), pp. 300–301.

55 Levine, *Economic Origins of Antisemitism*, pp. 183–90.

56 Dubnov, *History of the Jews*, p. 363.

emerging from this analysis can be presented. First, the period immediately after the First Partition saw the Central-East European region at peace. The Russo-Turkish War ending in the peace of Kuchuk-Kainardji in 1774 was winding down and in any event did not at this time directly involve the Poles. Indeed a major purpose of this and the later partitions was the avoidance of great power war.[57] An ongoing war that directly threatens state security may in fact be a necessary condition for genocide that no pre-genocidal antecedents can overcome.

Second, while ideational influence of the Roman Catholic Church fostered anti-Jewish feeling, there were clear limits to this antagonism. The Jews had experienced a protection of the Church if only to continue as 'witnesses' to the travails of a people that had refused to accept Christ as the Messiah. Roman Catholic theology explicitly rejected the outright murder of people, whatever their past 'misdeeds'.

Third, another ideational influence, this time from a very different direction, also militated against genocide. The Enlightenment in various countries including Germany immediately to the west and especially France further west was incorporating Jews into the polity and society. Clearly the Enlightenment was influential in Poland, as the constitutional efforts of the late eighteenth century attest. Even if incomplete, especially in the exclusion of Jews as a corporate entity, the influence of the Enlightenment simply would not permit wholesale efforts at mass murder.

Indeed, the (in)famous statement of Count Stanislaw de Clermont-Tonnerre to the French National Assembly in December 1789 presents the bases for both the Polish exclusion of Jews as a corporate entity from public life and the impossibility of genocide as the mass murder of individual Jews:

> As a nation the Jews must be denied everything, as individuals they must be granted everything; their judges can no longer be recognized; their recourse must be to our own exclusively; legal protection for the doubtful laws by which Jewish corporate existence is maintained must end; they cannot be allowed to create a political body or a separate order within the state; it is necessary that they be citizens individually.[58]

57 L.R. Lewitter, 'The Partitions of Poland,' in A. Goodwin, ed., *The New Cambridge Modern History*, vol. 8. (Cambridge: Cambridge University Press, 1965), pp. 333–59.

58 Quoted in David Vital, *A People Apart: The Jews in Europe 1789–1939* (Oxford: Oxford University Press, 1999), p. 44.

While the small Jewish communities of Paris, Bordeaux, and Avignon[59] did not present a citizenship problem for the National Assembly, that of the much larger Yiddish-speaking community of Alsace-Lorraine did. Only in September 1791 were all Jews granted full citizenship upon their willingness to take the 'civic oath' as provided in the Constitution. If even the Yiddish-speakers of Alsace-Lorraine could be granted recognition of their personhood in the form of full citizenship, certainly the inviolability of the lives of Yiddish-speaking Jews in Poland was not in question.

The fact of Jewish acceptance in revolutionary France established an affinity for Jews that likely would not permit great power and especially French approval of such a genocide. Ideas of the French *philosophes* and those emanating from the French Revolution were sufficiently widespread and influential in Poland to militate against any direct attack on a people that was currently being favored by revolutionary France, the soon to be continental hegemon.

Here is the crux of the matter. Revolutionary France, exponent of the Enlightenment and liberator of the Jews from their ghettoes and restrictive legislation, was in many respects the catalyst of the new Polish constitution. To offend this once again rising great power by a gross victimization of the Jews was simply out of the question. Effectively, France as the guardian of both the Jewish community and Polish liberalism, played the role of affine protector.

Britain and Ireland

Before tackling the question of Great Britain and Roman Catholic Ireland after the First World War – our second case of a genocide that might have been expected to occur but did not – a prior question must be addressed. Is it legitimate to suggest democracies as candidates for the commission of genocide? Clearly the histories of democracies have been vastly superior in this regard to those of autocracies.[60] Yet democracies have been known to commit genocide. The Melian genocide during the Peloponnesian War committed by democratic Athens is one case in point, as is the debated but nevertheless possible genocidal policy of successive US governments toward Native Americans in the 19th century. It remains an open question whether the use of smallpox-infected blankets given to vulnerable Indian tribes, or individual massacres such as

59 Paula E. Hyman, *The Jews of Modern France* (Berkeley: University of California Press, 1998), p.29.

60 Rudolph Rummel, *Power Kills: Democracy as a Method of Nonviolence* (New Brunswick, NJ: Transaction Publishers, 1997).

Sand Creek in Colorado were evidence of state-sponsored systematic mass murder. Nevertheless, the Melian genocide and the suspect US policy concerning Native Americans, certainly suggest the potential for democracies to commit genocide, especially against groups with ethnoreligious characteristics distinctly at variance with those of the majority.

The human rights program that developed in 19th century Britain also might have been influential in preventing genocide of the Irish Catholics, but for the retreat of this movement in the face of the unbridled realpolitik manifested by virtually all of the major powers at the First World War's end and the subsequent Greco-Turkish War of 1919–22.[61]

British Losses

One more issue needs to be addressed, namely the extent to which Britain was actually within the domain of losses at the time of the uprising. Although not nearly defeated, the British by April 1916 – the time of the Irish Easter Rebellion -- had not as yet won any major land victories, but did experience one humiliating defeat. This was the Gallipoli invasion of March 1915 through January 1916. With the naval bombardment of March 1915 and the April landings of British and mainly Commonwealth troops, Churchill's proposed shortcut to ending the war appeared soon to be realized. The tottering Ottoman Empire, defeated by Balkan states only three years earlier appeared to be by far the weakest major Central Power. Yet the determined stand of German-led Turkish forces forced the British to complete their withdrawal by January 1916.[62] To many observers this would appear to signify a further weakening of the British Empire, earlier evidenced by British difficulties in the Boer War against Afrikaner colonists some 17 years earlier.

Gallipoli signified the end to any illusions of a rapid Allied march to victory. Indeed, without significant land or sea victories (only the French had clearly won a victory on the Marne), and only a remote likelihood at that time of American entry into the War (Wilson was already campaigning for re-election on a platform of strict neutrality), defeat was a distinct possibility. Note the timing of the unwise and excessively harsh British response to the April 1916 uprising in Dublin, to be examined more fully below.

---

61 See, for example, Michelle Tusan, *Smyrna's Ashes: Humanitarianism, Genocide, and the Birth of the Middle East* (Berkeley: University of California Press, 2012), and my review of this book emphasizing realpolitik in the decline of British humanitarianism. This review is published in *The American Historical Review* (2014) 119 (1): 284–285.

62 Martin Gilbert, *The Straits of War: Gallipoli Remembered* (Stroud UK: Sutten, 2000).

Genocidal Solutions in Ireland

A genocidal solution of the 'Irish question' is found deep in Anglo-Irish history; it is most often associated with a period of English losses. As early as the late 16th century there were calls for genocide against the native Irish by English colonists who were driven out in the late 1590s. They wrote Elizabeth I, 'Lett the feete of yore forces treade and trample downe these bryars that will not suffer yore plantes to prosper. ... Lett them weare with theire heeles the very rootes out of the earth that they springe no more: soe shall you make Ireland a flourishing nursery for England.'[63] Edmund Spenser, one of the irate English colonists, suggested just such a genocidal program of deliberate starvation.[64]

After the Anglo-Norman invasion by Henry II in 1122, large numbers of English settlers arrived in Ireland. They took root in the Dublin area, in the Southeast and Southwest, and more sparsely throughout virtually the entire island. But by the 16th century English culture was in a state of decay. The counties Kerry and Tipperary were once 'studded with English settlements'[65] but wars with the native Irish and the absorption of many Old English into the majority Gaelic culture had sapped these communities of their number. The English imagined a 'golden age' of the late 12th and 13th centuries in which English culture reigned supreme at least in the areas of settlement, but by the end of the 16th were writing of 'the Irish problem.'[66] 'The English inhabitants of Ireland during the reigns of Henry VIII, Edward VI, Mary and Elizabeth I were convinced, correctly, that their world was shrinking day by day.'[67] Even in areas close to Dublin, the heart of the English settlement, English as a language had ceased to be used on a regular basis. It was in this context of shrinkage and loss that these genocidal sentiments were uttered by uprooted English settlers.

The Irish rebellion of the late 1590s and the general decline of English culture was, in the following century to be followed by a genuine effort at the 'root and branch annihilation of Irish customs' desired in the 1590s.[68] Oliver Cromwell's invasion of Ireland in 1649 led to this catastrophe. A three point strategy was adopted by Cromwell. First was the elimination of all military resistance to the Cromwellian Protestant reforms, effectively ending the chaos that had reigned in Ireland since 1641, and the rebellion that had its origin in

---

63 Quoted in Marcus Tanner, *Ireland's Holy Wars: The Struggle of a Nation's Soul, 1500–2000* (New Haven: Yale University Press, 2001), p. 30.

64 W.B. Yeats, *Essays and Introductions* (New York: MacMillan, 1961), p. 361.

65 Tanner, *Ireland's Holy Wars*, p. 28.

66 Ibid, p. 29.

67 Ibid, p. 33.

68 Ibid, p. 31.

Ulster. This was accomplished fairly quickly and with considerable loss of life, including the infamous massacres at Drogheda and Wexford. Second, all priests and landowners implicated in the insurrection were to be removed. This process eventually entailed the wholesale dispossession of all Catholic landowners out of the three provinces of Leinster, Munster and Ulster, effectively all of eastern Ireland, the most fertile region. Only small estates were to be allowed Catholic landowners to the west of the Shannon River. The infrastructure of the Catholic church was destroyed both organizationally and physically, entailing the murder of large numbers of clergy. Finally, Catholicism was to be replaced by Protestantism throughout the island. To this end, large numbers of Protestants were to replace Catholics, either murdered or forced to move to the west of the Shannon.[69]

This process yielded a loss of approximately 750,000 persons between 1600 and 1650, reckoned as follows. At the close of the 16th century, Ireland had roughly 750,000 persons,[70] while in 1650 it had about 800,000. Given a peacetime rate of fertility (suggested by the doubling of the Irish population between 1650 and 1700 to 1.5 million persons), the number of persons should have been 1.5 million in 1650, not roughly half that number.[71]

In addition to these human losses, the losses in land were equally catastrophic. Of the 7.5 million most arable acres, 5.2 million were transferred to Irish Protestants. Although some of that land did find its way back into Catholic hands, the net effect was a massive transference of landed wealth to the Protestants.[72] From that time the vast majority of Irish would be poor peasants, many without land, struggling to eke out a meager existence. The Protestant 'Ascendancy' dates from this time.

The third period that some have associated with genocide is that of the potato famine beginning in the late 1840s. Although the famine was not a genocidal act overtly planned by the British, it nevertheless took over 1 million Irish lives, mainly Catholics, and utterly transformed the sociopolitical face of Ireland. Just before the famine, the population of Ireland numbered some 8,175,124 in 1841. Of these, approximately 2.5 million were landless laborers and only 10% of farms had more than 30 acres.[73] In this setting of rural overpopulation, the failure of the principal crop was devastating in its consequences. In the

69 Nicholas Canny, "Early Modern Ireland, c. 1500–1700", in R.F. Foster, ed., *The Oxford Illustrated History of Ireland* (Oxford: Oxford University Press, 1991), pp. 145–48.

70 Ibid, p. 110.

71 Tanner, *Ireland's Holy Wars*, p.145.

72 Ibid.

73 Ibid, p. 241.

West of Ireland, the almost uniformly Catholic areas beyond the Shannon River, vast expanses of depopulation became apparent. In the words of one observer these empty villages were the 'tombs of a departed race.'[74]

Most importantly, after the departure of Lord Peel's relatively liberal cabinet, the new British government sought to allow laissez faire (i.e. Darwinian) economics to resolve the famine crisis, opening itself to accusations of genocide. The so-called Gregory clause of the Poor Law Amendment Act of 1847 forbade the distribution of any relief to poor who held more than ¼ of an acre of land[75] even in the midst of widespread starvation. It is no wonder that writers such as John Mitchel directly accused the British of formulating a consciously genocidal policy[76] in which the famine was artificially sustained. And John Mitchel was one of the first of the prominent Young Irelanders, forerunners of the Fenians who were to play a major role in the development of Irish nationalism.

Rise of Irish Nationalism

Originally known as the Irish Republican Brotherhood, (itself an amalgam of young Irelanders and Chartists, called Irish Confederates), the Fenians were actually founded in New York in 1858.[77] Many of the Fenians came from the pool of 150,000 or so Irish-American veterans of the Civil War, a large reservoir of young men whose Irish consciousness was raised first by the famine they had fled, and then by rampant anti-Irish and anti-Catholic prejudice in the United States. The Fenian movement spread to Great Britain and most crucially, Ireland.

And here we find one of the key elements in the development of an affine condition protecting the Irish Catholic community from systematic mass murder. The second major consequence of the Irish famine was the emigration of large numbers of mainly young people. The scale of the emigration can be gauged by the drop in Irish population from 8.5 million in 1845 to approximately 6.5 million six years later.[78] These numbers suggest that in addition to the number of deaths in excess of a million, another million or so had emigrated.

74 Quoted in R.F. Foster, 'Ascendancy and Union,' in R.F. Foster ed., *The Oxford Illustrated History of Ireland* (Oxford: Oxford University Press, 1991), p. 203.

75 Donald M. MacRaild, *Irish Migrants in Modern Britain, 1750–1922* (New York: St. Martin's Press, 1999), p. 31.

76 John Mitchel, *The History of Ireland: From the Treaty of Limerick to the Present Time* (New York: D. and J. Sadlier, 1868); Foster, 'Ascendancy and Union,' p. 209.

77 MacRaild, *Irish Migrants in Modern Britain*, p. 139.

78 Ibid, p. 32.

Additionally, this was no singular historical occurrence. A pattern had been set whereby families, especially in the Catholic west, designated certain family members to emigrate and where possible, return monies to their impoverished relatives in Ireland. This pattern had become so socially ingrained that 'by 1870 more than half as many natives of Ireland were living overseas as at home. Three-fifths of the three million emigrants were in the USA, a quarter in Britain, and about one-thirteenth in Australia as in Canada. The unique decline of Ireland's population for nearly a century after the famine was mainly caused by structural emigration, which removed up to half of each generation from the country.'[79]

Irish Affinity With the US

The nearly two million emigrants in the USA were to be crucial as we saw in the establishment of the Fenians, the prototypical militant Irish nationalist movement but also in subsequent key events. Between 1870 and 1914, at least a million pounds were to be sent home annually to Ireland. The Christmas 'American letter' became essential to the stability of the western rural economy.[80] And the maintenance of this relatively primitive economy was to ensure the perpetuation of this vast emigration throughout the period ending early in the First World War.

But Irish Americans were not only crucial to the Irish economy but also to the furtherance of Irish nationalism. As early as the 1860s 'republicanism was seeping into the country from Famine emigrants' new home in America, gnawing away at the fibres of loyalism.'[81]

The Easter Rebellion and the Excessive British Reaction

In April 1916, the Fenians, now known as the Irish Republican Brotherhood, staged its revolt. Although fought by Irishmen principally in Dublin, the funding was provided by the American *Clan na Gael*.[82] Given Fenianism's American roots, this source of financial support was to be expected. A participant in the uprising, Eaman de Valera, later to be Prime Minister of Ireland, probably was spared execution because of his American birth. He later urged an 'American' strategy in which Irish-Americans would be mobilized to seek American support for Irish representation at the eventual peace conference.[83] During the

79 David Fitzpatrick, 'Ireland Since 1870,' in R.F. Foster, ed., *The Oxford Illustrated History of Ireland* (Oxford: Oxford University Press, 1991), p. 213.
80 Ibid, p. 216.
81 Tanner, *Ireland's Holy Wars*, p. 250.
82 Fitzpatrick, 'Ireland Since 1870,' p. 237.
83 Ibid, p. 241.

postwar uprising, Irish public opinion in America was courted and heavily mobilized in favor of Irish independence, or at least a high level of autonomy. Given this profound connection between Ireland and America, how could the British even conceive of a genocidal solution to the 'Irish question', not to mention the large Irish communities in Britain's greatest cities including London, Liverpool and Glasgow.[84] The deep financial indebtedness of Great Britain to the United States after the First World War, as well as political obligations, should have ruled out any such possibility.

Yet there were strong influences in favor of a genocidal solution. Most important perhaps was the domain of losses noted earlier, but also to be considered is the failure of extensive British efforts to stem the tide of Irish nationalism. These included the Land Acts of 1870 and 1881, designed to reduce inequality, and the 1869 disestablishment of the Church of Ireland, the hated religious bastion of official Irish Protestantism.

Open rebellion occurred in 1916, suggesting that nothing short of a near genocidal solution, as in Cromwell's day, could alter Irish Catholic nationalist sentiments. And the over-reaction of the British authorities in 1916 is likely attributable to these considerations. Sixteen of the rebels were executed and 3500 people were arrested, court-martialed or interned in Britain. Given the initial extraordinarily negative reaction of most Dubliners who had little sympathy for the rebellion that led to the destruction of much of Dublin's center (rebels were pelted with tomatoes by the public after surrendering), the British overreaction was a gift. Instead of dealing with the rebels as dissident citizens, they were viewed by the British as traitors who had 'stabbed the Empire in the back'[85] and treated accordingly. All of the Irish Catholics were now viewed with great suspicion. The brutality of the British forces was indiscriminate in its application.[86]

Yet, as we know, despite movement in this direction in 1916, and another indiscriminate brutal response by the British (the infamous 'Black and Tans') to the postwar rebellion of 1920–21, genocide did not occur. The affine American connection simply was too strong for the British to even seriously consider this option.

Evoking the Affine Connection

Even the possibility of massacre raised red flags to incisive British observers. For example, Sir Henry Wilson, Unionist (favoring continued union between Great Britain and Ireland) Member of Parliament, and former Chief of the

84 MacRaild, *Irish Migrants in Modern Britain.*

85 Fitzpatrick, 'Ireland Since 1870,' p. 240.

86 Ibid.

Imperial General Staff noted in his diary in the summer of 1920: 'Winston Churchill suggested arming 20,000 Orangemen [hard line Unionists] to relieve the troops from the north. I told him this would mean taking sides. ... civil war and savage reprisals, and, at the very least, great tension with America and open rupture with the Pope. Winston does not realise these things and is a perfect idiot as a statesman.'[87]

It may be objected that Jews in Europe had an American affine population as well, yet this did not serve to deter Hitler. But there are several crucial differences. First the American Jewish community was of more recent vintage than the Irish Catholic, smaller in size, and less embedded within the overall polity and society. Irish Catholics began arriving in large numbers in the late 1840s; large-scale Jewish immigration dated from the 1890s. Whereas the Jewish community numbered approximately 4,000,000 in 1940, Americans of Irish Catholic descent numbered at least 20,000,000. More important, the hierarchy of the American Catholic Church was almost uniformly Irish Catholic in descent. As Marcus Tanner commented, 'the Catholic Church in America had become a vast extension of the Irish Catholic Church.'[88] To have outraged the second largest Christian denomination in America would have been extreme folly on the part of the British.

Still as implied above, the earlier relatively decent treatment meted out to Jews by the Nazis may have been pretty much due to the perceived exaggerated influence of the American Jewish community, in tandem with similar perceptions of influential Soviet Jewish officials. But in the final analysis, the Soviet Union could be conquered by the Nazis, or so ran their expectation, and America would eventually enter the war, thus rendering moot any fears of this double influence. The Holocaust could then proceed. The notion of the British conquest of America thereby nullifying Irish Catholic influence was absurd. That absurdity lies at the heart of the affine protection afforded the Catholic community in Ireland.

The Impact of War

Warfare though, may invert the affinity condition. While earlier, Eastern European Jews were protected by the existence of politically powerful Jews in the Soviet Union and Hitler's desire to avoid antagonizing the US, when the Nazis invaded the Soviet Union, the Jewish 'threat' had to be neutralized.

87 Quoted in Paul Bew, 'Versions of Murder,' *Times Literary Supplement* 5281 (June 18, 2004): p. 11.

88 Tanner, *Ireland's Holy Wars*, p. 298.

Armenians protected by the February 1914 agreement between the Ottoman Empire and Russia,[89] suddenly were transformed by the war into highly threatening Russian handmaidens that needed to be dealt with harshly. And when the United Nations as a local protector decided to withdraw its troops from Rwanda, this was the signal for the genocide to be enacted throughout the country.[90] Ottoman Greeks were saved from extinction not only by the affinity condition of extreme Allied, especially British protectiveness towards them, and existence of the Greek state itself, but by the emergence of Turkey as victorious in the later Greco-Turkish war that removed Turkey from the domain of losses. Genocide of the Vietnamese in Cambodia accelerated rapidly as the Khmer Rouge were being decisively defeated in the quickening border war with Vietnam.[91]

Precisely because the affinity condition restricts the decision latitude of the potential victimizer and in that sense magnifies the threat of both the potential victims and their affine protector, when war breaks out, these strictures no longer hold. Genocide then becomes a distinct possibility. This, perhaps, is the paradox of affinity – protection in peacetime, but much greater vulnerability in time of war.

Conclusion

Yet the ethnoreligious affinity of neighboring populations or protecting foreign governments is not the only way of preventing the genocide of threatened minorities. The existence of potential criminal proceedings against perpetrators of genocide by the International Court of Justice (ICC) is another, albeit still unproven, means of deterring potential perpetrators of genocide. In the absence of significant affine populations or protecting governments, and the willingness of a genocidal leader to risk an ICC indictment as in Sudan, there must be an additional deterrent.

This is the establishment and propagation of the R2P norm. If sufficiently grounded in international norms and expectations, then most any sizable country could be called upon to intervene in the event of a genocidal occurrence, even a large-scale massacre. Although this norm does not conform to

89 Alan Bodger, 'Russia and the End of the Ottoman Empire,' in Marian Kent, ed., *The Great Powers and the End of the Ottoman Empire* (London: George Allen and Unwin, 1984), p. 96.

90 Roméo Dallaire, *Shake Hands With the Devil: The Failure of Humanity in Rwanda* (Toronto: Random House Canada, 2003), p. 232.

91 Midlarsky, *The Killing Trap*, pp. 312–315.

contemporary realpolitik considerations, continued efforts at R2P could yield unexpected dividends. The 1975 Helsinki Accords among the US, Canada, and most European states including the Soviet Union, mandated respect for human rights and served as a barrier against Soviet mistreatment of minorities. It also enhanced Soviet willingness to allow them to emigrate, if they wished to do so. These successes of the Accords provide a model for the future protection of threatened populations.

More generally, these Accords may have been a progenitor of the influence of human rights concerns originating mainly in the West on governments that might not otherwise have accepted R2P. Because of the insistence on the rule of law by Western corporations and governments as well as major international organizations, many non-Western governments want to be seen as rule of law actors.[92] This image would make it easier for these governments to do business with the West either in the form of trade, investment, aid, or other economic necessities. In this sense, although not manifested in the form of international legal agreements, the French affine protection of Jews in late 18th century Poland may have been an even earlier instance of human rights protection in the West providing a model for countries further to the East.

Regrettably, Western human rights influence may extend more completely only to smaller countries with threatened minority populations. When confronted with larger powers like Russia with large militaries and extensive natural resources at their disposal, Western protection of minorities such as the Ukrainians and Crimean Tartars now absorbed into Russia, may not be as effective. Yet, the more the West – the US and EU – oppose this annexation of Crimea (short of war), the more reluctant Vladimir Putin will be to oppress these minorities for fear of needlessly antagonizing the West. Under these conditions, even the thought of genocide is exceedingly remote. In already according official status in Crimea to the Ukrainian and Crimean Tartar languages along with Russian, Putin may have been deflecting potential Western criticism of his treatment of minorities. Affine protection of minorities can assume many forms, including those inspired by considerations of a prudent realpolitik.

---

92 Karen J. Alter, *The New Terrain of International Law: Courts, Politics, Rights* (Princeton, NJ, Princeton University Press: 2014).

CHAPTER 5

Rethinking Approaches to Prevention under the Responsibility to Protect: Agency and Empowerment within Vulnerable Populations

Deborah Mayersen
University of Wollongong
mayersen@uow.edu.au

Abstract

Within the responsibility to protect (R2P) principle, there is an assumption that is rarely questioned. Beneath the statement that states and the international community are charged with the responsibility to protect populations from genocide, war crimes, crimes against humanity and ethnic cleansing, lies the implication that vulnerable populations cannot protect themselves. In periods of crisis, when the international community might consider mobilising a response under pillar three, this is often the case. Yet outside of such crises, when pillar one – the enduring responsibility of the state to protect its own populations – and pillar two – assistance from the international community to meet this responsibility – might be invoked in a preventive capacity, vulnerable populations may not be wholly reliant upon protection from external actors. In these circumstances, persecuted groups may actively seek to protect themselves, and may be successfully able to do so. In this paper, I challenge the current understanding of prevention within R2P as an externally imposed process, by considering how persecuted groups have themselves acted in ways that mitigate their vulnerability to mass atrocities. The paper considers a number of historical case studies in which targeted groups were able to leverage their own agency, often with assistance from others, to reduce this vulnerability. These include cases that culminated in genocide, namely the experiences of German and Austrian Jews under Nazi rule, and negative cases studies in which a demonstrable risk of mass atrocities was not realised, such as the experiences of Yemenite Jews in the first half of the twentieth century and those of the Bahá'í community in Iran since the 1979 Iranian revolution. These cases suggest that assisting persecuted populations to empower themselves can be an effective way to promote resilience to mass atrocities. In the final section of the paper, I explore why this approach is often overlooked, despite its capacity for some success. I consider the potential benefits and costs of a

 | DOI 10.1163/9789004299870_007

greater focus on utilising the agency of vulnerable groups in endeavours to prevent mass atrocities.

Keywords

genocide – genocide prevention – responsibility to protect (R2P)

Introduction

'Prompt, defensive measures are the most effective means for the prevention of genocide' concluded the 1967 Congress for the Prevention of Genocide.[1] Several decades later, the international community continues to wrestle with the difficult problem of preventing genocide and mass atrocities, most recently through the responsibility to protect (populations from genocide, crimes against humanity, war crimes and ethnic cleansing) principle. Yet the concept of persecuted groups utilising their agency to mitigate risk of mass atrocities is one that is now largely overlooked. The focus of major reports on mass atrocity prevention, such as *The Responsibility to Protect*, *Preventing Genocide: A Blueprint for U.S. Policymakers* and *Mobilizing the Will to Intervene* is centred at the level of the state, and preventive measures suggested in these reports, along with those of regular reports on R2P emanating from the UN Secretary-General, largely involve external actors.[2] The very concept of the responsibility to protect assumes a population in need of protection – that is, one unable to protect itself. While this may often be true during crisis periods, its applicability across broader situations in which there are opportunities for mass atrocity

---

1 V.V. Stanciu, 'Reflections on the Congress for the Prevention of Genocide', *Yad Vashem Studies* 7: 185–187 (1968).

2 International Commission on Intervention and State Sovereignty, *The Responsibility to Protect* (Ottawa: International Development Research Centre, 2001); Genocide Prevention Task Force, *Preventing Genocide: A Blueprint for U.S. Policymakers* (Washington DC: The United States Holocaust Memorial Museum, The American Academy of Diplomacy and the United States Institute of Peace, 2008); The Montreal Institute for Genocide and Human Rights Studies, *Mobilizing the Will to Intervene: Leadership and Action to Prevent Mass Atrocities* (Montreal: Concordia University, 2009); United Nations General Assembly/Security Council, 'Responsibility to Protect: State Responsibility and Prevention: Report of the Secretary-General', A/67/929-S/2013/399, 9 July 2013; United National General Assembly, 'Implementing the Responsibility to Protect: Report of the Secretary-General', A/63/677, 12 January 2009.

prevention measures is questionable. After examining the factors that have contributed to this assumption, this paper explores several historical cases in which vulnerable groups have been able to utilise their agency to ameliorate their risk or experience of mass atrocities. In two cases of mass atrocities, that is the experiences of German and Austrian Jews under Nazi rule, members of the targeted groups were able to utilise their agency to ensure that at least some of the group did not fall victim to genocide. In two 'negative' case studies, in which demonstrable risk of mass atrocities can be identified but did not occur during the period under consideration, Yemenite Jewry in the period 1900–1950 and the Bahá'í religious minority in Iran since 1979 were each able to utilise their agency to significantly reduce their vulnerability to such crimes. Following these case study examinations, the paper then analyses why the agency of persecuted groups is often overlooked as a potential contributor to mass atrocity prevention, despite its ability to have a real impact. The final section of the paper suggests that it is beneficial to consider how vulnerable populations can play an active role in mass atrocity prevention measures.

The Responsibility to Protect, Mass Atrocity Prevention and the Agency of Vulnerable Populations

The concept of a 'responsibility to protect' emerged out of the failure of the United Nations and the international community to respond effectively to the genocidal violence of the 1990s in Rwanda and the Balkans. The inaction of the UN Security Council in response to the 1994 genocide in Rwanda; and the 1995 genocidal killing of thousands of Bosnian men and boys who had sought UN protection in the 'safe area' of Srebrenica, severely damaged the credibility of the UN Security Council as the body primarily responsible for the maintenance of international peace and security under the UN Charter.[3] In the late 1990s, the war in Kosovo further challenged the Council. While it remained deadlocked over the crisis, the intervention of the North Atlantic Treaty Organisation (NATO) curbed the violence, but not without controversy. Subsequently UN Secretary-General Kofi Annan expressed his concern that 'unless the Security Council is restored to its pre-eminent position as the sole source of legitimacy on the use of force, we are on a dangerous path to anarchy'.[4] To this end, Annan

3 United Nations, *Charter of the United Nations*, https://www.un.org/en/documents/charter/, accessed 26 March 2014.

4 Cited in Stanley Meisler, *Kofi Annan: A Man of Peace in a World of War* (London: Wiley, 2007), p. 178.

called for efforts to resolve the impasse that had prevented UN action, that is, the dilemma between the principles of sovereignty and those of human rights.

In response to this call, the International Commission on Intervention and State Sovereignty (ICISS) was established. Its 2001 report, *The Responsibility to Protect*, recast the debate over sovereignty and intervention by focussing upon sovereignty as incorporating responsibility.[5] Nation states have a responsibility to protect their citizens, it asserted, and in the event that they are unable or unwilling to do so, this responsibility extends to the international community. This finding gained international acceptance at the World Summit in 2005, at which UN member states agreed 'Each individual State has the responsibility to protect its populations from genocide, war crimes, ethnic cleansing and crimes against humanity.'[6] The international community also accepted a responsibility to help protect populations from these crimes, through peaceful means. Should national authorities manifestly fail to protect their populations, however, nation states declared they were 'prepared to take collective action, in a timely and decisive manner, through the Security Council ... on a case-by-case basis.'[7] Such action could include non-consensual military intervention under chapter seven of the UN Charter.

The events that led to the establishment of the R2P norm have undoubtedly contributed to its focus on protecting groups from mass atrocities in times of crisis. As the ICISS report noted, R2P 'implies above all else a responsibility to react to situations of compelling need for human protection.'[8] Accordingly, the report gave the strongest emphasis to issues surrounding intervention.[9] Moreover, 'In academic, policy, and diplomatic circles, there is also a tendency to focus on this aspect of R2P and to evaluate and assess the effectiveness of the norm primarily, or even exclusively, in terms of whether a military response to a specific crisis took place and whether the military response was effective.'[10]

Certainly R2P also highlights the importance of prevention. The World Summit outcome document specifically identifies that each state's responsibility to protect its population from mass atrocities 'entails the prevention of such

5 ICISS, *The Responsibility to Protect*.

6 United Nations General Assembly, '2005 World Summit Outcome,' A/60/L1, September 15, 2005, paras. 138–140.

7 Ibid.

8 ICISS, *The Responsibility to Protect*, p. 29.

9 Alex Bellamy, 'The Responsibility to Protect and the Problem of Military Intervention', *International Affairs* 84/4: 615–39 (2008), p. 621.

10 Noha Shawki, 'Responsibility to Protect: The Evolution of an International Norm', *Global Responsibility to Protect* 3/2: 172–96 (2011), p. 180.

crimes, including their incitement, through appropriate and necessary means'.[11] The international community also committed to 'helping States build capacity to protect their populations ... and to assisting those which are under stress before crises and conflicts break out.'[12] Yet the predominant focus on situations of crisis limits the manner in which prevention is both conceptualised and practically envisaged.

The ICISS viewed prevention as 'an accompanying responsibility' implied by the responsibility to protect.[13] In some respects even the phrase 'responsibility to protect' implies a situation of crisis, in which external actors of some kind (international, national or local) are required 'to protect' a population or group unable to protect itself. In crises, where non-consensual international intervention may be proposed, this is typically the case. Yet in cases in which preventive measures may be appropriate, this implies a powerlessness and imbues a passivity upon vulnerable groups that may be both inaccurate and counterproductive.

More recently, a new term has entered the lexicon alongside 'protection' and 'prevention'. In his 2013 report on the responsibility to protect, the Secretary-General spoke of the need to build societies that are 'resilient' to mass atrocity crimes. Building national resilience can contribute to preventing mass atrocities, according to the report, and the Secretary-General called upon member states to 'conduct a national assessment of risk and resilience' which 'should include the identification of vulnerable populations'.[14] While protection, prevention and resilience are used almost as synonyms in this document, however, functionally they can involve very different pathways and lead to outcomes of varying desirability. An outcome in which a population is 'protected' for example, may still be one in which large-scale violence and displacement occurs; successful prevention would likely not involve a crisis of that magnitude. Resilience implies an ability to manage an ongoing and dynamic situation of risk, as previous research in this area demonstrates.[15] Distinguishing

11 UNGA, '2005 World Summit Outcome.'

12 Ibid.

13 ICISS, *The Responsibility to Protect*, p. 19.

14 UNGA, 'Responsibility to Protect: State Responsibility and Prevention', pp. 8–11, 16.

15 Deborah Mayersen and Stephen McLoughlin, 'Risk and Resilience to Mass Atrocities in Africa: A Comparison of Rwanda and Botswana,' *Journal of Genocide Research* 13/3: 247–69 (2011); Stephen McLoughlin and Deborah Mayersen, 'Reconsidering Root Causes: A New Framework for the Structural Prevention of Genocide and Mass Atrocities', in *Genocide, Risk and Resilience: An Interdisciplinary Approach*, ed. Bert Ingelaere, Stephan Parmentier, Jacques Haers and Barbara Segaert (New York: Palgrave MacMillan, 2013).

between these pathways and outcomes is particularly significant when discussing agency and empowerment within vulnerable populations. As the case studies below demonstrate, different contexts can constrain potential outcomes such that while goals of protection or partial protection may be feasible, those of prevention or resilience may not.

In this paper I utilise the conceptual prism of agency to examine the role of vulnerable groups and other key actors in cases of genocide and mass atrocities and cases in which there is demonstrable risk of mass atrocities. Agency, which can be defined as a capacity to act in a range of ways, is a concept often utilised in gender studies, and has been helpful in exploring the boundaries of women's capacity to act in situations in which they are vulnerable or constrained by difficult circumstances. While it has rarely been utilised in the context of mass atrocity prevention, it can similarly be helpful in exploring the (often limited) capacity of vulnerable groups to act in ways that may ameliorate risk of mass atrocities, typically in difficult circumstances.[16] Utilising this concept to examine mass atrocities or situations of potential mass atrocity also facilitates a deeper understanding of the role of different groups in contributing to violent or non-violent outcomes.

In any mass atrocity or potential mass atrocity, three primary categories of actors can be identified: persecutors/perpetrators, bystanders and targeted groups/victims. In a case of genocide such as the Holocaust, the Nazi perpetrators possessed a high degree of agency while the agency of bystanders, including allied nations, ordinary Germans and others, and that of victims, was severely circumscribed. In other genocides, such as the 1994 Rwanda genocide, the Hutu extremist perpetrators possessed a high degree of agency, and the Tutsi and moderate Hutu victims a very low degree of agency, but the agency of bystanders was more variable. While many bystanders within Rwanda had a limited capacity to act, the international community did not utilise their potential agency to intervene to curb the genocide. In cases in which mass atrocities have not occurred, but in which there are sufficient indicators of risk to deem prevention measures appropriate, the agency of each category of actor can be even more variable. The agency of persecutors may be circumscribed by fear of international intervention, for example, or a need to maintain good relations with other nation states for economic reasons. Persecuted groups or vulnerable minorities may have the capacity to respond to their circumstances in a range of ways that are less likely to be available on the cusp of

16 An important exception can be found in Erin Baines and Emily Paddon, 'This is How we Survived: Civilian Agency and Humanitarian Protection,' *Security Dialogue* 43/3: 231–47 (2012).

extreme violence. In Botswana, for example, the San Bushman have been recognised by Genocide Watch as being a vulnerable minority, potentially at risk of experiencing mass atrocities.[17] The strong rule of law in Botswana, however, means the San Bushman have been able to utilise their ongoing capacity to legally challenge government measures they consider oppressive, with some success.[18] With the assistance of international civil society organisations in this process, this has contributed to the ongoing resilience of the Bushmen despite their challenging circumstances.

This capacity of vulnerable groups to act in self-protective ways, however, and how it may contribute to mass atrocity prevention, has been largely overlooked in the slew of official reports that have been published on prevention in recent years. The ICISS, for example, reported 'Effective conflict prevention depends on disparate actors working together', but in the long list of 'actors' that follows, does not mention targeted groups themselves as a potential actor.[19] Even when highlighting the importance of local and detailed knowledge and understanding in root cause prevention efforts, there is a distinction made between 'helpers and those helped'.[20] Perhaps the closest it comes to recognising the potential capacity of vulnerable groups is through the recognition that 'when solutions are needed, it is the citizens of a particular state who have the greatest interest and the largest stake in the success of those solutions'.[21] *Preventing Genocide: A Blueprint for U.S. Policymakers* does only slightly better in considering the capacity of vulnerable groups to contribute to mass atrocity prevention measures. The only mention of such a capacity within the 'Early Prevention' section of the report is to suggest that 'popular resistance to mass violence by a broad cross-section of society, rather than solely vulnerable groups, can be a far more powerful response than international condemnation.'[22] *Preventing Genocide* recognises the importance of leadership in mass atrocity prevention, but misses the opportunity to specifically acknowledge that such leadership can also come from within vulnerable groups. The role of Nelson Mandela in promoting a nonviolent response to the oppression of black South Africans under Apartheid, for example, has been credited with

17 See Genocide Prevention Advisory Network, *Genocides, Politicides, and Other Mass Murder Since 1945, With Stages in 2008*, http://www.gpanet.org/content/genocides-politicides-and-other-mass-murder-1945-stages-2008, accessed 26 March 2014.

18 Mayersen and McLoughlin, 'Risk and Resilience to Mass Atrocities in Africa', pp. 247–69.

19 ICISS, *The Responsibility to Protect*, p. 25.

20 Ibid, p. 23.

21 Ibid, p. 17.

22 Genocide Prevention Task Force, *Preventing Genocide*, p. 41.

reducing the risk of mass atrocities there.[23] Elsewhere the report does consider that roles can be multifarious, such as that of women as both particularly vulnerable to atrocities and deeply involved in conflict mitigation efforts, highlighting the missed opportunity to consider the often similarly complex role of vulnerable groups.[24] Other reports are similarly focussed on preventive measures that are often externally-imposed, state-based, institutional, or at best, refer to 'local' actors without adequately defining this conception.[25]

In the broader scholarship examining the responsibility to protect, there have also been relatively few attempts to explore the agency of vulnerable groups in preventing or protecting themselves from mass atrocities. A notable exception is that Frédéric Mégret.[26] Across a large range of case studies of atrocities, Mégret identified that while the atrocities were underway, a large portion of those who survived or escaped did so through their own efforts, or through resistance movements.[27] That is, in Mégret's case studies at least, 'resistance by the victims of atrocities and by civil society more broadly has proven to be possibly the most significant factor in limiting, pushing back or even stopping atrocities.'[28] Numerous studies have also examined humanitarian self-protection in war or conflict zones, some of which can also be identified as locations at high risk of genocide or ethnic cleansing, or in which war crimes and crimes against humanity have occurred. Baines and Paddon identified three strategies used by civilians in a conflict zone in northern Uganda.[29] Civilians attempted to display neutrality in the conflict, sought to avoid soldiers or rebels through hiding upon their approach, and/or utilised strategies of accommodation, whereby limited cooperation was offered in return for protection.[30] Similarly, research commissioned by the Humanitarian Practice Network exploring self-protection in Myanmar, Sudan, South Sudan and Zimbabwe identified strategies including avoidance, often through forced displacement, and efforts to contain the threat, either through local leadership negotiating with power holders to contain the situation, or through 'silence

23 David Hamburg, *Preventing Genocide: Practical Steps Toward Early Detection and Effective Action* (Boulder: Paradigm Publishers, 2008), pp. 72–96.

24 Genocide Prevention Task Force, *Preventing Genocide*, p. 49.

25 UNGA, 'Responsibility to Protect: State Responsibility and Prevention'; UNGA, 'Implementing the Responsibility to Protect'.

26 Frédéric Mégret, 'Beyond the "Salvation" Paradigm: Responsibility to Protect (Others) vs the Power of Protecting Oneself', *Security Dialogue* 40/6: 575–95 (2009).

27 Mégret, 'Beyond the "Salvation" Paradigm', p. 583.

28 Ibid.

29 Baines and Paddon, 'This is How we Survived'.

30 Ibid, pp. 236–41.

and acquiescence to the demands of the powerful'.[31] An inventory published by The Cuny Center documenting how civilians protect their physical safety during violence also lists accommodation and avoidance prominently, alongside the use of protective social networks, links to patronage powers, and forms of armed resistance including community protection groups.[32] More broadly still, scholars have examined the role of civil resistance, both violent and non-violent. Stephan and Chenoweth, for example, have concluded that non-violent civil resistance can be more effective than violent resistance in political struggles.[33] From an atrocity prevention lens, however, it is difficult to gauge the relevance of this broader scholarship on humanitarian self-protection. Many of the case studies from which it has been developed are examples of conflict, war or political struggle, but these are not analogous with genocide, ethnic cleansing, or widespread war crimes or crimes against humanity. That is, avoidance or accommodation are potentially far more likely to be effective self-protection strategies in a conflict that is not specifically targeting inhabitants of the conflict zone, than in circumstances in which an ideologically motivated regime is deliberately seeking to destroy or remove a vulnerable group. It is therefore valuable to specifically consider the impact of agency of vulnerable groups in preventing and protecting themselves from atrocity crimes.

In the following section, I present four historical case studies demonstrating how the agency of vulnerable groups can be a significant and even critical factor influencing protection from, prevention of and resilience to mass atrocities. The first two case studies, of the experiences of German and Austrian Jews under Nazi rule, highlight that even in the most desperate of circumstances, the agency of persecuted groups can be somewhat effective in mitigating the impact of perpetrators and saving large numbers of lives. Case studies of genocide and mass atrocities, however, while most commonly utilised in the scholarship, inherently reveal much more about risk than resilience to such crimes. In these examples, processes of risk escalation have dominated, and those that may mitigate against genocide have become inoperable over time.[34]

31 Ashley South and Simon Harragin, with Justin Corbett, Richard Horsey, Susanne Kempel, Henrik Fröjmark and Nils Carstensen, *Local to Global Protection in Myanmar (Burma), Sudan, South Sudan and Zimbabwe*, Humanitarian Practice Network at the Overseas Development Institute, Number 72, February 2012, pp. 7, 11.

32 Casey Barrs, *How Civilians Survive Violence: A Preliminary Inventory*, The Cuny Center, November 2010.

33 Maria Stephan and Erica Chenoweth, 'Why Civil Resistance Works: The Strategic Logic of Nonviolent Conflict,' *International Security* 33/1: 7–44 (2008), p. 8.

34 McLoughlin and Mayersen, 'Reconsidering Root Causes', pp. 49–67.

To properly examine factors that promote resilience, therefore, the most illustrative case studies are those in which there is a demonstrable risk of mass atrocities, but in which such atrocities have not occurred (in the period under consideration). For this reason, the second two case studies, of the experiences of Yemenite Jewry in the first half of the twentieth century, and of the experiences of Iranian Bahá'í since the 1979 Iranian revolution, are 'negative' case studies, in which processes of resilience rather than risk have dominated.

Agency and Amelioration: Escaping Genocide and Preventing Mass Atrocities

German Jewry: 1933–1939

The experiences of German and Austrian Jews between 1933, when Hitler took power in Germany, and 1941, when the most intensive phase of the Holocaust began, highlight that persecuted groups are often intensely active in attempting to reduce their risk of experiencing mass atrocities. In 1933, there were approximately 525,000 Jews living in Germany.[35] Almost immediately after the Nazi government took power, discriminatory and persecutory measures commenced against them. Jews were progressively banned from employment in the civil service, academia, law, business and so forth. The 1935 Nuremberg laws banned marriage or sexual relations between Jews and non-Jews. Yet at the same time, it was not clear that these actions were a prelude to genocide, rather than a period of persecution and discrimination like that which European Jews had experienced many times previously. Nevertheless, about a quarter of the German Jewish population emigrated between 1933 and 1937.[36] In 1938 anti-Jewish measures intensified, including special marking of identity papers and passports, the expulsion of Jewish children from state schools, and the commencement of ghettoization.[37] Synagogues were destroyed, and on 9–10 November 1938, Nazi-organised riots erupted, in which thousands of Jewish-owned shops and synagogues were attacked and looted, and 91 Jews killed.[38]

35 Marion Kaplan, 'Persecution and Gender: German-Jewish Responses to Nazism, 1933–39,' in Jonathan Friedman (ed.), *The Routledge History of the Holocaust* (London: Routledge, 2012), p. 90.

36 David Engel, *The Holocaust: The Third Reich and the Jews* (Essex, UK: Longman: 2000), p. 41.

37 Ibid, p. 33.

38 Peter Longerich, *Holocaust: The Nazi Persecution and Murder of the Jews* (Oxford: Oxford University Press, 2010), pp. 109–113; Engel, *The Holocaust*, p. 34; John Dippel, *Bound upon a Wheel of Fire: Why So Many German Jews made the Tragic Decision to Remain in Nazi Germany* (New York: Basic Books, 1996), pp. 233–54.

Kristallnacht (the 'night of the broken glass'), as this event is known, contributed to intensified emigration, along with Nazi policy that also sought Jewish emigration. In 1938, 40,000 Jews left Germany, and that figured almost doubled to 78,000 in 1939.[39] By the outbreak of war, less than 200,000 of the 525,000 population of 1933 remained in Germany.

Austrian Jewry 1938–1939

In Austria, Jewish emigration was even more pronounced. Following the *Anschluss*, the March 1938 German annexation of Austria, Nazi policy strongly encouraged Jewish emigration. At the same time, Austrian Jews experienced discriminatory measures, violence, and terror. *Kristallnacht* was 'particularly brutal' in Austria.[40] In Vienna, where more than 90 per cent of Austrian Jews resided, most of the synagogues were destroyed, and Jewish businesses attacked.[41] Of the 192,000 Jews in Austria at the time of the *Anschluss* in 1938, 110,000 had emigrated by mid-1939.[42] These extraordinary levels of emigration, from both Germany and Austria, are even more remarkable when some of the obstacles to emigration are considered. The primary obstacle was the unwillingness of many countries to accept Jewish immigrants, motivated both by the economic crisis and high unemployment of the 1930s, and traditional antisemitism.[43] Additionally, there were significant financial costs. In Germany, for example, in order to emigrate a person had to pay a flight tax of 25 per cent of his property.[44] Further practical barriers included matters such as having to learn a new language, likely poorer economic prospects or lack of recognition of qualifications in foreign countries and issues of how to manage elderly or infirm relatives. Moreover, many German and Austrian Jews were highly assimilated and considered themselves primarily 'German' or 'Austrian' and only then Jewish, and there was often a real tension between feelings of patriotism and loyalty, and the pariah status accorded Jews.[45] Given these formidable

---

39 Engel, *The Holocaust*, p. 42; slightly lower figures are provided in Yehuda Bauer, *A History of the Holocaust* (New York: Franklin Watts, 1982), p. 109.

40 United States Holocaust Memorial Museum, 'Austria', in *Holocaust Encyclopedia*, http://www.ushmm.org/wlc/en/article.php?ModuleId=10005447, accessed 14 February 2014.

41 Ibid.

42 Ibid; Lee Igel, 'The Fate of the Jews in Austria, 1933–39,' in Jonathan Friedman (ed.) *The Routledge History of The Holocaust* (New York: Routledge, 2012), p. 109; Bauer, *A History of the Holocaust*, p. 109.

43 Bauer, *A History of the Holocaust*, p. 125.

44 Ibid, p. 123.

45 Ibid, p. 119.

obstacles, it is extraordinary that well over half of German and Austrian Jewry, within a few short years, were able to protect themselves from Nazi violence through emigration. While many of these Jews were subsequently caught up in the Holocaust due to the Nazi territorial conquests during World War Two, a substantial portion of these emigrants escaped the Holocaust altogether through these actions. For those Jews who did not emigrate prior to the outbreak of war, however, their agency quickly became very severely circumscribed. The relatively orderly emigration of the mid-1930s gave way to increasingly desperate attempts to flee by any means as the Nazi persecution intensified. By this stage, persecuted groups largely lacked sufficient agency to protect themselves.

Yemenite Jewry: 1900–1950

In circumstances in which persecution is less severe, and in which there are bystanders willing to assist, there may be even greater capacity for targeted groups to utilise their agency to prevent the commission of mass atrocities. The experience of Yemenite Jewry between 1900 and 1950 provides an illustrative example. A Jewish community had existed in Yemen since ancient times, predating the arrival of both Christianity and Islam to the region. When Islam came to dominate, Jewish communities in the area were either destroyed or subjugated.[46] Jews became *dhimmi*, a non-Moslem minority with some rights but an inferior status to Moslems. This longstanding arrangement continued under Ottoman rule of Yemen, and in areas of Yemen that came to be ruled as an independent Islamic kingdom. Aden, in the southern part of Yemen, came under British administration from 1839, and the Jews there enjoyed the protection of British authorities and equality before the law.[47]

In highland Yemen, under Islamic rule, the Jews experienced discrimination and some persecution. They also suffered alongside the Moslem population from drought, famine, locust plagues, and battles between Ottoman forces and Yemenite Iman Yahya ibn Muhammad for control over territory.[48] Following World War One, Yahya assumed control of much of the country (excluding areas under British administration), imposing Islamic Sharia law with vigour, although this was somewhat tempered by his relatively poor control over much of his territory.[49] Under Sharia, Jews were subject to a range of discriminatory

46 Tudor Parfitt, *The Road to Redemption: The Jews of Yemen 1900–1950* (New York: EJ Brill, 1996), p. 14.

47 Ibid, p. 23.

48 Ibid, pp. 35–37.

49 Ibid, pp. 41–42.

measures such as being forbidden to engage in the same commerce as Arabs. They had to pay special taxes, and they could not build a house higher than those of Moslems, brush against a Moslem in the street, bear arms or ride animals using a normal saddle.[50] The discriminatory measure that caused greatest distress to the Jewish community, however, was the forced conversion of Jewish orphans, introduced by the Iman in 1922. Under this custom, children whose fathers had died were to be seized and raised as Moslems.[51] These measures contributed to a rise in Jewish emigration to Aden, and to Palestine. In the 1930s, anti-Jewish feeling in Yemen, and to a lesser extent Aden, increased as a result of both anti-Zionist feeling amongst Arabs due to the increasing Jewish immigration into British Palestine, and the infiltration of Nazi propaganda. Jews in Yemen were forbidden to leave the country in an effort to prevent emigration to Palestine. Conditions deteriorated during World War Two, with one report noting 'deplorable conditions ... the death rate is particularly high, due to their impoverished condition, the lack of food and the lack of sanitary facilities, the heavy head tax levied on Jews only, the cruel and anti-Jewish laws, and the treatment accorded them by their Arab master as a degraded people'.[52] In 1947 an Arab riot against the Jewish community of Aden led to a pogrom that killed more than 80 Jews.[53]

The discrimination and violence against Jews suggests that there was a risk of mass atrocities being persecuted against them in this period. However a unique set of circumstances gave this vulnerable group sufficient agency to act decisively to protect itself. The establishment of the State of Israel in 1948, and the new nation's willingness to accept Jewish immigration, and that of Jewish and Israeli organisations to help finance and organise such immigration, provided an opportunity for Yemenite Jewry to seek asylum. Despite the process of emigration itself being very arduous, the overwhelming majority of the Jewish community in Yemen sought to emigrate as soon as possible. Between December 1948 and September 1950, 49,637 Jews from the Yemen and Aden were flown to Israel.[54] At the conclusion of the airlift, it was estimated that

---

50 Keren Hayesod, *The Exodus from Yemen* (Jerusalem: Keren Hayesod, [1950]); Parfitt, *The Road to Redemption*, pp. 41–42.

51 Ari Ariel, *Jewish-Muslim Relations and Migration from Yemen to Palestine in the Late Nineteenth and Twentieth Centuries* (Boston: Brill, 2014), pp. 117–136; Keren Hayesod, *The Exodus from Yemen*; Bat-Zion Eraqi-Klorman, 'The Forced Conversion of Jewish Orphans in Yemen,' *International Journal of Middle Eastern Studies* 33: 23–47 (2001).

52 Quoted in Parfitt, *The Road to Redemption*, p. 143.

53 Parfitt, *The Road to Redemption*, p. 167.

54 Reuben Ahroni, *Jewish Emigration from the Yemen 1951–98* (Richmond, UK: Curzon Press, 2001), p. 1; Parfitt, *The Road to Redemption*, p. 283.

1000–3000 Jews remained in the Yemen.[55] This mass emigration obviated the risk of mass atrocities being experienced. Subsequent events have highlighted the ongoing nature of this risk, with the remnant community suffering ongoing persecution, and many subsequently joining their brethren in Israel.[56] The vast majority of the community, however, had been able to utilise its agency to completely prevent any further risk of experiencing mass atrocities.

Iranian Bahá'í: 1979-Present

The Bahá'í community in Iran have also demonstrated the capacity to protect themselves from mass atrocities in recent decades. The Bahá'í religion was founded in Iran in the mid-nineteenth century and today there are around five million Bahá'í globally, with more than 300,000 in Iran.[57] The followers of the Bahá'í faith have experienced ongoing persecution since its inception.[58] Religious intolerance is the primary driver of the persecution of Bahá'í in Iran. The Bahá'í religion is perceived as illegitimate: 'Since Mohammed was the last prophet according to orthodox Islamic view to whom God revealed a message, no other religions which developed after his death are granted the right to exist'.[59] Since the nineteenth century the community has experienced sporadic violence and massacre, restrictions on marriage, employment and education; harassment, and limited legal recourse. However, the period of greatest concern has been since the 1979 Islamic revolution, when Iran became an Islamic republic with a religious legal foundation. According to one analyst, 'This differed qualitatively from the situation before 1979 in that whereas previously the Bahá'ís merely fell victim to sporadic government actions, there was now a specific and planned programme for the elimination of the Bahá'í community.'[60] In the early 1980s, prominent members of the Bahá'í community were targeted in a series of arrests, disappearances, and executions.[61] Bahá'í communal property was confiscated, and Bahá'í holy sites destroyed. Individual

55 Ahroni, *Jewish Emigration*, p. 2.

56 David Pinault 'Hidden Prayer in Yemen: Islam and the Problem of Religious Intolerance', *America* 201/17: 10–14 (2009), pp. 11–12.

57 Friedrich Affolter, 'The Specter of Ideological Genocide: The Bahá'ís of Iran', *War Crimes, Genocide, & Crimes against Humanity* 1/1: 75–114 (2005), p. 78.

58 Ibid.

59 Thomas Schirrmacher, 'Iran: Suppression of religious freedom and persecution of religious minorities', *International Journal for Religious Freedom* 2/1: 111–130 (2009), p. 117.

60 Moojan Momen, 'The Babi and Bahá'í community of Iran: A case of "suspended genocide"?' *Journal of Genocide Research* 7/ 2: 221–241 (2005), p. 224.

61 Roger Cooper, 'The Bahá'ís of Iran: A Minority Rights Group Report', (London: Minority Rights, 1985), p. 10.

Bahá'í were dismissed from government employment, summarily arrested and tortured, subject to harassment and violence, and by 1985 almost 200 had been killed for their religious beliefs.[62] Many of the risk factors for genocide can be identified in the experiences of this vulnerable religious group.

The Bahá'í community, both in Iran and internationally, decided to respond to the increasing persecution through a campaign to raise global awareness of the plight of Iranian Bahá'í. Bahá'í worked to bring the situation to the attention of the United Nations, the governments of many countries (particularly in the West), the Council of Europe and the European parliament, human rights groups, the media and the general public.[63] The community employed a public relations firm to develop the most effective strategies for reaching policy and decision makers.[64] The resulting efforts were very successful in obtaining the sympathy of the international community. Since 1980, various organs of the United Nations, including the General Assembly, the Commission of Human Rights and the Economic and Social Council have passed resolutions demonstrating concern regarding the situation of the Bahá'í community in Iran almost every year.[65] In 1997, for example, the General Assembly expressed its concern 'at the grave breaches of the human rights of the Bahá'ís', calling upon Iran to abide by its obligations under international human rights law.[66] A number of factors aided the Bahá'í community in their campaign. According to Bigelow, 'That the Bahá'í case is so straightforward has been an important component of the overall success of the publicity campaign.'[67] That is, it has been easy to demonstrate that the Bahá'í community has been persecuted on specifically religious grounds, with Iranian authorities offering to withdraw punishments should the victims recant their faith.[68] Additionally, the Iranian government has not been able to produce any evidence of sedition within the Bahá'í community, despite many accusations. The particular approach of the Bahá'í community to their oppression, one of 'constructive resilience' guided by Bahá'í religious beliefs, has also been productive in stabilising the situation.[69]

62 Ibid, p. 13.

63 Affolter, 'The Specter of Ideological Genocide', p. 100.

64 Katharine Bigelow, 'A Campaign to Deter Genocide: The Bahá'í Experience', in Helen Fein (ed.), *Genocide Watch* (New Haven, CT: Yale University Press, 1992), pp. 193–95.

65 For a listing of resolutions, see Bahá'í International Community, *The Bahá'í Question: Cultural Cleansing in Iran* (New York: Bahá'í International Community, 2008), appendix II.

66 Ibid, p. 71.

67 Bigelow, 'A Campaign to Deter Genocide', p. 195.

68 Cooper, 'The Bahá'ís of Iran', p. 13.

69 Michael Karlberg, 'Constructive Resilience: The Bahá'í Response to Oppression', *Peace and Change* 35/2: 222–256 (2010).

By 1992, genocide studies pioneer Leo Kuper suggested 'The international surveillance initiated by the Bahá'ís would seem to have restrained the large-scale massacres that earlier appeared imminent.'[70] In 2008, the Bahá'í International Community highlighted in a report that, 'This demonstration of international concern has played a critical role in moderating the actions of the Iranian authorities and providing a measure of security to the Bahá'í community.'[71]

The Bahá'í community has been credited with protecting itself from a precarious situation with a clear potential to escalate into genocide.[72] Yet while this is sometimes presented as the singular explanation for these events, a more nuanced analysis suggests there were a number of additional context-specific factors that contributed to the government being conducive to moderation rather than escalation by the mid-1980s, some of which have continued to play a stabilising role in the longer term. Most immediately, bad economic policies and falling oil prices meant the Iranian government faced significant economic pressures during this period, at the same time as the General Assembly and major trading partners were protesting over human rights.[73] There was thus a strong economic motive for the government to de-escalate the persecution of the Bahá'í minority in order to maintain agreeable trade relations with the West. Second, the Iranian government has long been limited by multiple power centres, ongoing tensions between clerical and more secular government institutions, and factional infighting.[74] While clerical authorities have often dominated, reformers have continued to challenge this, reducing the capacity for the kind of singular narrative and centralisation of power necessary for extremism to flourish. Additionally, during the 1980s the Iran-Iraq war commanded much of the government's attention. Finally, the government has targeted multiple minorities for discrimination and persecution, and while the Bahá'í have fared worst, persecution of intellectuals, reformers, Jews and others has perhaps diffused the focus of the regime. The Presidency of Mahmoud Ahmadinejad (2005–13), in particular, was characterised by vitriol directed towards Israel and the Jews. Together, these factors suggest that a

70 Leo Kuper, 'Reflections on the Prevention of Genocide', in Helen Fein (ed.), *Genocide Watch* (New Haven, CT: Yale University Press, 1992), p. 139.

71 Bahá'í International Community, *The Bahá'í Question*, p. 64.

72 Bigelow, 'A Campaign to Deter Genocide', p. 192; Momen, 'The Babi and Bahá'í community of Iran', p. 238.

73 Patrick Clawson and Michael Rubin, *Eternal Iran: Continuity and Chaos* (New York: Palgrave Macmillan, 2005), p. 103.

74 Patrick Clawson and Michael Rubin, *Eternal Iran: Continuity and Chaos* (New York: Palgrave Macmillan, 2005), pp. 93–98, 115–16, 127.

range of conducive circumstances played a considerable role in aiding the success of the publicity campaign in reducing the persecution of the Bahá'í.

In the late 1980s, the Iranian government appeared to alter its strategy from one of violent persecution to 'less visible and entrenched economic, social and cultural deprivation of rights.'[75] These have included ongoing efforts to prevent Bahá'ís from gaining a higher education, from earning a livelihood, and from being able to celebrate their cultural heritage.[76] Moreover, government-sponsored persecution of the Bahá'í community has re-intensified in the past decade. There have been 710 Bahá'ís arrested since 2005, and heavy prison sentences for crimes such as 'spreading propaganda against the regime'.[77] Crimes committed against members of the Bahá'í community often go unpunished, while the government has conducted an anti-Bahá'í media campaign.[78] Economic and educational discrimination continues. For the Bahá'í, the publicity campaign to reduce their persecution has been far from a panacea. Nevertheless, the resilience of the Bahá'í community is pronounced, and their ongoing campaign for self-protection continues to mitigate the risk of mass atrocities.

Agency and Controversy in Mass Atrocity Prevention

Collectively, the case studies above demonstrate that persecuted groups can play an important and even critical role in preventing and mitigating the impact of mass atrocities. This aligns with previous findings on the importance of resistance by vulnerable groups in protecting themselves from mass atrocities, and on the importance of agency and self-protection in conflict zones more broadly.[79] If agency can be such a powerful mitigating factor, however, it must be questioned as to why it is largely overlooked within rhetoric surrounding the responsibility to protect, and approaches to mass atrocity prevention more broadly. As Mégret has noted, 'There is a considerable gap between contemporary normative debates about what the international community should

75 Nazila Ghanea, *Human Rights, the UN and the Bahá'ís in Iran* (Oxford: George Ronald, 2002), p. 145.

76 Bahá'í International Community, *The Bahá'í Question*, p. 4.

77 Bahá'í International Community, 'Current Situation of Bahá'ís in Iran', 27 January 2014, http://www.bic.org/media/Current-situation-Bahais-in-Iran, accessed 18 February 2014.

78 Ibid.

79 Mégret, 'Beyond the "Salvation" Paradigm'; Baines and Paddon, 'This is how we Survived'; South et al., 'Local to Global Protection'; Barrs, 'How Civilians Survive Violence'.

do to save people, on the one hand, and the reality of what we know about how people have historically been saved, on the other.'[80] In many respects, this can be explained through recognising that the strategies available to vulnerable groups with limited agency are more likely to be protective, or partially protective, rather than preventative or resilient. As such, the solutions they offer are partial and flawed. In particular, within the international community there are strong negative perceptions concerning two of the most common, and historically sometimes the most effective, ways in which vulnerable groups attempt to protect themselves – through flight across borders and armed self-defence. Over time, this had led to the concept of promoting or assisting the agency of persecuted groups for self-protection to become very controversial.

Seeking refuge in foreign countries has long been a primary method through which persecuted groups have employed their limited agency in pursuit of self-protection. A wide range of historical case studies, including those examined above, demonstrate 'that the ability of potential victims of mass killing to flee across borders often has been a critical factor in limiting or averting mass killing.'[81] Indeed, the right to seek asylum was enshrined in the Universal Declaration of Human Rights following the Holocaust, in which many Jews seeking to escape Nazi persecution were turned away from other countries, subsequently becoming victims of the genocide. In the current international political climate, however, developed nations appear committed to discouraging refugees as much as possible. There are several reasons for this. First, there are very large numbers of refugees already. UNHCR, the UN refugee agency, notes there are 10.4 million refugees currently of concern to the agency.[82] Second, large numbers of economic migrants, including illegal immigrants, have contributed to conflation between the categories of refugee and economic migrant, and asylum seeker and illegal immigrant. Third, these factors have contributed to millions of refugees who are currently unable to obtain resettlement, and have little choice but to live in refugee camps, sometimes in very poor conditions. This is currently the situation for many refugees that have fled the genocide in Darfur and the mass atrocities in Syria, for example. As a result of these factors, issues surrounding the acceptance of refugees have become very political in many developed nations. Further, while it is recognised that an 'effective strategy to protect victims from mass killing without

80 Mégret, 'Beyond the "Salvation" Paradigm', p. 581.

81 Benjamin Valentino, *Final Solutions: Mass Killing and Genocide in the Twentieth Century* (Ithaca, NY: Cornell University Press, 2004), p. 249.

82 United Nations High Commissioner for Refugees, 'Refugee Figures', http://www.unhcr.org/pages/49c3646c1d.html, accessed 19 February 2014.

placing ground troops in combat would be to help potential victims of mass killing escape to safer areas,' developed nations are largely unwilling to absorb the large numbers of refugees such a process may create.[83] This highlights the tension between outcomes that may save lives in highly constrained circumstances (such as the current crisis in Syria), but which are deeply problematic both from the perspective of longer-term outcomes and from an ethical perspective whereby facilitating refugee flows can also be perceived as effectively facilitating ethnic cleansing.

A second measure utilised by vulnerable groups in pursuit of self-protection is that of armed self-defence. Historically, persecutors typically go to considerable lengths to disarm targeted groups prior to committing mass atrocities, rendering this option impossible for many. Nevertheless, targeted groups have attempted to defend themselves even when very poorly armed in comparison with their attackers, sometimes with surprising success. During the Holocaust, for example, an uprising in the Sobibor extermination camp led to the escape of around 600 prisoners, of whom around 50 ultimately survived the war.[84] The camp itself was then closed down, preventing further mass murder there. In other cases, self-defence has been utilised by vulnerable minorities to prevent mass atrocities. In the early 1890s, for example, the Armenian minority in Sassoun, in Ottoman Turkey, protected itself from the attacks of Kurdish brigands through armed self-defence.[85] This case, however, also demonstrates that this strategy is a high-risk one for vulnerable groups – in 1894, the Kurdish brigands obtained the support of the Turkish army for a fresh assault, and massacred approximately six thousand Armenians in the region.[86]

In recent decades, however, the idea of assisting persecuted groups to defend themselves, or even simply not impeding such self-defence, has become very controversial. The events in the former Yugoslavia in the early 1990s provide an

---

83 Valentino, *Final Solutions*, p. 249.

84 Jules Schelvis, *Sobibor: A History of a Nazi Death Camp*, trans. Karin Dixon, (Oxford: Berg, 2007).

85 Edwin Bliss, *Turkey and the Armenian Atrocities* (Boston: H.L. Hastings, 1896), p. 370; E.A. Brayley Hodgetts, *Round About Armenia: The Record of a Journey across the Balkans through Turkey, the Caucasus and Persia in 1895* (London: Sampson Low Marston, 1896), p. 91.

86 William Spry, *Life on the Bosphorus-Doings in the City of the Sultan. Turkey Past and Present, Including Chronicles of the Caliphs from Mahomet to Abdul Hamid II* (London: H.S. Nichols, 1895), pp. 281–282, reprinted in Vatche Ghazarian (ed.), *Armenians in the Ottoman Empire: An Anthology of Transformation 13th -19th Centuries* (Waltham: Mayreni Publishing, 1997), pp. 624–625; Richard Hovannisian, 'The Historical Dimensions of the Armenian Question, 1878–1923', in Richard Hovannisian (ed.), *The Armenian Genocide in Perspective* (New Brunswick: Transaction Books, 1986), p. 25.

illustrative case. The UN-imposed arms embargo on Yugoslavia was an attempt to reduce the violence of the Yugoslav wars there, but in practice the embargo cemented the military superiority of the Serbian aggressors. When Bosnia seceded from Yugoslavia, the embargo prevented Bosnian Moslems from acquiring the arms they needed to defend themselves, 'and thereby allowed the Serbs to perpetrate genocide against Bosnia'.[87] Even when this negative impact of the embargo became clear, there was disagreement amongst members of the Security Council about lifting it. There were concerns, particularly amongst nations with peacekeepers in the country, that lifting the embargo could intensify and prolong the fighting, and place peacekeepers at greater risk.[88] Yet as the historian and military analyst Norman Cigar has pointed out, 'An early lifting of the embargo could have stopped ethnic cleansing before much of the damage had been done.'[89] Successful resistance has de-escalated a number of other conflicts involving mass atrocities, according to de Waal and Conley-Zilkic.[90] Armed self-defence by persecuted groups can entrench conflicts and render them increasingly complex, however, contributing to the international community's negative perceptions towards this approach.[91] Demarcations between 'aggressors' and 'victims' become less clear, and perpetrators have a greater ability to presented a distorted image of the conflict to deflect intervention, for example by presenting it as a 'civil war'. Relatively successful resistance by a vulnerable group may even shift a conflict from potential genocide to civil war. Again, there is a tension between processes whereby vulnerable populations may successfully use resistance for self-protection, but resulting events may be perceived as deeply problematic by the international community.

Rethinking Agency in Mass Atrocity Prevention

The negative perceptions of the international community associated with these two common methods persecuted groups have employed in pursuit of self-protection have undoubtedly contributed to a general reluctance to

87 David Kopel, Paul Gallant and Joanne Eisen, 'Is Resisting Genocide a Human Right?' *Notre Dame Law Review* 81/4: 1275–1346 (2005–2006), p. 1288.

88 Norman Cigar, *Genocide in Bosnia: The Policy of 'Ethnic Cleansing'* (College Station, Texas: Texas A&M University Press, 1995), pp. 169–170.

89 Ibid, p. 177.

90 Alex de Waal and Bridget Conley-Zilkic, 'Reflections on How Genocidal Killings are Brought to an End', Social Science Research Council, 22 December 2006, http://howgenocidesend.ssrc.org/de_Waal/, accessed 30 May 2014.

91 Kopel, Gallant and Eisen, 'Is Resisting Genocide a Human Right?' p. 1319.

consider how the agency of vulnerable groups can contribute to mass atrocity prevention. Yet in situations in which the international community is unwilling or unable to prevent or curb mass atrocities, such as in the former Yugoslavia, this stance is difficult to justify. As Cigar has remarked, 'In certain scenarios, providing security assistance in order to enable the victims to protect themselves and to offer effective resistance to their victimisers may be the most effective, and the only realistic, means of inhibiting or stopping genocide.'[92] De Waal and Conley-Zilkic refer to this dilemma as the 'best of all worlds' trap, that is, 'the failure to advocate a realistic response, because it is not a perfect response'.[93] They highlight that '[i]f genocide is indeed an absolute evil, and it is justifiable to suspend other considerations in order to stop it, then support for those groups that are actively resisting genocide, however unattractive they may be in other ways, must be a serious option.'[94] At the same time, the very real and justified concerns regarding these measures should not be overlooked. In the following section, therefore, I evaluate the potential efficacy and limitations of mass atrocity prevention measures utilising the agency of vulnerable groups. I question whether rethinking the role and agency of vulnerable groups in mass atrocity prevention is prudent or foolhardy.

There are two key advantages of approaches to mass atrocity prevention in which vulnerable groups utilise their agency in pursuit of self-protection. First, many of the key barriers facing externally-imposed mass atrocity prevention measures become less critical. A lack of political will, for example, has been a major factor in determining international responses to mass atrocities. The Report of the Independent Inquiry into the Actions of the United Nations during the 1994 Genocide in Rwanda, for example, concluded 'The failure by the United Nations to prevent, and subsequently, to stop the genocide in Rwanda was a failure by the United Nations system as a whole. The fundamental failure was the lack of resources and political commitment ... there was a persistent lack of political will by Member States to act, or to act with enough assertiveness.'[95] Vulnerable groups, however, are often highly motivated to take a range of actions to stabilise and reduce their risk of experiencing mass atrocities. Similarly, the often critical barrier of *realpolitik*, by which states are primarily motivated to respond in their own best interests rather than to humanitarian

92 Cigar, *Genocide in Bosnia*, p. 166.

93 De Waal and Conley-Zilkic, 'Reflections on How Genocidal Killings'.

94 Ibid.

95 United Nations, *Report of the Independent Inquiry into the Actions of the United Nations during the 1994 Genocide in Rwanda*, S/1999/1257, 15 December 1999, p. 3.

precepts, is sidestepped.[96] Issues concerning sovereignty and intervention, and perpetrator denials of ongoing atrocities or attempts to present a distorted picture of aggressors on both sides of the conflict are also less likely to impede actions in pursuit of mass atrocity prevention. These issues may potentially resurface as persecuted groups seek international assistance. Nevertheless, the potential to circumvent factors that have proven critical impediments to alternative approaches to mass atrocity prevention merits further consideration.

The second advantage of considering approaches to mass atrocity prevention that utilise the agency of vulnerable groups is that historically, they rate highly in effectiveness in comparison with methods that rely on the international community 'to protect' such populations. The UN Security Council holds the ultimate 'responsibility to protect' populations from mass atrocity crimes, yet its record for doing so is mixed at best. In recent decades the Security Council has been unable to respond effectively to mass atrocities in Syria, Darfur, Sri Lanka, Kosovo, Rwanda and Bosnia, although arguably it has been more successful in preventing mass atrocity crimes in Kenya, Côte d'Ivoire, Libya and Mali.[97] Yet at best the UN Security Council typically only considers action when a situation has reached crisis point, and atrocities are imminent or already underway. This severely limits the options available for prevention. Measures typically employed at this stage have been only partially effective, or ineffective. Sanctions are a crude measure that can negatively impact civilian populations as much as the regime they target, and the record of even carefully targeted sanctions 'is ambiguous'.[98] Arms embargoes have typically proven ineffective or to aid perpetrators of mass atrocities, while 'safe areas' have also been discredited. Some measures have had greater success. Preventive diplomacy has proven effective in some cases, although attempts to negotiate with regimes committing mass atrocities, such as Sudan and Syria, are often fruitless.[99] The imposition of 'no fly zones' has also been successful in the past, but

96 Paul Bartrop and Samuel Totten, '*Realpolitik:* The *Major* Impediment to the Prevention and Intervention of Genocide', in Samuel Totten (ed.), *Impediments to the Prevention and Intervention of Genocide: Genocide: A Critical Bibliographic Review Volume 9* (New Brunswick, NJ: Transaction, 2013), pp. 7–30.

97 Bruce Jentleson, 'The Obama Administration and R2P: Progress, Problems and Prospects', *Global Responsibility to Protect* 4/4 (2012): 399–423, pp. 412–13.

98 David Cortright and George Lopez, 'Assessing Smart Sanctions: Lessons from the 1990s', quoted in Kopel, Gallant and Eisen, 'Is Resisting Genocide a Human Right?' p. 1282.

99 Robert Muggah with Natasha White, 'Is there a Preventive Action Renaissance? The Policy and Practice of Preventive Diplomacy and Conflict Prevention', Norwegian Peacebuilding Resource Centre, Report February 2013, http://www.peacebuilding.no/var/ezflow_site/storage/original/application/00175abccdb1df5f006c8e40da206643.pdf, accessed 23 July 2014.

the international community is not always willing to commit the necessary resources. The risk inherent in these approaches, however, is that should they fail, they are unlikely to be buttressed by international intervention. As a number of commentators have noted, 'Given that the United Nations has *never* ever stopped any of the many genocides that have taken place during the organisation's six-decade history, telling the genocide victims to wait passively until the United Nations rescues them is shockingly foolish and callous.'[100] In cases of mass atrocities such as the current crisis in Syria, the only protection available for civilians (at the time of writing) is that which they can utilise their own agency to provide – no matter how flawed it may be.

In acknowledging the merits of approaches that persecuted groups have utilised for self-protection, however, it is vital not to overlook the very serious limitations of these approaches, and the sometimes formidable barriers that potential victim groups face. As discussed in the preceding section, two common approaches vulnerable groups employ (usually in crisis situations) to try and protect themselves from mass atrocities, are to flee, becoming refugees, or to attempt self-defence. While these solutions may be somewhat effective, one of the reasons for the international community's reluctance to endorse them is that they rarely lead to good long-term outcomes. Only a minority of refugees are able to resettle in peaceful countries in a reasonable amount of time. The majority, indeed the vast majority, suffer high mortality rates during transit and often also in poorly equipped refugee camps, where they may remain for decades. Similarly, situations in which vulnerable groups attempt armed self-defence can lead to ongoing political violence and instability, civil wars and further atrocities. Even when vulnerable groups utilise their agency in pursuit of self-protection in a preventive capacity, significant barriers remain. Groups lack political power, most often lack necessary financial resources, and lack access to key articles, whether they be passports, visas, arms or communications equipment. Less tangibly but no less real are barriers they must overcome associated with stigma and the propaganda that regimes employ, both internally and internationally, against such groups. While the Bahá'í have thus far overcome many of these barriers to protect themselves with remarkable success, for example, both the context-specific factors that facilitated this success and the ongoing precariousness of their position in Iranian society must be considered before advocating a similar approach in other cases. These very real limitations of approaches to mass atrocity prevention utilising the agency of persecuted groups reinforce the ongoing need for the international community to fulfil its 'responsibility to protect', in both a reactive and preventive capacity.

100 Kopel, Gallant and Eisen, 'Is Resisting Genocide a Human Right?' p. 1320.

This analysis suggests therefore, that there are both significant advantages and substantial drawbacks associated with vulnerable populations utilising their agency as a primary strategy for mass atrocity prevention. In some, limited circumstances, it can be an effective measure to build resilience to mass atrocities, such as in the case of the Bahá'í in Iran described above. In other circumstances it can save lives, but lead to difficult ongoing situations such as large refugee populations and ongoing conflicts. At the same time, it should also be recognised that measures associated with the responsibility to protect also have a mixed, and sometimes poor record of preventing mass atrocities. For this reason, measures that utilise the agency of persecuted groups should not be overlooked, as they do offer some potential solutions.

In many respects, the best opportunities for this approach to mitigating risk of mass atrocities may be yet to be identified. The responsibility to protect, alongside other recent reports on mass atrocity prevention and intervention, have largely overlooked approaches to prevention that seek to work with vulnerable populations, promote their empowerment and utilise the agency of these groups to promote resilience to mass atrocities. Yet these groups themselves, with assistance from other nations, civil society organisations and others, may be best placed to identify the measures that they need in order to protect themselves. Working cooperatively may facilitate the identification and implementation of new mass atrocity prevention measures that are effective, lead to good long-term outcomes, and prevent escalation of crises into mass atrocities. In the current international climate, this is an approach to mass atrocity prevention that the international community cannot afford to continue to overlook.

Conclusion

Preventing mass atrocities is a formidable challenge for the international community. The responsibility to protect principle represents an ideal, but one which remains, to a large extent, an aspirational goal. Pathways to preventing mass atrocities have been identified, but this research has not always translated into improved responses in crises and pre-crisis situations. Genocide studies scholar Herb Hirsch has suggested that:

> Lessons concerning prevention have been learned and are quite clear … to save lives and prevent genocide and human rights atrocities, specified actions are required. These, in fact, have been spelled out in research … and publications. Yet … the actual implementation of programs derived

> from these lessons so seriously lag behind the academic discussion and means that slogans such as "never again" reverberate with a ring of insincerity.[101]

International reports such as *The Responsibility to Protect*, *Preventing Genocide: A Guide for U.S. Policymakers* and *Mobilizing the Will to Intervene* have identified key impediments to mass atrocity prevention, but the strategies they have proposed have not – to date – been sufficient to overcome them. *Realpolitik* and a lack of political will continue to dominate humanitarian concerns in the UN Security Council. This highlights the value of seeking and developing alternative approaches to mass atrocity prevention where possible. Utilising the agency of vulnerable groups to contribute to prevention efforts is one such alternative approach.

101 Herbert Hirsch, '"Paved with Good Intentions": Attempts to Design Mechanisms to Prevent Genocide in the Twenty-First Century and Why They Have Not Succeeded', in Samuel Totten (ed.), *Impediments to the Prevention and Intervention of Genocide: Genocide: A Critical Bibliographic Review Volume 9* (New Brunswick, NJ: Transaction, 2013), p. 247.

CHAPTER 6

Indigenous State-building: 'Local' Actors in Somaliland's Stabilization

Dr. Michael Walls, DPU, UCL

Abstract

Somaliland is often contrasted with southern areas of Somalia and offered as proof that democracy and stability are possible in a Somali context. While there is strong support for this position as far as it goes, this chapter argues that the causes of Somaliland's stability are far more complex and often paradoxically so than is often suggested. The Somaliland political settlement draws on a particular combination of customary and contemporary systems of governance that found fertile ground there. The chapter offers reflection on the specifics of culture and history, before considering the contextual definitions of externality and the roles that different 'external' actors have been able to play in facilitating the consolidation of a combined system of customary, discursive democracy with the representative politics of elections and the nation-state.

Specifically, Somaliland's success was built on the iterative and cyclical process of peace-building and debate that took place from 1991 until 1997; a process that continues to evolve today. The chapter explores that process, and also highlights the specific combinations of flexibility and intervention that permitted discussion, while also generating decision.

Key Words

Somaliland – Somalia – discursive democracy – representative democracy – peace-building – state-formation

1 Introduction

It should surprise no-one that analyses of crises at all scales, from state failure through conflict to mass atrocities, tend to focus on underlying problems, tensions and triggers. Not only does such a focus fulfil an apparently deep-rooted human fascination with dysfunction and antagonism, but it is also offers obvious reference points in the form of immediate causes and consequences.

 | DOI 10.1163/9789004299870_008

Trying to understand why bad things *don't* happen is both less superficially gripping, and requires patient engagement with a host of variables and uncertainties that shift the discourse outside the normal parameters of conflict studies into a more indeterminate, indeed interdisciplinary, arena that draws on a range of social science disciplines.

However, an unremitting focus on crisis and dysfunction is problematic precisely because it creates a picture of human action that is necessarily centred on the negative behavioural extremes of which we are undeniably capable, but usually able to resist. The reality is that, even in situations in which people have the ability, and possibly encouragement, to engage in violence, they usually do not do so. If we are truly to understand how atrocities are to be avoided, then it is even more important that, whatever the challenges involved, we understand why they don't occur than that we explore only or mainly the reasons that they do. The principle goes far further than that, though: an overly crisis-oriented understanding of conflicted peoples and territories presents a picture that obscures many of the positive foundations that might provide a basis for stability and the avoidance of crisis.

That situation certainly pertains in the Somali Horn of Africa, in which Somalia has endured more than a quarter of a century of conflict and repeated humanitarian disasters. The perception that Somalia is "the quintessential failed state" in which those engaged in trying to improve the situation hold a "pervasive doubt that the conflict will be resolved" is widespread.[1] This is in spite of the fact that many areas of the erstwhile Republic of Somalia are in fact notably stable, and boast relatively legitimate and functional systems of government or, at least, governance.

2 Contrasting Trajectories: Anarchy and State-Building in the Somali Horn

The received wisdom is that atrocities have been committed periodically by all sides, dating back to the dictatorial and, in its later years, particularly brutal regime of General Mohamed Siyaad Barre. While that representation is, in many respects, reasonable, it is far too broad in its scope. In practice, its focus on atrocity and failure misses important exceptions that pertain in many parts of the Somali Horn. If we are to better understand the mechanisms that tend to prevent mass atrocities then the tendency in the Somali Horn, as elsewhere, to focus on failure rather than relative success must inevitably lead to distorted

1 E. Leonard, and G. Ramsay. eds. *Globalising Somalia: Multilateral, international, and transnational repercussions of conflict.* (New York: Bloomsbury, 2013), p. 1.

policy frameworks and misguided intervention, especially on the part of non-Somali outsiders who are, by definition, most removed from the socio-political context within which differing trajectories take shape.

In that respect, Somaliland offers the most obvious and extensive example of a counter view: a territory in which local peace-building and political reconciliation has succeeded in supporting the gradual emergence of a stable and representative democracy, and in which there has been no widespread conflict since 1997. Somaliland still faces significant challenges, but while many, particularly in the eastern areas, are unconvinced by the Somaliland political settlement, the reality stands in stark contrast to the narrative of conflict and widespread crisis that pertains in other areas of the Somali Horn.

In fact, even beyond Somaliland, many of the Somali areas, including those subject to conflict, employ a system of customary, clan-based law that permits most people, most of the time, to go about their daily business in a manner that sustains GDP per capita at levels that are comparable to, and in some instances better than, those of their neighbours.

There are risks in that analysis too, though. For example, Peter Leeson argued the case strongly, noting that most development indicators for Somalia suggest that they have not only fared better than their neighbours, but also that improvements have generally accelerated since the fall of the central government in 1991.[2] Leeson rightly cautions against using this logic to 'romanticize' Somalia, but in arguing the cause of his finding, he falls into an almost precisely equivalent trap. Instead of romanticizing Somalia, he romanticizes what he calls 'anarchy'. Presuming a lack of central government to be anarchic, he presumes that relative Somali social and humanitarian success in the past two decades has rested on just such a condition.

The Somaliland case brings some balance to this view also, as the experience there clearly demonstrates not the efficacy of 'anarchy' in addressing socio-political issues, but the importance of order and agreed systems of governance.

There is a paradox here: not only has the Somaliland state, in contrast to culturally similar areas to the south, been successful in consolidating its position and in supporting a durable peace; but the establishment of that state itself occurred in the absence of existing representative political structures – what Leeson would presumably consider to be a state of anarchy. It is significant that, rather than permitting the continuation of statelessness, business, clan and political leaders drew on broad public support to institute a system of government. This offers an important counterpoint to the experience in other

2 Peter T. Leeson, 'Better off stateless: Somalia before and after government collapse', *Journal of Comparative Economics*, 35/4: (2007).

Somali areas, in which similar groups – popularly labelled 'spoilers' – have acted to subvert or prevent the emergence of such governance systems.

This focus on the emergence of state institutions holds a heightened significance with respect to the prevention of atrocities when we consider that the first of the three 'pillars' outlined by the UN Secretary-General in his 2009 report on the Responsibility to Protect underlines "...the enduring responsibility of the State to protect its populations, whether nationals or not, from genocide, war crimes, ethnic cleansing and crimes against humanity, and from their incitement".[3] This emphasis on the centrality of the state in protecting its citizens of course draws explicitly on the commitments made in the 2005 World Summit Outcome, which places primary responsibility squarely on "each individual state".[4]

If, indeed, such responsibility "lies first and foremost with the state",[5] what then of societies in which there is no effective state? Somaliland suggests strongly that such responsibility does not necessarily revert logically up the scale, but can in fact be exercised by local communities where international intervention can sometimes be an impediment to protection rather than its instrument.

The counter case of recognized states which lack the capacity to assume such a responsibility is well enough documented, though it bears noting that the Somali Federal Government falls more clearly into that category than most. In spite of enjoying universal international recognition, and receiving lavish funding support over many years, the government in Mogadishu continues to struggle to establish it's authority, and is powerless to protect a great many of its putative citizens, whether from the atrocities meted out by opponents such as the al-Shabaab militia, or those of allies including the African Union's AMISOM forces.[6] Once again, this underlines the significance of achievements in Somaliland.

This insight is important not least in that it runs counter to presumptions around the primacy of the state in initiating or assuming the primary responsibility for citizens that so clearly underpin UN statements on the responsibility to protect. There is an additional significance here in that many of the

---

3 Ban Ki-moon, *Implementing the responsibility to protect: Report of the Secretary-General*, A/63/677, 12 January 2009, p. 8.

4 UN General Assembly, *2005 World Summit Outcome*, A/RES/60/1, 24 October 2005, Para 138, p. 30.

5 Ban Ki-moon, *Implementing the responsibility to protect*, p. 9.

6 A number of of reports have detailed human rights abuses in Somalia, with the most prominent in recent years those of the international NGO Human Rights Watch: Human Rights Watch, *'The Power These Men Have Over Us': Sexual Exploitation and Abuse by African Union Forces in Somalia*, September 2014; Human Rights Watch, *Harsh War, Harsh Peace: Abuses by al-Shabaab, the Transitional Federal Government, and AMISOM in Somalia*, April 2010.

practical insights also work against the logic that states themselves will struggle to emerge 'spontaneously' as a result of the accretions of local action. Indeed, Somaliland shows that, while the challenges remain huge, such indigenous emergence is a possibility.

Somaliland is also useful in emphasizing many of the complexities of the situation. It is tempting to view the political settlement there through a romanticizing lens; one of autopoiesis, in which a complex political solution has been fashioned solely through indigenous efforts. Just as it points to the possibility of indigenous state-building, it is dangerously incorrect to present the process as wholly or even largely divorced from geopolitical events elsewhere or the actions of those outside the immediate area.

The essence of the argument in this chapter is that, on the one hand, it is *possible*, though not by any means inevitable, that indigenous action might effectively support the emergence of a legitimate state, while on the other, recognizing the importance of that state in perpetuating durable and reasonably just peace in the future. That, then, is a position that walks a line between the presumed efficacy of anarchy suggested by Leeson, and the common presumption that 'state-building' must be initiated or at least actively promoted from outside a given polity if it is to succeed. It is also a position, though, that notes the importance of external support for state-building, albeit in a context in which that support remains subservient to and embedded in broad local interests.

A key underlying presumption here is that a durable and inclusive political settlement that includes at least the essential and legitimate institutions of state will tend to minimize the risk that widespread atrocities will be committed in the long term. There are, of course, so many variables involved in defining legitimacy and the nature of the state, that it is nigh on impossible to demonstrate a clear causal link between those components and the absence of mass atrocity, but Somaliland does at least provide the minimum conditions in which there is an apparently positive link between the two. A second insight suggested by the Somaliland case is that the durability and effectiveness of such a system in preventing renewed conflict and crisis is enhanced where international links are diverse, deep and offer mutual benefit.

2.1 *Geopolitically Embedded Indigenous State-Building in Somaliland*

Since 1991, Somaliland has undergone a remarkable political transition which has seen methodical and incremental agreement on key issues, the cessation of widespread conflict and the establishment of what, by any measure, counts as a durable peace. But, while those achievements have indeed been led by Somalis, they have not occurred in isolation. In fact, various forms of 'external' intervention feature at every level, and on the part of a variety of actors.

To unpick the numerous paradoxes, one needs to start with at least a rudimentary understanding of culture and history. A key point here is that, far from being "a society addicted to congenital egalitarian anarchy",[7] Somali history shows strong forms of social and political organization, and has supported a number of enduring states through a millennium of history.[8] That Somali society is indeed egalitarian, if also profoundly patriarchal, does not inevitably result in anarchy or a chaotic politics.

In fact, Somali tradition strongly promotes a form of discursive decision-making that is fundamentally democratic. While international donor agencies tend to describe their political support programmes as promoting 'democratization',[9] that is far from an accurate portrayal. For adult male Somalis in particular, electoral systems of selection represent not an enhancement of democracy, but its diminution. Instead of the active consensus-building of traditions, elections require citizens to vote every few years, for representatives whose accountability is limited between each poll. It is not, therefore, surprising that the transition from a highly democratic discursive system to a representative form has proven difficult not just in the southern Somali areas, but also in Somaliland. A failure to understand this compounds the frustration of donors who largely hold unquestioningly to the view that their programmes should be welcomed rather than resisted, and therefore find it hard to understand the rationality of a people who, in some circumstances, see no government as preferable to the effective transfer of authority to a far less accountable political elite.

What is remarkable about Somaliland is that, in spite of understandable difficulties, its people have fashioned a viable and durable political settlement that accommodates many of these changes. This is important because, where Somali socio-political custom has long worked well in the context of fluid borders and a dispersed, largely pastoral, population, a representative polity is essential if Somalis are to enjoy success in a world of globally connected nation-states. Somalis have been traders throughout much of the millennium or so of identifiably Somali history. Living in a semi-arid environment, in which drought is a frequent occurrence, trade has provided a basis on which to accumulate sufficient assets and income streams to permit a reasonably resilient livelihoods system. That points too to the error in the myth of autopoesis: while

7 Said S. Samatar, 'Genius as Madness: King Tewodros of Ethiopia and Sayyid Muhammad of Somalia in Comparative Perspective', *Northeast African Studies* 10/3: 27–32 (2003), p. 29.

8 For examples, see Michael Walls, *A Somali Nation-State: history, culture and Somaliland's political transition.* (Pisa: Ponte Invisibile, 2014), pp. 69–78.

9 For example, IRI, *Strategy for International Democratisation Support to Somaliland* (London/ Washington DC: DFID/International Republican Institute, 2014).

Somaliland shows the importance of indigeneity in crafting viable political solutions, it does not demonstrate a need for disengagement from international systems.

In principle, a trade-based economic system should provide a readily transferrable base for profitable activity in a world in which business links are increasingly complex and widely distributed. Indeed, as already noted, Leeson's findings point to a remarkable resilience in that respect. However, the same observation also emphasizes the importance of a stable political settlement that permits formal and informal links with international business partners. While Leeson's observations show that a certain level of economic activity is possible in spite of conflict, in order to move beyond survival one must also assume the need for representative political structures that are capable of serving the interests of a body of citizens. Such a system would support a government that is capable, at the least, of negotiating and agreeing trade and other deals that facilitate the deepening and broadening of global links. In Somaliland, this form of representation remains a work in progress, but has nevertheless achieved, to a significant degree, a foundation based on local custom and leadership, that has seen an expansion in the economy and the accelerating development of ties with external partners, in business, politics and beyond.

2.2 *The Contextual Definition of the 'External' and Iterative Intervention*

There is value in continuing in this vein, and examining the nature of the 'external' in Somaliland's political transition. Importantly, it is vital to note that 'externality' itself is contextually-specific.

As is widely documented, Somali social structure rests on a highly sophisticated system of kinship groupings that include a number of levels of what are frequently described as clan-families, clans, sub-clans and so on.[10] IM Lewis firmly established himself as the leading anthropological authority on this 'segmentary' clan system, and although his work stood at the centre of a heated debate on the degree to which this segmentation could be seen to 'define' Somali society as opposed to changing and adapting over time, Lewis himself was at pains to point to the fluidity and pragmatism of those socio-political structures.[11]

10 Ioan M. Lewis, *A Pastoral Democracy: A Study of Pastoralism and Politics among the Northern Somali of the Horn of Africa* (Oxford: International African Institute/Oxford University Press, 1961); Walls, *A Somali Nation-State*, pp. 34–38.

11 Catherine Besteman, 'Primordialist Blinders: A Reply to I.M. Lewis', *Cultural Anthropology*, 13/1: 109–120 (1998); Ioan M. Lewis, 'Doing Violence to Ethnography: A Response to Catherine Besteman's "Representing Violence and 'Othering' Somalia"', *Cultural Anthropology* 13/1: 100–108 (1998).

In this context, then, a primary locus for external intervention in a conflict situation lies with clan elders from any clan grouping that is not directly involved in a specific dispute, but where the 'external' clan has some interest in the outcome. A neighbouring clan group is likely to be concerned that antagonists resolve their differences, for example, in order to avoid that conflict affecting their own lives. This sense of distance coupled with clear self-interest is vital in creating a context in which an external party is trusted yet sufficiently detached to permit good faith negotiation.

This can be illustrated in the Somaliland case with reference to the period after the Mogadishu government of Siyaad Barre had collapsed at the start of 1991. The Somali National Movement (SNM), the insurgent group composed of members of the largest clan-family in the erstwhile British protectorate of Somaliland, the Isaaq, followed the path of many successful insurgencies. No longer confronted with a common enemy to unify them, divisions amongst the constituent Isaaq clans of the SNM broke into outright conflict within about a year of the fall of the Mogadishu administration. While this was seen by some as an inevitable descent into internecine warfare, with a need for a strong state or international actor to step in to restore order, events took a very different path. In fact, so clear was the perception that the solution must start at a local level that the vigorous overtures of UNOSOM (United Nations Operation in Somalia) were emphatically rejected in favour of locally-based initiatives.[12]

With Isaaq groups at war with each other, it fell to two non-Isaaq clans who had been allied with the Siyaad government, to mediate. The Gadabuursi in the west and the Dhulbahante in the east sent representatives to broker a peace. This involved a painstaking series of conferences and meetings that focused firstly on agreeing the terms of local ceasefires, before moving on to address issues of increasingly broad governance.

That process had started many months previously, with overtures from a key Dhulbahante leader, Garaad Abdiqani Garaad Jaama, to the SNM. The Garaad had long shown sympathy for the Isaaq struggle, recognizing in spite of his clan's privileged position in General Siyaad Bare's MOD alliance,[13] the self-defeating brutality of the regime and its effect on the Isaaq clans. Emboldened by Abdiqani's overtures, the SNM leadership sought to agree peace terms with

12 Mark Bradbury, *The Somali Conflict: Prospects for Peace*, (Oxford: Oxfam, 1994), pp. 77–79.

13 The MOD abbreviation denoted the clans who were seen as providing the core of General Siyaad's support: his paternal clan of Mareehaan; his maternal kin in the Ogadeen clan; and fellow members of the Daarood clan-family, the Dhulbahante. David D. Laitin and Said S. Samatar, *Somalia: Nation in Search of a State* (Boulder: Westview Press, 1987), pp. 92–94; Abdisalam M. Issa-Salwe, *The Collapse of the Somali State: The Impact of the Colonial Legacy* (London: HAAN Publishing, 1996), p. 84.

opposing clans within the borders of the erstwhile British Protectorate. This policy of talking to antagonists saw a series of small meetings through 1990 and into 1991, first with the Dhulbahante in the Ethiopian border towns of Qaraaro, Dannood, Gowlalaale and Gaashaamo and then with other opposing clans in locations scattered through the eastern and western areas of Somaliland. Initially talks focused solely on agreeing the terms under which fighting could stop. In some instances, compensation was agreed, but often, a specific agreement was made to set aside compensation claims on the basis that the calculation would be too complicated and divisive after years of conflict.[14]

Only after a series of such agreements had been reached, establishing a meaningful if still fragile cessation of hostilities throughout most of Somaliland, was the 'Grand Brotherhood Conference of the Northern Clans' (*Shiirweynaha Walaalaynta Beelaha Waqooyiga*) hosted by the SNM in the town of Burco. All the larger clans residing within the borders of the old protectorate were invited and all sent delegates. It was at that conference, held in May 1991, that the announcement was made that Somaliland would henceforth be independent from other parts of Somalia. That momentous declaration, framed as the restoration of the sovereignty Somaliland had enjoyed for five days between their independence from Britain on 26th June 1960 and the union with Somalia on 1st July, did not come about through SNM leadership. In fact, the majority of the SNM Central Committee believed Somaliland to be non-viable as an independent state. Rather, secession was so clearly the determined will of the great majority of those living in Somaliland that the declaration was based explicitly on that popular pressure.[15]

With the Burco conference having confirmed the terms of peace, renewed conflict erupted amongst some of the Isaaq clans, with the consequence that the SNM itself collapsed. With fresh fighting in key cities, it was clear that the insurgent group could no longer maintain accord between it's own constituents, and so it fell to the Gadabuursi clan to offer to host a new reconciliation conference involving all the clans. Once again, a series of smaller meetings took place to agree the end of specific conflicts, and only once they were complete did the opportunity present itself for a new 'grand conference'. That conference was held in the first months of 1993 in the main Gadabuursi town of Booraame, with an explicit remit to both confirm the local peace agree-

14 Michael Walls et al., *Peace in Somaliland: An Indigenous Approach to State-Building. The Search for Peace Series.* (Interpeace/Academy for Peace and Development, Geneva/Hargeysa: 2008), pp. 16–18.

15 Walls, *A Somali Nation-State*, pp. 165–168.

ments that preceded it, and to address issues of political governance at the Somaliland level.

Proceedings in Booraame were extended when needed to allow for discussions to continue, and fund-raising continued amongst both local and diasporic communities in order to keep delegates and guests fed. At times when dissatisfaction amongst delegates seemed to be reaching a critical level, the chairing committee would declare an adjournment – sometimes on the pretext that one or other member was ill, or otherwise more explicitly to permit more time for agreement. In the event, negotiations took four months, with the principal chair explicitly privileging consensus-building over voting – urging against a vote until details had been thrashed out with the comment that "voting is fighting; let's opt for consensus".[16]

The conference resulted in two documents: the first, entitled *Axdiga Nabadgaladyada ee Beelaha Soomaaliland* (Security and Peace Charter of the Somaliland Clans), confirmed the terms of the peace; while the second, *Axdi Qarameed* (National Charter), was an interim Somaliland constitution which established a multi-party presidential system of government. On the basis of the latter document, the first civilian president of Somaliland's new era was elected, marking the transition from military rule.

Conflict again broke out after the Booraame conference in 1994, as one of the largest Isaaq clans, the Habar Yoonis, objected to the level of representation accorded to them in the conference. This led to the defection to Mogadishu of the ousted president and previous SNM leader, Abdirahmaan 'Tuur', where he had been enticed by a UNOSOM offer of representation in a 'unity' government. A period of conflict followed, but rather than fatally undermining the Somaliland settlement, renewed talks again brought the different clans to the negotiating table.

A fresh cycle of meetings and conferences was again employed, and although low-intensity conflict continued until 1997, that cycle eventually proved successful. A government-hosted conference in the capital city of Hargeysa saw often heated debate on a new constitution, and marked an evolution in the political settlement that has sustained peace to the present time.

In each instance of conflict, mediation and peace, hindsight reveals a clear pattern. Local peace agreements created the basis for further discussion, which addressed increasingly complex issues of governance. Third-party groups were often important in initiating or leading mediation efforts aimed at brokering

16 Michael Walls, 'The Emergence of a Somali State: Building Peace from Civil War in Somaliland', *African Affairs* 108/432: 371–389 (2009), p. 385.

local ceasefires, before moving onto more general governance, affecting increasingly large numbers of people.[17]

The result was that, between the start of 1991 and the end of 1997, a constitution had been debated, argued about and finally adopted, along with a commitment to electoral democracy and a strong executive wing. Militia had been largely demobilized, and although not fully integrated into a Somaliland army, significant steps had been taken in that direction.

This sequence, then, underlines two important themes: firstly the role played by 'external' clans in mediating a peace; and secondly the iterative and structured cycle of negotiation and agreement, which started with immediate disputes at the local level before progressing to wider issues of governance.

Recalling the point that 'externality' is contextually defined, it is worth considering a number of other groups who, depending on the circumstances, can and have played a role as 'outsiders' in promoting peace and helping to establish durable systems of governance.

Somali custom has long emphasized the role of Islam in promoting unity and arguing against conflict, with that role set explicitly against the divisive role of clan, which provides social support and many of the functions of justice, but within a context that emphasizes customary lineage divisions.[18] Men of religion, or wadaad, have long been accorded special respect, along with poets, women and children, all of whom are expected to be spared from the most harmful effects of conflict and, in turn, to urge their fellows to follow more peaceful methods.

There are apposite examples involving each of these groups, but it is that provided by Somali women that are the focus of the following paragraphs. Adult women hold an invidious position in Somali society in that they are not seen clearly to belong to any one clan. Instead, their loyalties are presumed divided between the lineage of their fathers and those of past, present or future husbands. This has made it particularly difficult for women to break into representative electoral politics, as female candidates struggle to persuade voters driven by clan loyalty that they will act in the interests of one clan or another, thus being deserving of their votes. However, this perceived division in loyalties also has the counter-effect that women can, in some circumstances, act as communicators who are able to cross conflict lines or argue for a greater good. Since 1991, this has translated on a number of occasions into space for women

17 Walls et al., *Peace in Somaliland.*

18 For a detailed study on this, see Ioan M. Lewis, 'Sufism in Somaliland: A study in tribal Islam' in Akbar S. Ahmed, and David M. Hart (eds.), *Islam in Tribal Societies: From the Atlas to the Indus.* (London: Routledge and Kegan Paul, 1984), pp. 127–168.

as activists who actively promote not just a cessation of hostilities, but sometimes quite detailed development objectives. This could be seen in the lead up to the 1993 Booraame conference, when groups of female activists organized themselves outside meeting venues to maximize pressure on male delegates to agree on the points prioritized by the activists. On at least one occasion, women were unsuccessful in arguing for representation inside a meeting, so purchased cheap microphones and speakers, so they could monitor proceedings nonetheless. They then situated themselves immediately outside the venue with placards displaying their demands, and refused to allow delegates to leave the meeting until those demands had been discussed formally.[19]

Interestingly, their demands included a specific insistence that a letter be sent by the Somaliland government to the UN, rejecting deployment of UNOSOM forces in Somaliland. The rejection of UN intervention reflected the popular mood, and underlines the commitment of Somalilanders to retaining local control of their peace process. This was not simply reflective of a romantic attachment to local solutions: Somaliland's very identity is based to a great degree on a call for the rest of the world to recognize their sovereignty and allow them integration with global trade, financial and other systems. On the contrary, it is indicative of a clear-headed analysis of UN intervention in the south in which it was recognized that the model for that involvement differed fundamentally from the iterative and bottom-up approach being employed in Somaliland. For that reason, UNOSOM's enthusiasm at the time to intervene in Somaliland was treated with deep and deserved distrust.[20] Those women also demanded that the meeting delegates agree a means of integrating militia groups into a viable police force and of rehabilitating municipal water systems: each a highly specific and clearly important objective that enjoyed wide support amongst Somaliland communities.

The theme here, then, is that external intervention is not only possible but culturally sanctioned. But equally that intervention per se is not welcomed: the terms under which it is offered matter materially. Accepted and successful spaces for the involvement of 'outsiders' need to be both culturally and circumstantially appropriate, building on or supporting local efforts. Thus far, the interventions cited have involved Somalis with close connections with the local context. But it is equally possible to offer examples in which those much further afield have been involved in the Somaliland political space with considerable benefit.

---

19 Walls et al., *Peace in Somaliland*, pp. 48–49.

20 Bradbury, *The Somali Conflict*, pp. 77–79.

Diaspora members are often seen by non-Somali policy-makers and other agents as intimately connected with the Somali context, but in fact experience a much more challenging relationship with relatives and others in the Horn. Yet the involvement of diaspora Somalis in local politics, business and social life is important and far-reaching. There was a particularly notable diaspora-led effort that started in 1995, with a view to mediating in a complicated period of conflict. A group based in northern Europe met with colleagues in the Horn in Addis Ababa, and so commenced almost three years of negotiations between the Somaliland government and their opponents at the time. In the final analysis, this self-titled Peace Committee were not successful in brokering the broad-based agreement they had aimed for, but they played an important role in maintaining dialogue at a difficult time, and in helping establish small-scale local agreements that ultimately helped lay the foundation for the government-organized peace conference in Hargeysa. That 1997 conference is still frequently criticized as having been too closely controlled by the government of President Igaal, but it marked the final conclusion of broad inter-clan conflict in Somaliland; a peace which continues today. As already noted, it also agreed the basis of the Somaliland Constitution which is in place now.[21]

Finally, in this list of 'external' agents, we must address the role played by a group of non-Somalis over the years. Whether colonists, diplomats or development professionals, this diverse group have also played significant roles in Somaliland's political development in one way or another. The UNOSOM example cited above is illustrative of some of the pitfalls in that relationship, and it is commonplace for that relationship to be presented in malign terms. However, that is by no means the whole story, and the argument that runs through this chapter is that, when formulated carefully and with due concern for and understanding of the local context, this group has played an important and constructive role. The formative period of 1991–97 offers a number of examples of such engagement, though because of the geopolitical machinations associated with Somaliland's unilateral declaration of sovereignty, those examples are more limited than they might be. Those that do exist tend to focus on the actions of non-governmental developmental agencies, who were able to build strong local operations, in large part precisely because Somaliland had become an isolated region in a difficult area. The likes of ActionAid's work in Sanaag, and that of the Catholic Institute for International Relations (CIIR – then operating in Somaliland as ICD or International Cooperation for

21 Matt Bryden and Dr. Ahmed Yusuf Farah, *The Peace Committee for Somaliland: Case Study of a Grassroots Peace Making Initiative*, (Addis Ababa: UNDP Emergencies Unit for Ethiopia, 1996); Walls, *A Somali Nation-State*, pp. 185–198.

Development, and now as Progressio) were successful in these early years in building incrementally on local efforts, supporting development projects based on local initiatives.[22]

A particularly useful instance in which members of the international diplomatic community played a pivotal and successful role in resolving a significant Somaliland crisis in the political realm, though, comes from more recent years.

One of the most contentious contemporary political issues in Somaliland has related to the counting of people – either in the context of a general population census, or in the form of a register of voters. This sensitivity is not by any means confined to Somaliland. Siyaad Barre's government conducted two censuses: one in 1975 and another in 1985–6.[23] The results would certainly have upset the delicate balance of power between different clan groups, based as they were on historic formulae that purported some connection with the population of each sub-clan. Consequently, neither set of census results was published in full, and population estimates throughout the area of the old Italian and British Somalilands remain uncertain and politically charged.

One result of that situation is that Somaliland elections prior to 2010 were each run without a voter register, relying on finger-inking, local identification in person and general goodwill to prevent multiple and ineligible voting.[24] There was, however, a ready acknowledgement that this relative informality could not continue indefinitely. Each election was accompanied by promises that the next would be held with a full register, and by 2008, the need had become sufficiently urgent that a process of registration was commenced.

That process ran into serious problems motivated by the same concerns over feared changes in the power structure as those that prevented the publication of census results after the 1975 and 1985–6 Somalia censuses. As the registration process continued in Somaliland through 2009, reports of multiple and fraudulent registration became increasingly widespread. By its conclusion, some regions recording a majority of voters as having been registered without the mandatory provision of usable fingerprints or photographs. This resulted in heated arguments over the usability of the register, into which the

22 Mark Bradbury, *Somaliland Country Report.* (London: Catholic Institute for International Relations, 1997); Sujai Shivakumar, *ActionAid Somaliland: Programme Review – Institutional Analysis*, (London: ActionAid, 1998).

23 K.E. Vaidyanathan, *Population Statistics of Somalia*, (Nairobi: UNDP Somalia, 1997), p. 3.

24 Adan Yusuf Abokor et al., *Further Steps to Democracy: The Somaliland Parliamentary Elections, September 2005*, (London: Progressio, 2006); Michael Walls and Steve Kibble, *Somaliland: Change and continuity: Report by International Election Observers on the June 2010 presidential elections in Somaliland*, (London: Progressio, 2011).

donors who had funded the process, along with the implementing agency, Interpeace, were plunged.[25] With the crisis worsening to the point where significant, though locally contained violence occurred and more widespread conflict became a real possibility, a small group of foreign diplomats intervened. This time, the intervention was led by the UK Deputy Ambassador to Ethiopia, working in tandem with Ethiopia's Deputy Foreign Minister. Negotiations were fraught and heated with the donors seen by Somali antagonists as having a strong stake in the outcome given their heavy investment in electoral support. Eventually, and with the support of others in the Somali-focused foreign diplomatic community and also active engagement from key local civil society groups, the Ethiopian and UK representatives tabled a 'non-paper' containing six points aimed at resolving the political impasse. That non-paper was slightly adapted before being re-presented as a memorandum for agreement between each of the key antagonists. Each of the Somaliland parties signed the document, thus committing to use of a 'cleaned' version of the voter register in an election to be held as soon as practicable.[26]

That agreement brought to a close a period of significant crisis, and made possible an electoral timetable that, a few short weeks earlier, had looked to be unachievable in the extreme.

This example is again useful in that it points to a number of critical components that contributed to the success of the intervention. Firstly, while the initiators were not Somali, they drew on significant and deep engagement in the issues of the moment, working behind the scenes and drawing on the support of respected local actors to facilitate discussion and, eventually, agreement. As with the work of ActionAid, CIIR and the like, this non-Somali engagement sought to maintain a low profile, working behind the scenes, and seeking every opportunity for the principle protagonists to 'own' the outcome as their own. This was not a trivial position: the outcome was never assured until those protagonists had signed up to it, making local acceptance much easier for the supporters and officials of each of the political parties. In many ways, this supports the common-sense view that politics must be locally legitimated to succeed in the long term, but it flies in the face of efforts to prominently 'brand' the work of international agencies.

25 Michael Walls, 'Somaliland: Democracy Threatened – Constitutional Impasse as Presidential Elections are Postponed', *Chatham House Briefing Note* (2009).

26 Walls, *A Somali Nation-State*, pp. 273–282.

3 Conclusion

In each of the examples cited, there are a number of common factors. The sequence of peace conferences between 1991 and 1997 built incrementally on agreements that addressed local disputes first before moving up the chain to tackle issues of governance.

That process unravelled on a number of occasions, resulting in renewed conflict, but rather than abandoning the incrementalist approach, the fresh conflict was addressed using similar principles. In every case, the efforts of mediators or external agents were not bound to succeed: the individuals and groups involved invested significantly in an open-ended situation. In the case of the diaspora-based Peace Committee, their efforts did not lead to clear success, but they did support dialogue in a manner that contributed to agreement in the future.

Women too, although excluded from formal proceedings, were seen to hold genuine and deep-seated interests in the processes with which they were engaged. That engagement was specific and demands were practical, detailed and enjoyed wide support.

The cultural-embeddedness of the interventions cited most obviously opens the way for Somali involvement, but there is room too for internationally-based, non-Somali initiatives. In common with the roles played by women, clan elders and diaspora groups, that form of external engagement is far more likely to succeed where it builds on local custom and context, involving people with a clear investment in the situation. There is ample room for robust engagement: the issue is not that the actors involved must play a passive or compliant role, but that whatever role is assumed is not seen to dominate proceedings.

Overall, the cyclical process of peace-building, and then state formation, has taken pragmatic advantage of interventions from a number of external sources: sometimes clan elders external to a given dispute; at other times women, diaspora groups or non-Somali diplomats. Externality itself is contextually defined and in each case, the intervention occurred at a level that worked within, rather than overwhelming locally-based processes. As such, customary space for external interventions of differing sorts has been used constructively and in full awareness of both the customs themselves and the politics of the moment.

That approach has the significant disadvantage that it is slow, and the intervenor cannot easily establish objectives or meaningful deadlines prior to an intervention. Combining as it does, discursive Somali traditions with those of representative government, it also tends to be crisis-driven as, at the societal level, it takes a crisis to bring people together and to focus minds sufficiently to provide the impetus for resolution.

In that context, Somaliland shows the importance of external intervention, and also the potential for it to support resolution of immediate crises, and in the long run, a durable and reasonably inclusive political settlement.

It is precisely in the inclusivity and legitimacy of that settlement that we find the basis for an argument around the prevention of atrocity. Somaliland still has a considerable distance to travel in those respects, with disputes over the very existence of Somaliland unresolved in some quarters, and a number of significant minority groups still excluded from the political sphere. However, there can be no question that the incrementalist approach adopted there has achieved vastly greater progress than has been the case with the more 'top-down' state-building in the southern Somali areas. There is no need to argue that the Somaliland process is complete to look for important lessons. The durability of the Somaliland peace, with no widespread conflict since 1997 stands in clear contrast to the situation in the south. Importantly, too, in the almost three decades of that peace, and in the years that laid its foundations, Somalilanders – both the wider public and elites – have learned how to manage crisis in a manner that has, so far, allowed them to step back from the brink time and again.

It is Somaliland's success in iteratively establishing a durable peace, followed by increasingly sophisticated institutions of government that provide the clearest indication as to the reasons that underpin their avoidance of the sustained conflict and associated abuses experienced by many Somalis further south. Not only are constructive external links a part of the story, but they are essential to it, with the mutual benefit offered by business and political partnerships important in providing a basis for cooperation. This is far from the 'anarchy' imagined by some commentators, but in the long term, peace alone is not enough either: Somaliland's success also shows the importance of a stable and legitimate system of government.

CHAPTER 7

Iran 1998–2008: Insight on the Containment of Risk

Sara E. Davies

Abstract

In the decade from 1998 to 2008, Iran experienced a period of continued political contestation and upheaval. During this period there were a number of political events that challenged the authority of Iranian regime (1999 student protests, Afghanistan and Iraq border conflicts, and the 2005 Presidential election). This chapter explores why two particular events, the 1999 student protests and the post-Iraq post-2005 Presidential election, did not 'trigger' a situation where the Iranian state engaged in mass atrocities to (re)assert regime stability. The use of violence to quell political opposition is a rational choice that many regimes engage in, with immediate and resounding success. However, the Iranian regime – despite consistently identified as having a high risk of genocide – has appeared reluctant to publicly sanction police and army to carry out mass atrocities. This chapter contends that the fragmented but hierarchical political system provides a delicate power balance that, for now, provides greater benefit for political and security sector in maintaining the status quo and avoiding bloody confrontation with Iranian citizens.

Keywords

Hierarchy – authoritarianism– ethnicity – resources – protest – human rights

1 Introduction

The Islamic Republic of Iran (Iran) exhibits many features of a country with a high risk of mass atrocities being perpetrated against its citizens, particularly those of minority faith (Christian, Jewish, Sunni and Bahai), ethnicity (Azari and Kurd), and those who express strong political opposition to the Islamic Republic.[1] In the decade from 1998 to 2008, the focus in this chapter, Iran

1 Minority Rights Group International, 'Iran', World Directory of Minorities and Indigenous Peoples, 9 July 2014. http://www.minorityrights.org/?lid=5092.

 | DOI 10.1163/9789004299870_009

experienced a period of continued political contestation and upheaval. During this period there were a number of political events that challenged the authority of Iranian regime. The most dramatic event during this decade was the university student protests in 1999 – Iran's most significant and sustained public protests since the Islamic Revolution.[2] Before these protests, and after, there were (sometimes violent) efforts by the conservative establishment within the Republic to curtail the reforms enacted by President Khatami, who was popularly elected in 1997.[3] The 2005 election of Ahmadinejad,[4] an extreme ideological conservative, saw Iran take a further backward step in terms of the rule of law and democratic processes, particularly for women and minority groups.[5] Unemployment and inflation increased during his first term. This internal political instability was potentially further intensified with the geopolitical impact (refugee flows, presence of rebel insurgents and religious/ethnic rivalry) from the United States-led coalition intervention in Afghanistan (2001) and Iraq (2003).

This chapter explores why these events, combined with a history of social, economic and political exclusion, have not 'triggered' a situation where the Iranian state has engaged in mass atrocities[6] to assert regime stability during two particular events when its authority was threatened: the 1999 student protests and the post-Iraq post-2005 Presidential election. The use of violence to quell political opposition is a rational choice that many regimes engage in, with immediate and resounding success.[7] However, the Iranian regime – despite being identified by one genocide watchlist as having a high risk of

2 The 2009 Presidential Election Protests were larger in number, but the focus in this chapter is on 1998–2008.

3 Reformist President Khatami in 1997 returned with the largest majority and highest turnout of any presidential election since the 1979 Islamic Revolution.

4 Public Broadcasting Service (PBS), 'Mahmoud Ahmadinejad's Victory in Iran's Presidential Runoff Election', *Online NewsHour*, 27 June 2005, http://www.pbs.org/newshour/bb/middle_east/jan-june05/ahmadinejad_6-27.html, accessed 15 January 2014.

5 Committee on the Elimination of Racial Discrimination (CERD), 'Consideration of reports submitted by States parties under article 9 of the convention. Concluding observations of the Committee on the Elimination of Racial Discrimination – Islamic Republic of Iran', Advanced Unedited Version, Seventy-seventh session, CERD/C/IRN/CO/18-19, 27 August 2010.

6 This chapter defines 'mass atrocities' as crimes against humanity, act of genocide and war crimes. See Office of the Special Advisor for the Prevention of Genocide and Responsibility to Protect, 'Framework of Analysis for Atrocity Crimes: A Tool for Prevention', New York: United Nations, 2014, p.1-2. http://www.un.org/en/preventgenocide/adviser/pdf/framework%20of%20analysis%20for%20atrocity%20crimes_en.pdf

7 Benjamin A. Valentino, 'Why We Kill: The Political Science of Political Violence against Civilians', *Annual Review of Political Science*, Vol. 17 (2014): 89–103.

genocide/politicide[8] – has appeared reluctant, on the streets at least, to sanction police and army to carry out brutal acts of domination and violence to silence political opposition. This chapter examines the reasons why.

In attempts to understand the conditions that lead to regime-induced mass atrocities, regimes with centralized authority have been identified as less prone to mass atrocities, however these regimes are not resilient against this risk. When the regime is seriously threatened, authoritarian regimes are attached to a high risk of mass atrocities.[9] Iran is an interesting authoritarian regime case, as it appears to have a relatively fragmented political system, with authority and institutional power spread widely across different parts of the elite. At the same time, there is a clear hierarchical structure to this devolved authority. The state is ruled according to the *velayat-e faqih,* or guardianship of the juris consult. In descending order of political hierarchy there is the Supreme Leader, the Guardian Council, the Assembly of Experts, the President, the Majlis (Parliament), the Expediency Council and the Supreme Court (who are appointed by both the Supreme Leader and the Guardian Council). Each of these have their own centres of power and differing degrees of influence over the state's various armed wings, which include the Revolutionary Guard, the Iranian Army, the police, the religious police and the *Basij* militia.

This chapter contends that this fragmented but hierarchical political system provides a delicate power balance that allows, presently, political and security actors to access resources to ensure their own survival. Any risk to the present regime would not be a net gain for all, and so there is (for now) greater benefit from maintaining the status quo. This finding is reflected in the fact that while Islamic Republic has been identified as having a 'high' risk of genocide/politicide, it has at the same time, a very low risk of future political instability. 'Harff makes this argument with another case, China. Despite a history of political and social marginalization, human rights violations and a high score on the genocide/politicide list, China is 'less worrisome' because of the stability of its authoritarian rule.'[10] This chapter explores whether this

8 Barbara Harff, 'Assessing Risks of Genocide and Politicide: A Global Watch List for 2012', Genocide Watch (2012), Table 6.1 Accessed at: http://www.genocidewatch.org/images/Global_Watch_List_-_Harff_2012.pdf, accessed 15 January 2014. Harff places Iran ninth out of 20 states in the 2012 genocide/politicide watchlist.

9 Matthew Krain, "State-Sponsored Mass Murder The Onset and Severity of Genocides and Politicides." *Journal of Conflict Resolution* Vol. 41 (3) (1997): 331–360; OECD, 'Concepts and Dilemmas of State Building in Fragile Situations: From Fragility to Resilience', OECD Discussions Paper (2008), http://www.oecd.org/dac/governance-peace/conflictandfragility/docs/41100930.pdf, accessed 15 January 2014.

10 Harff, Assessing Risks of Genocide and Politicide, p.54.

claim may also pertain to the history of the Islamic Republic after the 1978 Revolution and the key moments of crisis during the 1998–2008 period. The purpose of examining this period is that it has been identified as a key moment when individuals and younger population, in particular, sought to challenge the regime's authority. This chapter seeks to understand why the regime stopped short of employing mass atrocities when this authority was being challenged.[11] This chapter does not attempt to argue that the Iranian state has not and does not engage in oppressive, violent acts against its citizens. The regime regularly employs violence to compel and coerce Iranians, particularly in the arrest and treatment of political prisoners. But the state tends to carry out public acts of violence and repression in a limited and carefully calibrated fashion. Popular uprisings in support of reform are harshly repressed but the level of violence employed between 1998 and 2008 was significantly less than in the past, in situations where public demonstrations were less active than during this decade we examine.[12]

2 Brief Economic, Political and Social Background of Iran

The Islamic Republic of Iran (Iran) is a Persian state that sits on the periphery of both Asia and the Arab Middle East. Its unique geopolitical existence on the border of two regions has produced a history of geostrategic vulnerability, an oxymoronic contrast with the material power it could command due to its population size (largest in the Middle East) and material resources (it is estimated to have the world's fourth largest reserves of oil) and its long history as a territorial state.[13] Iran has a long cultural, linguistic and political history and the borders of the contemporary state are almost identical to borders drawn a

11 Kamran Taremi, 'Iranian Foreign Policy Towards Occupied Iraq, 2003–2005,' *Middle East Policy* 12 (4) 2005, p.28–47; Nikki R. Keddie, *Modern Iran: Roots and Results of Revolution. Updated Edition*, with section by Yann Richard (New Haven: Yale University Press, 2006); Vali Nasr, 'When the Shiites Rise', *Foreign Affairs* 85 (4) 2006, p.58–71, 73–74; Ali M. Ansari, 'Iran and the United States in the shadow of 9/11: Persia and the Persian question revisited,' in *Iran in the 21st Century: Politics, economics and conflict,* eds. Homa Katouzian and Hossein Shahidi (London: Routledge, 2008); Ervand Abrahamian, *A History of Modern Iran* (Cambridge: Cambridge University Press, 2008).

12 There was a three month long political prisoner execution spree in 1988 in which between 3,000 and 10,000 political prisoners were killed. There earlier killings were carried out near the end of the Iran-Iraq war. Abrahamian, *Tortured Confessions*, p.210, 215–216; Shirin Ebadi, *Iran Awakening: A Memoir of Revolution and Hope* (New York: Random House, 2006), p.90.

13 Sanam Vakil, 'Iran: Balancing east against west,' *The Washington Quarterly* 29/4 (2006): 51–65.

thousand years ago.[14] Iran also has significant ethnic minorities within its citizenship. Just over half of the population is of Persian ethnicity (61%), ethnic Azaris make up 16% of the population, Kurdish population comprise 10%, Lur 6%, then Arab, Turkmen and Baluchis make up approximately 2% each.[15] Iran hosts nearly 1 million refugees from (mostly) Afghanistan and Iraq.[16] Iran's own history has been punctuated by internal conflicts amongst feuding tribes and rival dynasties, conflicts against those with colonial ambitions in Persia including the Ottomans, British, French and Russians, and sectarian conflicts produced by the fact of a Shiite dominant Persian state in a predominantly Arab Sunni region.

The Islamic Republic of Iran was founded after months of revolution against the Shah Reza Pahlavi in April 1979. The Iranian Army did not automatically recognize the rule of the Islamic Republic or Ayatollah Khameni, but came into the fold within months to ensure that the creation of the Islamic Revolutionary Guard Corps did not entirely supersede its power and access to air, sea and land defence operations and equipment. The popular uprising promised to improve living conditions, redistribute wealth and address political inequalities that had been exploited by the Shah. The vision of Islamic Republic was one that could acknowledge and include citizens of different ethnicity and religious faith. However, this has not been the case in practice. Those of the Bahai faith were particularly targeted for discrimination and violet attack, as were the Christian population. The Kurds and Azeris were originally supportive of the creation of the Islamic Republic; however, the attempts by Kurdish populations across Iraq and Iran to form an autonomous state during the early stages of the Iran-Iraq War (1980–1988) led to violent reprisals against the Iranian Kurds.

Despite the devastation of the Iran-Iraq War, and the US-led international sanctions against the Iranian regime (who supported the Shah), the standard of living in Iran has improved markedly over the past few decades. Adult literacy increased from 36.5% in 1976 to 65% percent in 1991 and 82% in 2006.[17] Infant mortality fell from 156 deaths per 1000 lives births in 1965 to 64.4 in 1985,

14 Abrahamian, *A History of Modern Iran*, p.1–2.

15 Minority Rights Group International, 'Iran', *World Directory of Minorities and Indigenous Peoples*, July 2014, http://www.minorityrights.org/?lid=5092#minorities, accessed 02 August 2014. See also: Eliz Sanasarian and Avi Davidi, 'Domestic Tribulations and International Repercussions: The State and The Transformation of Non-Muslims in Iran', *Journal of International Affairs*, 60/2: 55–69 (2007), p.56; Hussein D. Hassan, 'Iran: Ethnic and Religious Minorities,' CRS *Report for Congress*, updated 25 November 2008 (Washington: Congressional Research Service, 2008), p.CRS-3.

16 UNHCR, 'Islamic Republic of Iran', 2014 UNHCR Country Operations Profile. http://www.unhcr.org/pages/49e486f96.html, accessed 12 August 2014.

17 World Bank, *Islamic Republic of Iran*. http://data.worldbank.org/country/iran-islamic-republic, accessed 15 January 2014.

and 25.9 in 2009. The poverty count (percent of population earning less than $2 a day) dropped from 13.83 in 1986 to 8.03 percent in 2005.[18] The state has delivered significant improvements to public infrastructure such as water, housing and electricity.[19] As one commentator put it, 'The Islamic Revolution has been as a whole a very successful anti-poverty endeavour'.[20] However, discriminatory practices against minority groups continue to this day, and the Islamic state has adopted erratic patterns of discrimination and violence against minority groups. This is a point I return to later when I discuss, in particular, the Kurdish political agitation for autonomy during this period.

Under the Shah, the Iranian economy was dependent on its ties to the US; with the removal of US investment the Revolutionary government has had to continually deal with a foreign investment vacuum.[21] The need for international investment intensified after the devastation of the Iraq-Iran war. During the Khatami years (1998–2005), the regime became eager to secure external investment. To sustain its welfare provisions, the regime at first pursued foreign investment, especially from the European Union.[22] Some rapprochement was achieved with the reformist Khatami seeking to reform human rights, media and election processes, vital to secure European investment. However, over the period of time examined, the Iranian economy increasingly pulled away from the West with the dramatic increase of Chinese and Indian investment. This has had the effect, over this decade, of making the regime less sensitive to Western criticism of its nuclear program and human rights record.[23] The imposition of Western sanctions also, ironically, made the Iranian government less vulnerable to global financial crisis.

Nonetheless, the continued imposition of sanctions has badly hurt the economy, leading some analysis to predict a major economic collapse is imminent. Inflation is high, wages are low, unemployment amongst the youth continues to increase and too much of the economic sector is state owned to allow competition and investment.[24] Across a range of indicators, the Iranian economy deteriorated during the 1998–2008 period, saved only by its strengthened

18 Ibid.

19 Djavad Salehi-Isfahani, 'Poverty, inequality, and populist politics in Iran,' *Journal of Economic Inequality* 7/1: 5–28 (2009).

20 Ibid, p.6–7.

21 Parsi, *Treacherous Alliance*, Part Two.

22 Sanam Vakil, 'Iran: Balancing east against west'; Elliot Hen-Tov, 'Understanding Iran's New Authoritarianism,' *The Washington Quarterly* 30/1: 163–179 (2007).

23 Vakil 2006.

24 Bradley, 'Iran's Ethnic Tinderbox', p.182; Hen-Tov, 'Understanding Iran's New Authoritarianism', p.172.

relations with China and India.[25] The economic fortunes of the Iranian state are closely tied to its political system and who is in control of vast and complex political institutions.

Since the Islamic Revolution against the Shah Pavlavi dynasty in 1979, Iran has been governed by a theocratic constitution that vests political authority and material power in a number of different institutions. The way in which the authority and power of the various arms interact is very much predicated on informal networks that shift over time. The current Supreme Leader Khamenei was appointed in 1989 by the Assembly of Experts after Supreme Leader Khomeini's death. Khamenei's rule is absolute across the diverse political institutions that govern Iran. He has the power to appoint jurists to the Guardian Council, to appoint the highest judicial authorities in the country to the Supreme Court, hold supreme command over the armed forces with the power to appoint and dismiss officers and controls the Supreme Defence Council. The Supreme Leader must certify the appointment of the President after the general election, and has the power to dismiss the President. In addition to commanding the armed forces, the Supreme Leader also has a private militia.[26]

At this point, power appears to dissolve across the various institutions with each having some influence in each other's remit. The Guardian Council has the right to veto parliamentary resolutions, oversee national elections (though, despite its best efforts, not local elections) and has the right to veto candidatures.[27] Like the Guardian Council, the Assembly of Experts is composed of Islamic jurists. The Assembly elects and has the theoretical right to dismiss the Supreme Leader. It also monitors his and Clerics adherence to Islamic law. These bodies are dominated by conservative minded clerics who continue to monopolize the administration of justice, the military, parliamentary participation and procedure, and economic institutions. While the President is responsible for appointing Cabinet Ministers, the Guardian Council is permitted to block such appointments. The Council is most protective of key portfolios such as the ministries of oil, foreign affairs and intelligence, as well as the armed forces and judiciary.[28] The clerics also tend to display clear preferences for Shia practising, Persian males.[29]

25 Vakil, 'Iran: Balancing east against west'.

26 Asghar Schirazi, *The Constitution of Iran: Politics and the State in the Islamic Republic*, translation by John O'Kane (London: I.B.Tauris, 1997).

27 Ibid, p.13.

28 Gheissari and Nasr, *Democracy in Iran*, p.136.

29 Schirazi, *The Constitution of Iran*.

The Majlis is one of the system's more democratic institutions, although the Guardian Council's does bear the right to block candidatures. Its members are elected from representative regions, with representation set aside for ethnic and religious minorities (except for those of the Bahai faith who face most intense discrimination).[30] Under Khatami, it was progressively filled with reformists but, prior to the 2004 election, the Guardian Council vetoed 2,000 candidates including an unprecedented 80 parliamentary deputies.[31]

While Iran is not one of the worst offenders when it comes to disrespect for the electoral process, President Khatami's period of rule (1997–2005) (which covers most of the decade explored), the capacity of the Supreme Leader and Guardian Council to block Majlis legislation and reformist candidates and influence Supreme Court decisions compromise the more democratic components of Iran's political system.[32] Most notably, in the period under consideration this power was used to scupper President Khatami's reform efforts, despite the President's historic 1997 election victory where he secured 69% percent of the vote and the 2000 Majlis election which sent 80% of votes to reform oriented candidates.[33]

A further impediment to Iranian democracy is the absence of transparent civilian control of the security sector. The *Basiji* militia (also known as Army of Mobilization) and the Islamic Revolutionary Armed Corps are directly tied to the authority of the Supreme Leader, and have separate ranks, uniforms and economies to the regular Iranian army. The Revolutionary Corps and the *Basiji* were established to protect the Islamic state from both internal and external opponents and stand apart from the regular armed forces. *Basiji* local bases (over 70,000) across Iran act as the local enforcer of Islamic code, a form of moral police, especially appointed by the Supreme Leader to be 'present in all public spheres particularly to protect revolutionary-Islamic values'.[34] The regime leadership has preferred to funnel support to the *Basiji* and Revolutionary

30 Human Rights Watch, 'Iran,' *World Report 2012: Time to Abandon the Autocrats and Embrace Rights*, 2012, http://www.hrw.org/sites/default/files/iran_2012.pdf, accessed 15 January 1014.

31 Keddie, *Modern Iran*, p.327.

32 After the introduction of Sharia law post-Revolution, the Judiciary works with 'two constitutional axes: the obvious administration of justice and the supervisions of proper rule of law' which has increasingly seen contradictions in courts findings from prosecution to appeal as the judiciary attempts to blend an Islamic and civil law interpretation (Arjomand 2009: 49). Appointees to the Judiciary are a mix of traditionally trained (civil law) lawyers and jurist clerics or religious jurists. The Supreme Leader appoints the Chief Justice of the Supreme Judiciary Council (Arjomand 2009: 47).

33 Abrahamian, *A History of Modern Iran*, p.186, 188.

34 Arjomand, *After Khomeini*, p.59.

Guard, deliberately at the expense of the regular army.[35] Since the 1979 Revolution, the regular army has remained politically weak in comparison to the Revolutionary Guard and *Basiji* because its past association with the Shah makes it an unreliable partner in the eyes of the revolutionary leaders. The Revolutionary Guard and *Basiji* were at least in part therefore established to balance the military capacity of the unreliable armed forces. These tensions have subsided a little, particularly in the wake of the Iran-Iraq War, leading to attempts to integrate the Revolutionary Guard into the regular army (President Rafsanjani in 1992), which were blocked by the Supreme Leader. Limited integration occurred in 2008, but this has only further blurred the line between their separate functions as (respectively) morality policy, militia and regular soldiers.[36] Since 2005, the *Basiji*, of which President Ahmadinejad is a member, has been significantly strengthened. The *Basiji* and Revolutionary Guard were pivotal supporters of his candidacy and have been rewarded financially with exclusive government contracts for development projects in steel, oil and gas. The *Basiji* was 'credited' with securing Ahmadinejad's election wins in 2005 and 2009 by employing violence, coercion and bribery through their local bases to secure support for the president.[37] The absence of strong democratic institutions, the division and absence of accountability in the security sector, and the constitution's capacity for arbitrary executive rule, undermines the rule of law in Iran.

Ideologically driven government, weak democratic institutions and practices, and limited rule of law creates a high degree of impunity for human rights abuses, monitored only by a small number of civil society activists in Tehran who are repeatedly harassed by the regime.[38] The regime imposes harsh legal penalties for those deemed to be 'acting against the state', activities that include overt political opposition, investigative journalism, and lawyers representing oppressed minority groups and political prisoners. Torture and forced confessions are routine in Iran's prisons, as are the use of threats and violence against family members and the execution of political prisoners.[39]

From this brief survey of the political, economic and social structure that characterized the Iran period from 1998–2008, it seems clear that the source of

35 Greg Bruno, Jayshree Bajoria, and Jonathan Masters, 'Iran's Revolutionary Guards, Council on Foreign Relations, 14 June 2013. http://www.cfr.org/iran/irans-revolutionary-guards/p14324.

36 Arjomand, *After Khomeini*, p.153.

37 Arjomand, *After Khomeini*, p.151–152.

38 CERD, 'Concluding observations of the Committee on the Elimination of Racial Discrimination – Islamic Republic of Iran'.

39 Ebadi, *Iran Awakening*.

potential instability stemmed from three key areas: the absence of democratic institutions and practices (with the attendant absence of rule of law), a history of human rights violations against religious, political and ethnic minorities – including a relatively recent history of atrocities (1988), and weak economic unstable economic growth. On the other hand, the regime has improved basic quality of life conditions for most Iranians, engaged in reform processes that saw limited amounts of political participation offered to (some) minorities, and has tried to avoid prolonged patterns of internal and external conflict (as we will see in the case of the Afghanistan 2001 and Iraq 2003 wars). The combination of these factors appear to have helped mitigate the risk of mass atrocities occurring despite a context of relatively high underlying risk that is exacerbated in crises situations, as will be examined in the following section.

3 Crises

There were two major crises between 1998 and 2008 that led to an escalation of violence and the potential for imminent mass atrocities. The first was the 1999 July student protests that followed in the wake of the 'Serial Murders case' (or Ministry of Intelligence assassins list) and the forced closure of the *Salam* newspaper that had reported the Ministry of Intelligence's culpability in the targeted assassination of writers and political dissidents in 1998–1999. The 1999 protests were the largest since the 1979 Revolution and generated the first direct calls for Supreme Leader Khamenei to step down. Fearing that the President would support the protests, the Revolutionary Guard threatened Khatami with a coup on 12 July and the country fell into deadlock for six days until the President distanced himself from the protests and deplored their actions. Though this was widely interpreted as a sign of weakness by President Khatami, the events also revealed the conservative establishment's reluctance to simply force Khatami from office. In other words, the fragmentation of power and authority across the regime forced conservatives to build coalitions and coerce Khatami rather than employ coercive force against the students and Khatami. This desire for a political compromise appeared to stay the hand of the security forces and mitigated the risk of atrocities.

The second major crisis occurred in the aftermath of the 2003 US-led invasion of Iraq. The subsequent overthrow of Saddam Hussein's regime threatened Iran's internal political stability in two ways. First, Iran's Kurdish and Sunni Arab minorities were encouraged by the US government to challenge the regime. US rhetoric placed these minority populations at great risk, weakened Khatami's reformism and provided a pretext for conservative attempts to regain control of the presidency to quash Kurdish and Sunni opposition. As in 1999, however, though violence was employed to quell few instances of rebellion within the outer provinces of Iran where Kurdish and Sunnis lived in greater number, conservatives did not advocate mass violence. Elite fragmentation played a role once more in shaping this response, more important in this case was the regime's sensitivity to its internal legitimacy – especially the need to maintain peace and security within the state.

3.1 *Serial Murders and the 1999 Protests*

In the wake of Khatami's historic election victory in 1997, Supreme Leader Khomeini consolidated his political power through the Guardian Council, Judiciary, Revolutionary Guard, various militias led by the *Basiji*, and the Ministry of Intelligence. The appointment of the conservative Ghorban Ali Dorri Najafabadi to the intelligence ministry was directed by the conservatives. In the first two years of Khatami's presidency, four investigative journalists and dissident writers were murdered.[40] The killings were preceded by an alleged attempt to kill a busload of writers from the Iran Writers Association in 1996. The writers were returning from a conference on a government chartered bus when the driver steered the bus towards a cliff and jumped out. Tragedy was averted by the quick thinking of one of the writers able to apply the brake. The authorities instructed the writers not to publicize the incident.[41] In November 1998, husband and wife Dariush Forouhar (former Minister for Labour in the revolutionary government) and Parveneh Eskandari (intellectual) were stabbed to death in their home, having been visited the previous night by Ministry of Intelligence officials.[42] Shortly after, journalist Akbar Galnji, a former Revolutionary Guard member and Ministry of Intelligence operative, published a series of articles in the newspaper *Salam* revealing that at least nine murdered dissidents (including Forouhar and Eskandari) were named on a Ministry of Intelligence assassination list. In January 1999, Khatami ordered an investigation into the killings and within a week the Ministry identified 'rogue elements' acting alone as being responsible.[43] The only Ministry official identified as

40 Some report four: Los Angeles Times, 'Iran Orders Retrial Over Killings of Dissidents', 19 August 2001. http://articles.latimes.com/2001/aug/19/news/mn-35909; some have reported nine: Nikki R. Keddie and Yann Richard. *Modern Iran: Roots and Results of Revolution* (New York: Yale University Press, 2003), p.275.

41 Boroumand, 'The Untold Story of the Fight for Human Rights', p.71.

42 Ibid, p.68–69.

43 Mehdi Moslem, *Iran: Factional Politics in Post-Khomeini* (NewYork: Syracuse University Press, 2002), p.265.

responsible for the killings – deputy minister Sa'id Emami – committed suicide in prison in June, 1999 (under suspicious circumstances: death due to ingestion of hair removal cream). His wife was also imprisoned after his death.[44] After this publication, the conservative Minister of Intelligence, Najafabadi, proposed a new law restricting press freedom in the Majlis.[45]

The judiciary then ordered the immediate closure of the *Salam* on 5 July. Three days later, thousands of Tehran University students conducted a peaceful sit-in protesting both the bill and the closure of *Salam*. That night, the Revolutionary Guard, the police and members of a militia funded by the conservative establishment, *Ansar-e Hezbollah*, stormed a student dormitory: killing one student, injuring many and arresting hundreds.[46] This attack was denounced by Khatami and the following day emboldened protestors gathered on the streets to protest.[47] The protests then spread to many universities around the country. In response, the police and militias clashed with protestors, beating and arresting unspecified number who sought to join the rallies.[48] Six days of unrest caused three reported deaths and left 200 people injured. A further seventy students remained unaccounted for after their arrest. Across the country, a further 1,200–1,400 people were arrested, mainly university students.[49] On 12 July the government announced a ban on demonstrations – which was ignored by students. The crisis ended when Khatami denounced the protests on 13 July.[50] On 14 July, Conservatives organized counter-demonstrations, and allegedly, placed *Basiji* and Revolutionary Guard members within the crowd as a pretext for a violent crackdown if confrontations with students occurred.[51]

Why the President denounced the protestors on 13 July remains a key point of contention; but there is no doubt it took away the students' political momentum – they were risking their lives for his attempt at reform. Keddie argues that the Revolutionary Guard threatened to launch a brutal repression on the

44 Cyrus Bina, 'The Hot Summer of Defiance: The Student Protests for Freedom and Democracy in Iran', *Journal of Iranian Research and Analysis* 15/2: 47–62 (1999), p.49; Ebadi, *Iran Awakening*, p.138–139.

45 Moslem, *Iran*, p.265; Abrahamian, *A History of Modern Iran*, p.189.

46 Keddie, *Modern Iran*, p.276; Arjomand, *After Khomeini*, p.95.

47 Keddie, *Modern Iran*, p.277.

48 Jahangir Amuzegar, 'Khatami's First-Term Presidency: An Outsider's Assessment', *SAIS Review* 22/1: 1–21 (2002), p.5; Boroumand, 'The Untold Story of the Fight for Human Rights', p.72.

49 BBC News, 'Six Days that shook Iran', 11 July 2000, http://news.bbc.co.uk/2/hi/middle_east/828696.stm, accessed 10 December 2010; Keddie, *Modern Iran*, p.277.

50 Gheissari and Nasr, *Democracy in Iran*, p.139; Arjomand, *After Khomeini*, p.95.

51 Bina, 'The Hot Summer of Defiance', p.51–52.

protestors if Khatami did not denounce them and demand their end.[52] If this report is accurate, then Khatami's actions potentially averted an atrocity.

Keddie argues that immediately after the protests ended a form of rapprochement occurred between the Khatami and Khamenei camps.[53] Both were allegedly surprised by the speed and size of the protests.[54] Khatami again deplored the protests, arguing that such clashes would only undermine democracy and lead to extremism.[55] Most protestors arrested were released without charge; although some were not and they were subjected to torture and long prison sentences.[56] One hundred policemen were prosecuted for brutality in the dormitory attack, but no members from *Ansar e-Hezbollah* (cleric sponsored militia), the Revolutionary Guard or the *Basiji* were charged. The hardline conservative head of the Judiciary, Yazdi, who led the crackdown on reformist newspapers, journalists and reformist politicians, was replaced with a more 'pragmatic conservative'.[57]

Whatever the reason for Khatami's decision to denounce the protests and the rapid return to order that followed, a massacre was potentially averted in this situation. There is evidence that the Revolutionary Guards wished to use extreme violence to end the protests, especially if there had been a large-scale confrontation between demonstrators and the 'counter-demonstrators' on 14 July.

What restrained these events from further escalation? First, fragmentation within the political system meant that no single group enjoyed complete control over how the state would respond to the student protests – except for Khamenei. The threats made by the Revolutionary Guard to Khatami, were then followed by Khatami's efforts to deplore the protests. There were two to three days when the crisis could have escalated because different strands of the governing elite could not reach a consensus. While the *coup d'etat* threat by the Revolutionary Guard to Khatami was an ostensible show of strength, it also revealed the regime's fundamental weakness. Bina argues that, on the one hand, the Revolutionary Guard's desire to brutally suppress the protestors and remove Khatami from the Presidency, if he did not distance himself from their actions, revealed the Guard's capacity to unleash unlimited indiscriminate

52 Keddie, *Modern Iran*, p.277.

53 Keddie, *Modern Iran*, p.276–277.

54 Ali Akbar Mahdi, 'The Student Movement in the Islamic Republic of Iran', *Journal of Iranian Research and Analysis* 15/2: 5–46 (1999), p.25–26; Ebadi, *Iran Awakening*, p.154.

55 Abrahamian, *A History of Modern Iran*, p.192.

56 Boroumand, 'The Untold Story of the Fight for Human Rights', p.73.

57 Keddie, *Modern Iran*, p.277.

violence suggesting authority came from the Supreme Leader.[58] On the other hand, Bina argues, the Guard's initial strong-arm reaction had not delivered the political consensus (and silence) it had presumed was assured.[59] Khatami's eventual concession to the Revolutionary Guard appears not to have been a simple knee-jerk reaction to their demands. This was made clear by the fact that Khatami did not – in the first instance – give in to the Guard's demands to denounce the protests. He took several days to consider his position. During this interregnum, many Majlis members and Cabinet ministers condemned the brutality of the police force to domestic and international media sources. It was not until three days later that Khatami publicly denounced the protests. During this time, the conservative forces had slowly escalated their response to the protestors, with the organization of the 'anti-protestors' sent out to chant 'Death to America'. By 12 July the deployment of Guards, along with the *Basiji* and *Ansar e-Hezbollah*, amongst the protestors was kettling protestors into certain parts of the cities (by this stage the protests had spread beyond Tehran and into Tibriz, Shiraz and other major cities).[60] This was when President Khatami backed away from his support for the protestors.

Khatami was reportedly worried that the protests would strengthen the core arguments of the conservative establishment about the potential of reformism to sow the seeds of chaos and disorder. Having voted for a reformist government, protestors demonstrated their preparedness to challenge the regime directly. But at the same time, this placed the reform effort at risk if the situation was not quickly brought under control. Although there was no shortage of violence and torture in the regime's response to the protestors, there was no mass killing of political prisoners on the level that was recorded in 1988. Second, there were charges laid against the police for their role in the dormitory raids. Third, there was the removal of Yazdi, who had ordered the shutdown of the *Salam* newspaper which led to protestors taking to the streets. Khatami ultimately had to concede, but he was able to do so – it appears – without being co-opted into arguments for violent force and retribution against protestors.

The second important factor that mitigated the risk of mass atrocities in the wake of the protests was the détente established between the two rival political groups – the conservatives and the reformists – which was based on a shared interest in protecting the regime's legitimacy and Khamenei's authority. While there were hardliners within the militia keen to teach the protestors a lesson by issuing reprisals against them and their families, the senior conservative

58 Bina, 'The Hot Summer of Defiance', p.51.

59 Ibid, p.57.

60 Ibid, p.51.

establishment was reported as shaken by the protestors' challenge to regime's legitimacy. The demographic that had been crucial for the 1979 Revolution were opposing the regime twenty years later. Conservatives also recognized that there could be a popular backlash against the forced removal of Khatami.[61] In addition, some clerics were aware of the critical vulnerability to their powerbase if the protests continued and Revolutionary Guard were the only ones who could restore order. Clerics were eager to return to normalcy as quickly as possible.[62] In short, leading conservatives gathered around Khamenei wanted to suppress the reformist opposition, but not at the cost of creating a fractured state where power base shifted and support for the regime further divided between conservatives and reformists.

The 1999 crisis was the culmination of a political struggle that had been developing since the 1997 elections, which Khatami won with overwhelming – but unexpected – popular support. Khatami's push for legal, economic and social reform threatened the conservative hold over political institutions, the judiciary and the economy. The inevitable political resistance came through Khomeini's refusal to reform the security sector, his insistence upon conservative appointments to key Cabinet positions such as the Intelligence Ministry, and the appointment of hardline conservatives to the Judiciary and Special Court for Clerics, created a significant degree of political division and tension that bubbled over in 1999. The role of the Ministry of Intelligence – and in turn the conservative clerics and the Supreme Leader himself – in the serial murders, the forced closure of the reformist newspaper *Salam* and the push for conservative legislation in the Majlis, brought these tensions to a head. Who precisely ordered the morning crackdown on the peaceful student protest remains unanswered. There is, however, no doubt that the crackdown was an attempt to intimidate those demanding further reform and undermine popular support for Khatami.[63] Whether the Revolutionary Guards ever intended to unleash full scale violent repression against the students as they threatened to Khatami is also unknown, but the threat was a credible one and it existed within a context of growing tensions: the protestors made a direct challenge to the legitimacy of a non-democratic government, the establishment and use of militia against students and other opposition groups, the violent targeting of independent media, the escalation of popular dissent and protest from the regime's use of violence, threats of a wider repression by the Revolutionary Guard, and the threatened forced removal of the President.

61 Mahdi, 'The Student Movement in the Islamic Republic of Iran', p.16.

62 Mahdi, 'The Student Movement in the Islamic Republic of Iran', p.26.

63 Moslem, *Iran*, p.265.

The 1999 student protests may never have resulted in the breakout of mass violence, but there appears to be two factors that mitigated its escalation, the location of authority and material power within the regime, and sensitivity to popular legitimacy on the part of some members amongst the leadership. First, the fragmentation between conservatives and reformists meant that the regime was unable to articulate and execute a united political front in response to the protests. Indeed, the leadership itself was institutionally divided on the question of the legitimacy of the protests. Khamenei was undisputedly in control of the situation, but his allies were not united on how to proceed. The Revolutionary Guard undoubtedly desired one course of action, but his powerful assembly of clerics were cautious to give too much power to the military wing of the regime. One of the effects of this was that although a degree of impunity was certainly evident, there was not a *culture of impunity* among those who used violence to suppress the students. This was most obviously demonstrated by criticism from some parts of the regime after the assault on the student dormitories and the fact that some of the perpetrators were indeed prosecuted for crimes committed against the students. Albeit it was the police officers, and not *Basij* militia members, who were charged and prosecuted. Second, because the crisis was rooted in an intra-regime political struggle, the principal target of attack for the conservatives was not the public, but the President. The militias and the police certainly had the material power to quell the protests with extreme force on the very first night. The fact that they did not do so, suggests to some that, that the real goal was to quash reformism whilst preserving the regime's popular legitimacy, this meant that the target was not the protestors but the authority of President Khatami. As Bina argues,[64] this was made clear by the Revolutionary Guard's decision to deliver a threat to President Khatami rather than immediately target the protestors – a move we noted above was both a sign of the Guard's capacity to coerce the President and its inability to marshal the whole regime. The attacks on the dormitories were an example of what could happen if Khatami did not back down. This reinforces the view that conservatives were keenly sensitive about the need to protect popular legitimacy in a context of diminishing popular support for the conservative establishment and its militia.

The 1999 crisis reached a point at which *Basiji* militia and the police committed egregious human rights violations against individuals, but events did not escalate further. One reason appears to be that challenges to authority were not emanating only from the public but from within the regime, and containing this internal power struggle was essential. However, it appears the

64 Bina, 'The Hot Summer of Defiance'.

struggle had to be resolved without one branch of the regime succeeding over the other – Khamenei's pushed back on reform but did so through the (coerced) assistance of Khatami rather than ceding power to the Revolutionary Guard and militia (though matters may have come to this if Khatami had refused to back down). There was also sensitivity within the regime to maintain popular legitimacy and national cohesion. This influence particular comes to the fore again after the 2003 US-led invasion into Iraq.

3.2 *The 2003 Invasion of Iraq and the Question of Territorial Integrity*

The 2003 invasion of Iraq and subsequent armed conflict and instability there created another potential source of conflict and escalation in Iran.[65] In the years that followed the 1999 protests there were two important changes to the internal dynamics of the Islamic Republic. First, popular turn out for the Majlis, municipal and Presidential elections weakened markedly. Nonetheless, the Majlis election in 2000 election and Khatami's re-election to the presidency in 2001 demonstrated that, despite the government's crackdowns, there remained strong popular support for the reformists. The reformists' hold on the Majlis diminished only because the Guardian Council disqualified a higher number of reformist candidates than in the past. The second major change was Khatami's retreat from a reformist foreign policy. A reformist foreign policy based on the non-use of force and international dialogue, ostensibly aimed at attracting foreign investment and forging stable regional relations, gave way to conservative rhetoric as the United States and Israel moved in a conservative, anti-Iran, direction during Khatamis' second presidential term. President George W Bush's declaration that Iran was one of three states forming an 'Axis of Evil', during his now famous State of the Union address in the wake of the 11 September 2001 terrorist attack on New York and Washington, dramatically undermined Khatami's fledging attempts to promote Iranian diplomatic and economic engagement with the West. Furthermore, it polarized the Iranian public, prompting many to question whether Khatami's engagement with the West had delivered better relations and satisfied Iranian interests. This speech undermined the success of foreign engagement during Khatami's first term and made it almost impossible for Khamati to persuade the regime to continue in a reformist direction. At the same time, Israel's majority Likud party stepped up its rhetoric against Iran, focusing especially on its pursuit of nuclear weapons that threatened both the Jewish state and Arab neighbours, who were traditionally hostile to the Islamic Republic and needed little convincing to

65 Keddie, *Modern Iran*, p.284.

further isolate the regime.[66] These external factors weakened the reformists hand and lent domestic legitimacy to hardliners.

The ramping up of external threats also prompted the regime to step up its military preparations for defence. Iran also began aggressively pursuing development of its ground to air missile stockpile and nuclear enrichment program.[67] Of course, what some in Iran saw as necessary defensive measures to respond to over US and Israeli threats was read by others in the international community as a threat to regional and international security, as well as violation of international law, establishing a debate in Europe about the imposition of sanctions and discussion in the US about further strengthening anti-Iranian sanctions. Iran embarked on a foreign policy balancing act of seeking to project strength against the Bush Administration's increasingly vocal demand for regime change in Iran, without undermining foreign investment in its oil and gas sectors, as well as in other parts of its flagging economy. This balancing act pushed Iran towards engagement with countries that would be less interested in its domestic politics, namely China and India, effectively reducing Western economic leverage over the Islamic Republic.

All of this, it is important to underscore, significantly strengthened the hand of the conservatives vis-a-vis the reformists. In line with Khatami's foreign policy of engagement – Iran had supported the US invasion of Afghanistan in November 2001 and provided diplomatic assistance with the creation of the new government in Afghanistan. Known as the 'Geneva Channel' talks, Iranian diplomats had provided intelligence on the Taliban and al-Qaeda, offered air bases to the United States and instigated talks between the Northern Alliance and the US.[68] The Iranian delegation at the Bonn Conference in December 2001, a UN led conference to discuss the composition and direction of the new Afghanistan government, proved crucial in securing the Northern Alliance's support for the new Afghan government.[69] Of course, it was in Iran's interests to see the Taliban defeated in Afghanistan. The Taliban had murdered eight Iranian diplomats in September 1998, which escalated tensions between the Sunni dominated Taliban and the Islamic Republic to the point where the Iranian army was mobilized on the Iran-Afghanistan border. Iran was also host to at least two million Afghan refugees and had been profoundly affected by Taliban's black market poppy (raw material for heroin) trade, which had

66 Parsi, *Treacherous Alliance*.
67 Ibid.
68 Parsi, *Treacherous Alliance*, p.228.
69 Ibid, p.229.

almost single handedly created a huge increase in heroin addiction.[70] But this reformist effort to engage positively with the West produced no discernible improvement in Iran's global position – especially no reduction in the US Congress-sponsored sanctions against Iran investments and no movement on the renegotiation of arms sales. Supporters for the continuation of sanctions would, and did, point to the fact that Iran had continued to financially support Shiite extremist groups such as Lebanon's Hezbollah and the Palestinian Hamas in an attempt to weaken relations within Arab states and weaken the state of Israel.

Conservatives ridiculed Khatami's government and denounced the willingness of the Iranian Foreign Ministry to assist the US in Afghanistan for so little in return.[71] The Revolutionary Guard sought to use Bush's speech as justification for declaring a 'state of emergency' on the grounds that Iran was directly threatened by the US. Reform debate within the Majlis was overtaken by discussions about the ineptitude of the Iranian Foreign Ministry and external threats to Iranian security.[72] Khatami lost his influence over the Majlis, with municipal elections showing Iranian opinion moving back towards the conservatives. The conservatives persuasively argued that Khatami's rapprochement efforts with the US had left the Iranian state weak and vulnerable.[73]

But US policy in the Middle East came to pose a more direct threat to Iran's territorial integrity, establishing a renewed threat of atrocities there. As it became clear that the US was intending to invade Iraq in early 2003, some within the Iranian regime became genuinely concerned that the US would also invade Iran to bring about regime change there. Certainly, this is where the logic surrounding the 'axis of evil' and rhetoric about 'regime change' in Iraq seemed to be pointing.[74] Iranian concerns were heightened by a switch in Israel's position under Ariel Sharon – from opposing the Iraq invasion to unequivocal support for it and endorsement of a follow-on invasion of Iran.[75]

US invasion of Iraq exacerbated the Iranian regime's sense of geostrategic vulnerability.[76] The effect of the rapid fall of Saddam's regime sharpened Iranian fears about being subjected to similar treatment.[77] There were also

70 Adam Tarock, 'The Politics of the Pipeline: The Iran and Afghanistan Conflict,' *Third World Quarterly*, 20/4: 801–819 (1999).

71 Ibid.

72 Ansari, 'Iran and the United States in the shadow of 9/11,' p.114–115; Abrahamian, *A History of Modern Iran*, p.193.

73 Abrahamian, *A History of Modern Iran*, p.193.

74 Keddie, *Modern Iran*, p.284.

75 Parsi, *Treacherous Alliance*, p.240.

76 Parsi, *Treacherous Alliance*, p.240.

77 Taremi, 'Iranian Foreign Policy Towards Occupied Iraq, 2003–2005,' p.35.

concerns that sectarian strife in Iraq would exacerbate the Sunni-Shiite divide in Iran, the Baluchi Sunnis aligning with their Arab neighbours, replicating the division religious division in Iran that was seen in Iraq after the US invasion.[78] Above all, though, it raised concerns about the potential for instability in Iraq to exacerbate ethnic cleavages in Iran. In particular, it was feared that Iran's Kurds (10% of the population) would align with their counterparts in Iraq and seek to create an independent Kurdistan – taking a considerable part of Iran's northern territory.

Although less acute than the 1999 protests as an imminent threat of atrocities, the instability caused by the collapse of the Iraqi state and onset of sectarian war created the potential for a process of escalation of political tensions within Iran, especially given the cross-border nature of the ethnic and sectarian conflicts. In the section that follows, I identify two reasons why conflict, particularly with the Kurdish population, did not intensify during this period: (1) the Iranian regime shied away from attempting to aggressively exploit the situation in Iraq because it was concerned about the potential spill over effect; (2) the regime – especially its reformist elements – attempted to engage with ethnic minorities, especially the Kurds, in order to avoid the emergence of a consolidated ethnic political bloc that could pose a direct threat in some regions.

During the rule of the Shah, the Kurdish educated elite in Iran were the primary drivers of the Kurdish Republican movement. This group's principal grievances related to their exclusion from important positions of government and the military. Though the Kurdish population were allowed to retain ownership of their land under the Shah's 1962 Land Reform act (which has been important factor to this day in shaping Kurdish tribal resistance to the nationalist movement in the rural provinces), and were given some positions in the army and representation in the Majlis, there was always a limit to the number of Kurds who could reach such positions. Under both the Shah and the Islamic regime, the vast majority of Kurds were barred from positions of wealth and power in Iran, with the Kurds faring much worse than other ethnic minorities such as the Azeris as well as the predominant Persian population.[79]

Kurdish nationalists had been against the Shah in 1979 and supported the revolutionary movement. The Islamic revolutionary clerics rewarded this support with promises of greater rights for the Kurdish minority in the new Constitution.[80] The Kurdish Democratic Party of Iran (KDPI) presented

---

78 Taremi, 'Iranian Foreign Policy Towards Occupied Iraq, 2003–2005,' p.28; Parsi, *Treacherous Alliance*, 241–242.

79 Shaffer, 'The formation of Azerbaijani collective identity in Iran,' p.172; Kooh-Kamali, The Political Development of the Kurds in Iran, p.171.

80 Atabaki, 'From multilingual empire to contested modern state,' p.54.

Khomeini with a request for substantial Kurdish autonomy, with only the currency, foreign policy and defence remaining under the authority of Iranian state. Khomeini immediately rejected the proposal. When it became clear that the more moderate Islamic revolutionaries were losing power to the hardliners in the development of the Constitution and the formation of the first Parliament, Kurdish militia returned to arms. In the ensuing conflict which lasted from 1980–1983, some 10,000 Kurds, including many civilians in this number, were killed.[81] After the effective defeat of organized armed resistance, the Kurdish struggle continued in the form of low-level guerrilla and terrorist attacks but enjoyed little success. Having repulsed Saddam's initial offensive, Iran continued its offensive against the Kurds in Kurdistan. This region was heavily shelled with heavy losses of civilian life.[82] The violence prompted a split in Kurdish opinion, with some claiming neutrality in the war, and others siding with either Iran or Iraq. Ironically, as a means of weakening Saddam, the Iranian regime provided strong support to Iraqi Kurds, offering political assistance, refuge and military arms.[83] However, neither Iran nor Iraq were interested in addressing Kurdish demands for autonomy, leading one analyst to reason that the Iran-Iraq war provided just 'another opportunity for repression of the Kurds in both countries' (Ibid: 195).[84]

In 2003, acutely aware that an escalation of conflict inside Iraq had the potential to spill over into Iran, the conservative establishment, especially former President Hashemi Rafsanjani as Head of the Expediency Council (established to resolve the legislative impasse between Majlis and Guardian Council), was most anxious to tacitly (though not publicly) acknowledge their willingness to assist the US in establishing democratic rule in Iraq.[85] Rafsanjani led the drive towards diplomatic rapprochement with the Bush Administration after the Iraq invasion.[86] Referred to as the 'grand bargain', in return for its support the Islamic Republic sought the lifting of economic sanctions, removal from the 'axis of evil' and 'sponsors of terrorism' lists, recognition of Iran's security interests in the region, and access to peaceful nuclear technology.[87] For

81 Sam Dagher, 'Kurds', *New York Times*, 3 May 2010, http://topics.nytimes.com/top/reference/timestopics/subjects/k/kurds/index.html?scp=2&sq=iran%20kurdistan&st=cse, accessed 14 January 2011.

82 Michael Rubin, 'Are Kurds a Pariah Minority?' *Social Research* 70/1: 295–330 (2003), p.319.

83 Koohi-Kamali, *The Political Development of the Kurds in Iran*, p.190–191.

84 Ibid, p.195.

85 Taremi, 'Iranian Foreign Policy Towards Occupied Iraq, 2003–2005', p.33; Parsi, *Treacherous Alliance*, p.241–243.

86 Gheissari and Nasr, *Democracy in Iran*, p.153–154; Ansari, 'Iran and the United States in the shadow of 9/11', p.116.

87 Parsi, *Treacherous Alliance*, p.341.

this, the Iranians would support US attempts to establish democracy in Iraq, permit nuclear inspections, cease its support for terrorist organizations (within Iraq, Palestine, Lebanon or elsewhere), and accept the two-state solution to the Israel-Palestine conflict. This approach was made through a Swiss diplomat intermediary, Tim Guldimann. There are conflicting reports about who instigated the initiative, no doubt due to pragmatic conservative efforts to distance themselves from the negotiations, especially when it became clear that the Bush Administration had no intention of accepting the grand bargain.[88] There are reports that it was President Khatami, and not Rafsanjani who led the initiative.[89] Regardless of who in Iran led the initiative, there is much agreement that it was first initiated by the Iranians,[90] and this diplomatic attempt to engage indicated that the regime was acutely aware of the potential risks posed by the instability in Iraq.[91]

After the failed 'grand bargain' with the US, pragmatic conservatives steadily gained control of the Majlis and Assembly of Experts, and by 2005, the ideological conservatives would have their own President (Ahmadinejad).[92] In the interim, the Iranian government sought a 'positive neutral' stance on Iraq. Ironically, Iran had started to enjoy some economic relief with the high priced oil sales from the Middle East turmoil.[93]

In response to the potential threat to Iran's precarious ethnic and sectarian relations, the regime was quick to diffuse possible tensions by immediately seeking to support elections in Iraq. Importantly, the Iranian regime never treated post invasion Iraq as an opportunity for reviving the Khomenei dream of Iran rule over all Shiites in Iraq.[94] Instead the regime sought to instil its political, economic and religious influence in the Shiite dominated (and religiously significant) regions of Najaf and Basra. The regime also extended support to secular parties, moderate Shiite political parties and Kurdish parties. Ayatollah Rafsanjani summed up the new Iranian position in April 2003:

> As far as Iran was concerned, the dissolution of the Baath regime *per se* was neither good nor bad; it all depended on the kind of regime that replaced it. If the United States succeeded in establishing a client state in

88 Ansari, 'Iran and the United States in the shadow of 9/11', p.116–117.

89 Parsi, *Treacherous Alliance*, p.243.

90 Ibid.

91 Parsi, *Treacherous Alliance*, p.245.

92 Gheissari and Nasr, *Democracy in Iran*, p.153–157.

93 Parsi, *Treacherous Alliance*, p.257.

94 Nasr, 'When Shiites Rise'.

> Iraq, that would be extremely detrimental to Iran's national security. On the other hand, if elections were held and an independent government emerged, that would be in Iran's interests because it was bound to be dominated by a Shiite majority. Such a government, Iranian leaders believed, would inevitably align itself with Iran.[95]

As mentioned above, from 2003 the Iranian regime sought diplomatic relations with the major political factions in Iraq in an attempt to mitigate potential sources of instability. Moreover, whilst parts of the regime – especially the Revolutionary Guards and *Basij* – undoubtedly supplied arms and other support to Shiite militia, other part of the regime provided counsel and sought to alleviate tensions between Shiite militias and the more moderate Shiite political parties.[96] The influence that Iran had sought in Iraq was evident when it was its diplomatic intervention that enabled Iraqi leaders to form parliament in late 2010 after an election stalemate had left the Kurd, Sunni and Shiite political parties unable to form government.[97] Of course, this role has had consequences in recent times with religious and ethnic divisions within Iraq creating a political and security sector vacuum from May to September 2014 that has enabled the Islamic State of Iraq and Levant (IS) to siege key territory and terrorise populations.

Prior to this, immediately after the 2003 invasion by the US-led coalition, the Iranian regime's decision to nominally address the ethnic and religious divisions in Iraq related to implications for its own Kurdish population. The Iranian Kurds are a predominantly Sunni minority (there are some Shiite Kurdish areas). They are estimated to make up around 10% of Iran's population and live mostly in three provinces – Kurdistan (where the majority live), Western Azerbaijan and Kermanshah.[98] As with Iran more generally, there are significant cultural, economic and political differences *within* the Kurdish population which has, historically, hampered successful secessionist attempts within

95 Taremi, 'Iranian Foreign Policy Towards Occupied Iraq, 2003–2005', p.35–36.

96 'Iranian Foreign Policy Towards Occupied Iraq, 2003–2005', p.37–38; Robert Grenier, 'Iraq: Threats of foreign influence', *Al Jazeera* 11 January 2011, http://english.aljazeera.net/indepth/opinion/2011/01/201111014225474996.html, accessed 11 January 2011.

97 In fact, Iran has been accredited for pressuring the Cleric Muqtada al-Sadr to support the establishment of the secular Prime Minister Nuri al-Maliki to form government by giving his crucial 12 percent of the Council of Representatives seats (won by al-Sadr's Jaysh al-Mahdi militia/political party in March 2010 elections) to the coalition government. Greiner, 'Iraq'.

98 Farideh Koohi-Kamali, *The Political Development of the Kurds in Iran: Pastoral Nationalism* (Hampshire: Palgrave Macmillan 2003), p.31.

that community. At one end of the spectrum, some Kurds adhere to tribal culture and practices, live in villages that derive their subsistence and income from agricultural and pastoral farming. At the other end is a large population of 'urban Kurds', comprising a much higher number of professionals and traders. The latter group have tended to have a history of accommodating the Iranian regime. Another source of division is between Kurds living in Kurdistan and those living in other regions. The Kurdish nationalist leadership in Iran is mostly dominated by the Kurdistan Kurds, but even here there are divisions between those who are content to pursue autonomy and those holding out for a Kurdish state.[99]

By the time of Khatami's presidency, the main grievance amongst the Kurdish population related to socio-economic discrimination, with only a relatively small political group still calling for outright independence.[100] President Khatami acknowledged these grievances by discussing rural development projects, devoting higher health and education expenditure in the region, and addressing cultural grievances.[101] During his first term, there was also a relaxing of various restrictions. The publication of Kurdish language literature and newspapers was permitted as was minority representation in local councils (where the Guardian Council has been less successful in blocking candidates). These measures dampened (growing) agitation for secession.[102]

However, at the same time, across the border the Iraqi Kurds were being granted semi-autonomous rule in northern Iraq by the US-led coalition. The Iranian regime, reportedly, became concerned that the experience of autonomy in Iraq would inflame the militancy of Iran's Kurdish separatists (however, there is little evidence of a strong military or political relationship between two Kurdish populations.[103] Nonetheless the Iranian regime was discomforted and alarmed when the George W. Bush administration hinted at allowing Iraqi-Iran Kurdish nationalism to flourish together through funding Kurdish separatist groups in Iran).[104] Given the brief history of Kurd-Iran tensions outlined above, Iran acted quickly in 2003 to prevent opportunity for Kurdish separatists to intensify. First, once US victory was clear, Iran sought to promote and assist the holding of general elections in Iraq – and, reportedly, used its special ties formed

99 Ibid.

100 Roger Hardy, 'Profile: Iran's Jundullah militants', *BBC News* 20 June 2010, http://news.bbc.co.uk/2/hi/middle_east/8314431.stm, accessed 10 December 2010.

101 Keddie, *Modern Iran*, p.332–333.

102 Atabaki, 'From multilingual empire to contested modern state', p.60.

103 Koohi-Kamali, *The Political Development of the Kurds in Iran*, p.170; Atabaki, 'From multilingual empire to contested modern state', p.60–61.

104 Parsi, *Treacherous Alliance*.

with the Iraqi Shiites and Iraqi Kurdish groups from the 1980s to seek agreement on the inclusion of the autonomous Kurdish region into the new Iraqi government. The Iranian regime reportedly played a prominent role in supporting autonomy for Iraqi Kurdistan in the hope that this would divert them from seeking independence and inciting similar sentiment in Iran. Iran has also tried to establish positive relations with Kurdish Iraqi President Jalal Talabani, who had been a refugee within Iran along with around a million other Iraqi Kurds during the Iran-Iraq war and Saddam's notorious 'Anfal' campaigns.[105]

However, recognition of Kurdish civil and political rights were not replicated in Iran itself and the election of President Ahmadinejad further stalled earlier efforts to recognize the rights of the Kurds within Iran. For all of Khatami's reformism, Kurdistan and Western Azerbaijan (where Kurdish militancy has increased in the last five years) remains extremely poor in comparison to their Persian dominated neighbouring provinces.[106] This contributed to increased militancy, especially by the Kurdistan Free Life Party (Pejak) – the Iranian 'sister' to Turkey's Kurdistan Workers Party (PKK), after Ahmandinejad's election in 2005. In response, Iran supported a Turkish offensive against Kurdish rebel bases on the Iran-Iraq-Turkish border in August 2006. This was justified on the grounds that Pejak had carried out attacks against Revolutionary Guard bases in Kurdistan and Western Azerbaijan, one of which killed at least eight soldiers.[107] Increased unrest amongst the Kurdish nationalists, as well as the Sunni Baluchis who claimed responsibility for a number of bombings in Sistan-Baluchistan province, has been attributed to the increased repression of minorities by Revolutionary Guard and Basij under Ahmadinejad. Despite his 2005 election promise to deliver more development projects and recognize ethnic grievances in the outer provinces, little had been delivered by the end of 2008 (this chapter's final year of analysis) and violence against minorities was starting to rise at disturbing levels in the immediate years that follow (briefly discussed below). In fact, Ahmadinejad further alienated the Kurdish and Baluchi population in particular with his appointment of Persians from outside the province as governors of these provinces.[108]

These acts of renewed repression did encourage al Qaeda and Sunni Arab extremists in Iraq to further exploit Tehran's mistreatment of ethnic minorities

105 Dagher, 'Kurds'.

106 Keddie, *Modern Iran*, p.333.

107 Michael Howard, 'Kurds flee homes as Iran shells Iraq's northern frontier', *The Guardian*, 18 August 2006, http://guardian.co.uk/world/2006/aug/18/iraq.iran.html, accessed 14 January 2011.

108 Keddie, Modern Iran, p.333; Bradley, 'Iran's Ethnic Tinderbox', p.184–187.

by fostering instability. The Iranian regime responded by intensifying the Revolutionary Guard's presence within these regions, exacting harsh punishment against the Kurdish and Baluchi population, especially those who engage in protests, and continually supporting *Basiji* militia and Shiite militia within Iraq. Witness reports of an August 2005 protest stated that twenty Kurds were shot by the Revolutionary Guard.[109] Fourteen Kurds were summarily executed in 2009 after being accused of armed struggle against the regime, after their alleged involvement in attack on Iranian police officers that left ten officers dead in Ravansar, Kermanshah Province.[110] Eleven Baluchis were hanged in December 2010, for alleged membership to Jundullah (founded in 2003, the Sunni-faith Jundullah (Soldiers of God) claim to be fighting for the autonomy – not separatism – of the ethnic Baluch people).[111] The eleven were charged with the attack a week before on a Shiia mosque in Sistan-Baluchistan province, which killed thirty-nine people. In both the Kurdistan and Baluchistan cases it is not clear whether those executed were actually involved in the attacks or protest or whether their execution was a form of collective punishment.

To date, the political, ethnic and religious fragmentation in Iraq had not been replicated in Iran. It has managed to avoid 'spill over' largely due to a combination of 'good' fortune (the political and social fragmentation of the Kurdish minority), but also because during the period of reformism under Khatami, Kurdish culture and political autonomy was (slowly) encouraged. This period of Khatami rule was vital at the same time that Iraq was reconfiguring its constitution and its relationship to autonomous Kurdistan. However, emerging differences within the regime – between reformists and convervatives – remain regarding acknowledgement of the rights of minority groups. There also remain deeper structural forms of discrimination that remain unaddressed – the accommodation of ethnic minorities in local council and (tightly managed representation) in the Majlis, but the complete absence or accommodation within clerical, executive, judicial and military institutions.

4 Conclusion

Why has a regime such as Islamic Republic, in possession of common risk factors (history of human rights violations, history of conflict, capacity to commit

109 Bradley, 'Iran's Ethnic Tinderbox', p.184.

110 Dagher, 'Kurds'.

111 BBC News, 'Iran hangs 11 Jundullah Sunni militants', 20 December 2010. http://www.bbc.co.uk/news/world-middle-east-12039745, accessed 20 December 2010.

atrocities) and specific risk factors (history of crimes against humanity and genocide), not committed the mass atrocities forecasted?[112] From 1998–2008, many of Iran's underlying problems – including its economic problems – actually worsened and the country faced two potential crises for its leadership: the 1999 student protests crisis and the more indirect threat of conflict 'spill over', especially amongst Kurdish population, posed by instability in Iraq in the wake of the fall of Saddam. Despite the combination of apparent common risk and specific risk, the Iranian regime did not use mass violence on either occasion to mitigate the risk to the regime. This is not to say that Iran has not and does not engage in human rights abuses against individuals and groups, but at moments of crisis we saw a preference for political solutions to publicly end crises. What often followed were private acts of violence, retribution and intimidation.

What prevents Iran's reflexive use of violence as a rational tool to quell political opposition when it arises? First, despite appearances to the contrary, the regime is actually sensitive about the need to protect its domestic legitimacy. This manifests in a variety of ways. For example, the regime is fixated on the need to deliver economic development and improve the material conditions in which Iranians live. For much of the period under discussion, the need to secure European investment to achieve these goals made the regime sensitive to – though of course not entirely compliant with – investors' concerns about political and human rights reform. However, the country's growing isolation with its pursuit of nuclear enrichment, particularly under Ahmadinejad, saw the reform efforts give way, enabled somewhat with investment from China and India: over this period there was a reduction in the extent to which international economic leverage could moderate Iran's domestic behaviour.

However, a second related point is that the Iranian regime is increasingly fragmented – consolidated action requires the building and maintenance of consensus across different institutions and sources of authority. Even the security sector is fragmented. In other situations this could have been seen as a tremendous source of instability but in the Iran case there are two unique overlapping factors. On the one hand, it sensitized leaders to the possibility that they may not have full political and security support – not everyone may follow the same set of orders. More importantly, power is still centrally located with Ayatollah Khamenei. Often, this meant that during crises different parts

112 Harff, Assessing Risks of Genocide and Politicide; 'Common' and 'Specific' risk terms used in UN Office on Genocide Prevention and the Responsibility to Protect, 'Framework of Analysis for Atrocities Crimes: A Tool for Prevention', July 2014. http://www.un.org/en/preventgenocide/adviser/pdf/framework%20of%20analysis%20for%20atrocity%20crimes_en.pdf, accessed 15 August 2014.

of the Iranian political regime – and its security forces – are as concerned with competing for internal political power and approval from Ayatollah Khamenei as with the events themselves. This appears to have established limits on what risks political leaders are willing to take to diffuse tensions. The degree of regime fragmentation appears to result in caution as would-be perpetrators are not assured of freedom from future prosecution.

A subsidiary factor underpinning this argument is the 'authoritarian peace'. In both the crises examined in this chapter, the regime was able to prevent the escalation of dissent through a combination of rhetoric, diplomacy, tangible concessions and limited violence. In doing so, the regime prevented the escalation of existential risks, obviating the need to commit mass atrocities. The question of whether the regime could muster the unity needed to sustain a campaign of mass atrocities in the face of an existential threat remains an open one.

Iran is a cautionary tale for the international community. Indeed, 2009 saw intense violence and gross human rights violations against citizens who expressed dissent with the Presidential (re)election of President Mahmoud Ahmadinejad. People were shot in the streets; there was physical and verbal intimidation of peaceful protestors by security forces, particularly the *Basij* paramilitary forces. There were large-scale arrests and reports of sexual and physical violence against detainees.[113] The events in 2009 directly contradicts the argument of this chapter – that the Islamic State tends to carry out acts of violence and repression in a limited and carefully calibrated fashion to avoid creating a pattern of atrocities. There appeared to have been three unprecedented factors in 2009: President Ahmadinejad's authority was particularly tied to his identity as an Iran-Iraq War veteran, a former *Basij*, with political and security connections. This situation appeared to create impunity for the actions taken by security forces. Second, Ahmadinejad was not a Cleric. As such, he did not demonstrate any indication of allegiance to the Guardian Council, even Supreme Leader Khamenei. This situation saw the power and authority of the President weaken over the ensuring years, the marginalization of his authority via select appointments by the Guardian Council and the *Majlis*; culminating in his preferred successor losing to President Rouhani (a Cleric) in June 2013.[114] Third, populations were willing to challenge the result of an authoritarian regime and not go away quietly.

113 Human Rights Watch, 'The Islamic Republic at 31: Post-election Abuses Show Serious Human Rights Crisis' (2010). Accessed at: http://www.hrw.org/sites/default/files/reports/iran0210web.pdf.

114 Jon Lee Anderson, 'Understanding Basij', The New Yorker, 19 June (2009), http://www.newyorker.com/news/news-desk/jon-lee-anderson-understanding-the-basij, accessed 14 April 2014; Abbas Milani, 'Is Ahmadinejad Islamic Enough for Iran', *Foreign Policy* 29

International actors need to ensure that efforts to promote or support reform do not have the unintended consequence of weakening one political group over another within a country to such an extent that it weakens them irrevocably. The most promising avenues for achieving this seem to be by identifying reformists within the regime itself and helping them to deliver on the policy items that can strengthen their domestic legitimacy – in Khatami's case the securing of foreign investment and the normalization of relations with the West. Those who support reform in the Iran case seem best disposed to seek reform within Iran, in particular focused attention on reform to permit minority groups to live in safety. Strengthening reform through international engagement appears to open opportunities for long-term transformation in a way that can mitigate ongoing human rights violations. But the source of security to date – regime fragmentation and dependence on one source of authority (Ayotollah) – could easily become a source of instability with the inevitable succession of an Ayotollah. Furthermore, the ongoing regional instability in the Middle East creates a risk that multiple (competing) security actors within Iran may start to adopt different stances on quelling internal conflicts and regional disputes – from rivalry between the police and the *Basiji*, to Revolutionary Guard and the Iranian Army. These remain potential sources of instability in Iran the longer regional instabilities continue.

(2011)., https://abbasmilani.stanford.edu/wp-content/uploads/2014/10/Is-Ahmadinejad-Islamic-Enough-for-Iran.pdf, Accessed 12 January 2014; Mark Gollom, 'Why Ahmadinejad's greatest enemies may be in Tehran', CBC News, 15 March (2013), http://www.cbc.ca/news/world/why-ahmadinejad-s-greatest-enemies-may-be-in-iran-1.1341886, accessed 12 January 2014; Geneive Abdo, 'Ahmadinejad Shows No Signs of Going Quietly', Spotlight, Stimson Centre, 16 May (2013)., http://www.stimson.org/spotlight/ahmadinejad-shows-no-signs-of-going-quietly/, accessed 14 January 2014; Geneive Abdo, 'The end of Rouhani's honeymoon', Aljazeera America, 18 February (2014), http://america.aljazeera.com/opinions/2014/2/hassan-rouhani-iranalikhameneinuclearnegotiations.html, accessed 18 April 2014.

CHAPTER 8

Azerbaijan 1998–2008: Ceasefire, Stalemate and Simmering Tensions

Stephen McLoughlin

Abstract

Between 1998 and 2008, Azerbaijan contained a very high risk of mass atrocities. Pogroms against the Armenian minority, and disputed claims over Nagorno-Karabakh saw escalating violence erupt into war between 1992 and 1994, where atrocities were committed against both Azeri and Armenian populations. Since then, an uncomfortable stalemate has ensued, with the OSCE observing a ceasefire line between the Azerbaijani and Armenian militaries. This chapter examines how and why a re-escalation to conflict, and further atrocities were avoided in this decade, particularly when leaders on both sides resorted on many occasions to nationalist and exclusionary rhetoric to shore up domestic political support. It argues that the country's changed demographics, more stable regimes in Azerbaijan and Armenia, and international mediation efforts were factors that helped push the country back from the brink of atrocities, albeit without any success in achieving a more lasting rapprochement.

Key Words

Azerbaijan – Armenia – conflict – ethnic cleansing – ethnicity – Nagorno-Karabakh

1 Introduction

The purpose of this chapter is to investigate why mass atrocities were avoided in Azerbaijan in the decade 1998–2008. In 1998, Azerbaijan demonstrated a high risk of committing future atrocities. The country had recently emerged from a bitter conflict with Armenia over the Azerbaijani territory of Nagorno-Karabakh, a territory that had been under Azerbaijan's sovereignty during the Soviet era, but ostensibly administered by members of the majority Armenian population. Between 1988 and 1994, tension and violence between ethnic Armenians and Azeris escalated throughout Azerbaijan, prompting massacres,

 | DOI 10.1163/9789004299870_010

mass displacement and forced deportation. These atrocities were committed during a period of profound political upheaval. The Soviet Union was collapsing as two former Soviet Socialist Republics – Azerbaijan and Armenia – emerged as independent states, both spurred by exclusionary nationalist ideologies, and both laying claim to Nagorno-Karabakh. This was the third time in the twentieth century that Armenians and Azeris had committed atrocities against each other, and like the recent conflict, each previous episode also occurred following major political upheaval.[1] Although the territory is officially within Azerbaijan's sovereign borders, by 1994 Armenian militia groups, aided by Armenia's national army, occupied Nagorno-Karabakh, along with a large swathe of Azerbaijani territory, forming a land bridge between Nagorno-Karabakh and Armenia. On the edge of this occupied front, a ceasefire agreement was forged in the same year, but there remains little prospect of a political settlement. Yet despite the ongoing tensions along the ceasefire line, no atrocities were committed between 1998 and 2008.

The chapter is divided into two parts. The first part provides historical background to the preconditions that led to the most recent atrocities in Azerbaijan between 1988 and 1994. It then examines how these preconditions escalated into violence and atrocities during the political upheaval of the collapse of the Soviet Union – it was this violence that defined the high level of risk in the decade between 1998 and 2008. The second part then provides an account of why this risk did not escalate once again into violence and atrocities during this ten-year period. The general argument is that greater international mediation, and more stable political regimes in Azerbaijan and Armenia have resulted in a sustained, albeit uncomfortable stalemate. In addition, the recent conflict saw the mass displacement and forced deportations of minority populations in both Azerbaijan and Armenia. As a result, populations in both countries were dramatically homogenized, reducing the possibility of inter-ethnic violence. However, the ongoing tensions along the frontline of the unresolved conflict, and the increasingly authoritarian character of the Azerbaijani regime meant that by 2008, the various factors which mitigated the risk of atrocities in the short term may not sustain effective mitigation into the future.

2 Background

Azerbaijan is a small state located at the southern end of the Caucasus region, occupying the Southwest coast of the Caspian Sea. It shares borders with Iran

1 Atrocities were committed following the Russian revolutions of 1905 and 1917.

to the south, and Georgia to the north, with Armenia to the west. Prior to 1918, the territory comprising the modern state of Azerbaijan had been under the control of various empires – Seljuk, Monghol, Ottoman, Persian, and Russian. As a result, over the last thousand years, it has undergone numerous transformations, altering the language, culture and composition of peoples over time.[2] Azerbaijan's history as an independent state is short – its first steps into nationhood came in the wake of the Russian Revolution, but lasted only two years, after which it was subsumed by the Bolshevik invasion of the South Caucasus.[3] Following the Soviet Union's collapse in 1991, Azerbaijan re-asserted its independence, with its currently recognized borders matching the boundaries delineated by the Soviets in 1923.[4] The nature of social division between ethnic Azeris and Armenians, discrimination, a history of past atrocities and long-standing autocratic rule that both exacerbated and ignored ethnic divisions took shape gradually from the mid-nineteenth century to the present day. The conflict between 1988 and 1994,[5] its ensuing atrocities, and the subsequent impasse between Azerbaijan and Armenia over the territory of Nagorno-Karabakh are direct products of the social, political and economic dynamics that unfolded over this period.

Azerbaijan contains seven preconditions associated with the long-term risk of mass atrocities – politicized divisions, discrimination, recent atrocities, loss of territory, limited rule of law, limited democracy and economic inequality. Divisions between ethnic Azeris and Armenians have been highly politicized for more than a century. This has been exacerbated by entrenched discrimination of the ethnic Armenian minority living in Azerbaijan, through displacement, as well as denial of employment and social welfare. The recent conflict between the nascent states of Azerbaijan and Armenia was characterized by mass atrocities committed by and against members of both groups. Azerbaijan's army lost the battle over the disputed territory of Nagorno-Karabakh, which

2 For an account of the origins and influences of the Turkic (as well as pre-Turkic) speaking Azerbaijanis, see Audrey L. Altstadt, *The Azerbaijani Turks: Power and Identity under Russian Rule* (Stanford, CA: Hoover Institution Press, 1992), pp. 1–15; Suha Bolukbasi, *Azerbaijan: A Political History* (London: I.B. Tauris, 2011), pp. 16–45; Charles van der Leeuw, *Azerbaijan: A Quest for Identity* (Surrey: Curzon, 2000).

3 Stephen K. Batalden and Sandra L. Batalden, *The Newly Independent States of Eurasia: Handbook of Soviet Republics* (Phoenix: Oryx, 1997), p. 111; Stuart J. Kaufman, *Modern Hatreds: The Symbolic Politics of Ethnic War* (Ithaca: Cornell University Press, 2001), p. 51.

4 The most recent conflict over Nagorno Karabakh (1988–1994) ended with a ceasefire after Armenian forces took control of large tracts of Azerbaijani territory, although this land is still recognised as being part of Azerbaijan.

5 The conflict escalated to full-scale war from 1992.

remains under the de facto control of Armenian forces. These atrocities and the broader conflict occurred amidst the breakdown of the rule of law, following the collapse of the Soviet Union. While the coming to power of Heydar Aliyev in 1993 precipitated an eventual stabilization of the country, his autocratic hold on power was brutal in punishing dissenters and rewarding a small cadre of supporters. His son and successor, Ilham Aliyev adopted virtually the same approach to leadership after Heydar retired in 2003. Since the mid-1990s, Azerbaijan's economy has benefitted from oil and natural gas. However, this windfall has enriched a small minority while the vast majority of citizens live in poverty. This long list of preconditions is an indication that the risk of future atrocities remains very high.

2.1 *Social and Political Factors*

Although the demography has undergone substantial changes over the last two centuries, the territory has been characterized by a majority population of ethnic Azeris, and substantial Armenian and Russian minorities.[6] In the last twenty years there has been a dramatic exodus of these minority groups, with the exception of Armenians living Nagorno-Karabakh.[7] Currently, Azerbaijan's population comprises 92 per cent ethnic Azeris, with ethnic Armenians and Russians comprising 1.3 per cent each.[8] At the advent of the Soviet Union, Armenians comprised 5 per cent of the population, settled mostly in and around Baku, and in Nagorno-Karabakh.

During the Soviet era, ethnic Armenians suffered discrimination within the Soviet Socialist Republic of Azerbaijan. Most significantly, in Azerbaijan-controlled Nagorno-Karabakh, ethnic Azeris were relocated there in an attempt to dilute Armenia's claim to the contested territory. Initially comprising 94 per cent of the local population in 1923, but by 1989 had been reduced to

---

6 Other minority groups such as Kurds, Jews and Daghestanis have also had a presence in Azerbaijan. As tension in conflict in Azerbaijan have largely been the product of dynamics between Azeris, Armenians and Russians, this chapter limits the discussion of social division to these three groups.

7 Alec Rasizade, 'Azerbaijan after Heydar Aliev,' *Nationalities Papers: The Journal of Nationalism and Ethnicity* 32/1: 137–164 (2004), p. 142. Rasizade also points out that along with the exodus of Azerbaijan's minority groups, the economic hardship endured by all citizens has precipitated mass emigration from ethnic Azeris as well. He claims that three million Azeris left Azerbaijan between 1989 and 1999.

8 See Central Intelligence Agency, 'Azerbaijan,' *The World Factbook* (2014), https://www.cia.gov/library/publications/the-world-factbook/geos/aj.html, accessed 21 July 2014.

76 per cent.[9] Tension between Armenian and Azeri populations centred on this disputed territory, which had been allocated to Azerbaijan and not Armenia, despite an overwhelming majority of ethnic Armenians living there. Armenian claims on Nagorno-Karabakh never fully disappeared during the Soviet era, and after Stalin's death they resurfaced sporadically in the form of petitions requesting the transfer of the autonomous oblast to the Armenian Soviet Socialist Republic. Moscow repeatedly rejected these requests.

Between 1920 and 1991, Azerbaijan was part of the Soviet Union – one of three Soviet Socialist Republics in the Transcaucasus region. Territorial disputes between the two nascent (and short-lived states) of Azerbaijan and Armenia were papered over following the Bolshevik invasion of the South Caucasus, which meant that contested claims to the territory of Nagorno-Karabakh were never resolved. Moscow's decision to allocate the territory to the Azerbaijan Soviet Socialist Republic was a compromise aimed at seeking a balance between the desires of the Russian/Armenian dominated Azerbaijan Communist Party (AzCP) and local Azerbaijani leaders. The desire was to ensure that the ethnic Azerbaijani leadership would remain in favour of the Communist Party, and to appease the new Kemalist state of Turkey, who supported Azerbaijani claims to the territory.[10] It also formed part of Stalin's tactic of divide and rule in the Caucasus – making the region part of Azerbaijan meant that Armenians within Nagorno-Karabakh could be used as 'hostages' to guarantee the cooperation of the Armenian Soviet Socialist Republic. For Azerbaijan, the existence of a semi-autonomous region of ethnic Armenians within its borders meant a 'possible pro-Soviet fifth column in the event of disloyalty by the Azerbaijanis.'[11] To further solidify this division, Stalin delineated the borders in such a way that separated Nagorno-Karabakh entirely from Armenia, leaving a channel of Azerbaijani territory between the two.[12] In

9 Bolukbasi, *Azerbaijan*, p. 60. Bolukbasi points out that the population of both ethnic groups had grown during the Soviet era. The change in demographic representation arose out of a far greater rate of increase of the local Azeri population, a fact attributed by Armenians to a strategy by the Azerbaijani administration to establish a number of new Azeri-populated villages in Nagorno Karabakh. See Kaufman, *Modern Hatreds*, p. 55.

10 Bolukbasi, *Azerbaijan*, p. 76; Alec Rasizade, 'Azerbaijan's Prospects in Nagorno-Karabakh,' in *Mediterranean Quarterly* 22/3: 72–94 (2011), p. 76; Thomas de Waal, *Black Garden: Armenia and Azerbaijan Through Peace and War* (New York: New York University Press, 2003), p. 130.

11 Michael P. Croissant, *The Armenia-Azerbaijani Conflict: Causes and Implications* (Westport, CT: Praeger, 1998), pp. 19–20.

12 Croissant, *The Armenia-Azerbaijani Conflict*, p. 20.

short, this was an arrangement that pleased no one, and left the dispute over Nagorno-Karabakh unresolved over the entire duration of Soviet control.

For the remainder of Stalin's tenure as leader of the Soviet Union, complaints regarding the status of Nagorno-Karabakh were not tolerated by Moscow. Indeed, the economic reforms and Stalin's 'Great Terror', which lasted until the Second World War, relegated any tensions over territory as a secondary concern in Azerbaijan.[13] Two petitions during Krushchev's period of rule – one from prominent Karabakh leaders, and the other signed by 2500 Armenians from within Nagorno-Karabakh Autonomous Oblast – were ignored.[14] However, although the issue of Nagorno-Karabakh rarely surfaced during the Soviet period, the Soviet system itself preserved the dispute through its original creation of administrative structures that linked ethnic identity and territory.[15] The refusal of the Soviet leadership to address outstanding tensions in the region merely delayed their resurfacing. This became evident during Gorbachev's period of *Glasnost* and *Perestroika* in the late 1980s.

The issue of Nagorno-Karabakh re-emerged during *glasnost* in the late 1980s, when Gorbachev encouraged greater political expression throughout the Soviet Union. Large rallies were organized in Yerevan, as well as throughout Nagorno-Karabakh, campaigning for the oblast's separation from Azerbaijan. In 1989, ethnic Armenian deputies in the local soviet in Nagorno-Karabakh requested the territory undergo a transfer of jurisdiction to the Armenian Soviet Socialist Republic – this was immediately rejected by the Politburo.[16] This precipitated growing tension with Baku, as well as between ethnic Armenians and Azeris throughout both Azerbaijan and Armenia. From the late 1980s through to 1994, these tensions escalated to anti-Armenian pogroms in and around Baku, and provoked mass displacement of minority populations in both countries. Virtually all of Azerbaijan's Armenian population (with the exception of those in Nagorno-Karabakh) fled the country by 1991.

These tensions stemmed not only from discrimination during the Soviet era, but also from discrimination and persecution that occurred in the Ottoman Empire, which prompted a growing diaspora community in Yerevan, Nagorno-Karabakh and Baku. Armenian nationalism – inevitably shaped by persecution

13 Altstadt, *The Azerbaijani Turks*, pp. 131–132.

14 Croissant, *The Armenia-Azerbaijani Conflict*, p. 20.

15 de Waal, *Black Gardern*, p. 131.

16 Following declarations of independence in 1991 by Armenia and Azerbaijan, Armenians in Nagorno Karabakh also declared the territory to be independent and separate from Azerbaijan. See Thomas de Waal, *The Caucasus: An Introduction* (Oxford: Oxford University Press, 2010), pp. 109–115.

and genocide – took form when notions of pan-Turkism and national unity were gaining popularity amongst the Azeris in the same region. Both groups were threatened by each other, and these threats materialized into violent conflict and atrocities by both groups during times of upheaval.

2.2 *Economic Factors*

Azerbaijan's economy is heavily dependent on oil and gas, which comprises ninety per cent of its export revenue; the petroleum and natural gas industries account for 60 per cent of GDP.[17] Following the cessation of violent conflict in 1994, and the subsequent political stabilization under Heydar Aliyev, foreign investment in oil and gas increased dramatically, providing much greater revenue in the mid-late 1990s.[18] This provided the basis for strong economic growth, which contrasted with decades of economic stagnation during the Soviet era. However, inequality has commonly accompanied economic growth in Azerbaijan – it was this inequality that deepened social divisions in the late 1800s. Even in the 1990s, the country's renewed economic growth created new divisions, this time between a small and well-connected elite, and the rest of the population to whom improvements in economic growth bestowed little or no benefit.[19]

The close relationship between the oil industry and social inequalities goes back to the industry's initial growth period in the 1800s, under the Russian Empire. The Russian state had a monopoly on the oil industry, and as a result, Russian and Armenian entrepreneurs benefitted more. By 1888, fifty-four companies were involved in the extraction of oil, yet only two were owned by Azeris.[20] The richest oilmen and merchants were Armenian, then followed by Russians. By 1901, the oil industry in Azerbaijan was bigger than in the United States.[21] As the region rapidly grew wealthier, Azeris became further marginalized from the greatest source of wealth in their territory. Armenians and Russians gained increasing influence and wealth by the beginning of the twentieth century, as many Azeris were further marginalized economically. This deepened social divisions, and sowed greater tension, particularly between Armenians and Azeris.

---

17 Central Intelligence Agency, 'Azerbaijan', in *The World Factbook,* 2012, https://www.cia.gov/library/publications/the-world-factbook/geos/aj.html, Accessed 5 July 2012.

18 Alec Rasizade, 'Azerbaijan Descending into the Third World after a Decade of Independence,' *Journal of Third World Studies,* 21/1: 191–219 (2004), p. 196.

19 Rasizade, 'Azerbaijan after Heydar Aliev,' pp. 140–142.

20 Bolukbasi, *Azerbaijan,* p. 24.

21 Batalden and Batalden, *The Newly Independent States,* p. 110.

During the Soviet era, economic policies continued to be dictated from Moscow. Under the rubric of central planning the discrimination of wealth that had developed in the late nineteenth and early twentieth centuries became much less salient. Azerbaijan's economy performed poorly, and the wealth generated from the Republic's oil revenues did not directly benefit the region. Widespread corruption and poor leadership within the Azerbaijan Communist Party were blamed for the Republic's decades-long economic stagnation.[22] Under the leadership of Veli Akhundov and then Heydar Aliyev, the last four decades of the Soviet regime entrenched in Azerbaijan a culture of patronage that sustained a system of elite advantage for the connected few, and hardship among most Azerbaijanis.[23]

The culture of patronage that flourished during the Soviet era continued post-independence. With the opening up of further investment in oil and natural gas, Azerbaijan's dependence on these resources remained high. The windfall from renewed international investment strengthened Aliyev's government and heralded a new period of political stability. However, such revenue and subsequent economic growth benefitted a small minority of political and entrepreneurial elites. Poverty remained widespread – by 2002, 78 per cent of the population lived on less than two US dollars a day, and 56 per cent lived on less than one US dollar a day.[24]

By 1998, the economic situation in Azerbaijan had brought the country mixed blessings. It experienced a dramatic increase in revenue as a result of the post-Soviet opening up of the oil and natural gas industries to foreign investment. The ensuing economic growth helped to stabilize the country's political environment, and to consolidate the Aliyev government's hold on power, mitigating the risk of further upheaval and violence in the short to medium term. However, the government's management of this economic growth has resulted in further inequities, with most of the population receiving no benefit from it at all. This, combined with the repressive autocratic government of both Heydar Aliyev and son his Ilham has provoked widespread dissatisfaction with the current regime, and the growing perception that the regime's patronage networks are the main beneficiaries of the country's wealth. This increased the long term risk of political instability – from 1998 to 2008, these inequalities remained salient in a climate

22 Ibid, p. 111.

23 Ibid, p. 111.

24 See Rasizade, 'Azerbaijan after Heydar Aliev', p. 144; The World Bank, *Social Assessments for Better Development: Case Studies from Albania, Azerbaijan and Moldova* (Washington: World Bank, 2002), p. 36.

of growing intolerance of political dissent. However, the inequalities that existed between 1998 and 2008 did not correspond with historical ethnic-based inequalities that had contributed to tensions in the early twentieth century.

3 Absence of Atrocities between 1998 and 2008

The years leading up to and following the collapse of the Soviet Union were clearly tumultuous ones for Azerbaijan, and indeed the whole of the South Caucasus. Mass killings, ethnic cleansing, mass deportation and displacement saw the conflict between Armenia and Azerbaijan over Nagorno-Karabakh play out amidst widespread atrocities. However, since the 1994 ceasefire, mass violence has not occurred. Indeed, the decade from 1998 to 2008 was significant for its absence of atrocities, despite the lack of resolution and the ongoing risk of mass atrocities that existed. This section will provide an account of why atrocities were not committed between 1998 and 2008. First, I provide an outline of the social, political and economic circumstances that unfolded in the years following the ceasefire in 1994. Following this, I contend that there were three key reasons why atrocities were avoided: the absence of minority groups to target, a relatively stable regime, and improved international mediation. Accounting for the absence of atrocities in Azerbaijan over this period demonstrates the great complexity of conditions that have been protective against the possibility of such violence. As this section will point out, often preconditions associated with long-term risk (such as the absence of democracy) can be instrumental in risk mitigation in the short to medium term. This means that although there has been an absence of atrocities, the circumstances that have enabled greater calm are not indefinitely sustainable.

3.1 *Stalemate and Mediation 1994–1998*

The first few years following the ceasefire of 12 May 1994 were characterized by a virtual absence of violence,[25] an entrenchment of the military positions on both sides, and an absence of progress in mediation efforts. The OSCE-initiated 'Minsk Group' was unsuccessful in bringing the parties to a resolution, despite its greater engagement in the negotiation process. Nevertheless, while efforts to forge a lasting resolution did not materialize, neither did a breaking of the ceasefire and a return to war and mass violence. In this way, the impasse

25 With the exception of isolated exchanges of fire that occasionally resulted in casualties.

that was becoming entrenched by 1998 was as much a product of the irreconcilability of political differences between Armenia, Nagorno-Karabakh and Azerbaijan as it was a product of the lack of enthusiasm any side had for entering into a new chapter of fighting.

Given that military failures in the conflict had already been responsible for the fall of two presidents, Aliyev was reluctant to risk a political backlash that such future failure would inevitably have brought. Instead, he spent the next few years consolidating his position as president by forging a 'suffocating order.'[26] This involved removing from office anyone who was considered to be a possible opponent, especially from within the military. He dismissed a number of commanders who had surrendered battles during the conflict, and later removed Prime Minister Husseinov, accusing him of plotting an overthrow.[27] He then resumed negotiations with international corporations to develop the oil and gas deposits in the Caspian Sea, heralding a windfall of billions of dollars.[28] The development of these oil projects prompted cooperation with both Russia and the West, especially the United States. Aliyev's strengthening of power and the country's developing trade relationships with key international actors marked a period of greater internal stability, at least more than had been known since the advent of *glasnost*. However, the resolution of the Nagorno-Karabakh conflict remained politically difficult – there was no enthusiasm for inviting the uncertainty of another military strategy, nor was there any currency in conceding any part of Azerbaijani sovereignty through a mediated resolution. For Azerbaijan in the mid-to-late 1990s, the safest option was ceasefire and impasse.

Overcoming this impasse has hitherto proved impossible for the main mediators. However, the establishment of a lasting ceasefire was an achievement in itself, which put an end to mass violence and mass displacement that had characterized the conflict in Nagorno-Karabakh. The two main mediators to the conflict were the CSCE and Russia – both actors were active from 1992, but both initially had fundamental weaknesses. In its overt support for Armenia in the conflict, Russia was clearly not an impartial player and was regarded as such by Azerbaijan. While the CSCE was impartial, its initial weakness was a product of its lack of knowledge of the conflict.

The CSCE's active interest in the conflict commenced when both Armenia and Azerbaijan became new members in 1992. Given the organization was then expected to become involved, it dispatched a fact-finding mission to the

26 de Waal, *Black Garden*, p. 251.

27 Ibid, p. 251.

28 Ibid, p. 252.

Transcaucasus. Member states then resolved to hold a peace conference in Minsk to bring the parties together. While the conference did not go ahead,[29] the 'Minsk Group', comprising at the time of Azerbaijan, Armenia and nine other states, became the chief mediating bloc. However, the Minsk Group was initially ineffective, and was regarded by both sides at the time as being ill-equipped to engage with the conflicting parties, due to an alleged virtual absence of knowledge of the conflict and the region.[30] Further complicating the process was lack of consensus on how to deal with Nagorno-Karabakh as a party to the conflict. Azerbaijan was opposed to giving the territory any recognition as a distinct political actor for fear of affording it with sovereign legitimacy, yet no peace agreement could work without facilitating dialogue between Baku and the Karabakh Armenians.[31] These challenges complicated the CSCE's attempts to bring all parties to the negotiating table.

Further complicating matters was Russia's involvement. In 1993, Yeltsin declared Russia to be the logical choice for guaranteeing peace in the region, and was the only country willing and able to provide peacekeepers to enforce a ceasefire agreement. Prior to May 1994, the Russian foreign ministry mounted pressure on both sides to cease fighting, dictating its own terms in the process. Neither Russia nor the CSCE were able to broker a ceasefire in 1993. Throughout the early months of 1994, Russia increased its pressure on both sides to end fighting, and using the Commonwealth of Independent States (CIS) as the main diplomatic vehicle, leaders from Azerbaijan, Nagorno-Karabakh and Armenia were persuaded to meet in Bishkek to discuss terms of a possible ceasefire. Although Azerbaijan opposed the possibility of a Russian peacekeeping contingent patrolling the frontline, an agreement was reached, which premised the cessation of violence on further negotiations in the future. The absence of a peacekeeping force between the two sides resulted in what de Waal referred to as an unpatrolled, 'self-regulated' cease-fire line.[32] Subsequently, both Armenia and Azerbaijan fortified their battle lines, 'turning the front line into one of the most impregnable borders of the world.'[33] While the Azerbaijani leadership was reluctant to engage in a Russian-led mediation process, the failure of the CSCE to provide an alternative, and Aliyev's reticence to provoke a diplomatic confrontation with Russia resulted

29 Due to renewed fighting in Nagorno Karabakh.

30 de Waal, *Black Garden*, p. 229.

31 Ibid, p. 230.

32 de Waal, *Black Garden*, pp. 229–230.

33 Ibid, p. 253.

in Moscow becoming the chief negotiator, albeit through the veil of the CIS.[34] Hence, Armenia (as well as Nagorno-Karabakh) and Azerbaijan, exhausted from fighting, agreed to the ceasefire brokered through the CIS in Bishkek in early May. The ceasefire itself provided very little basis for a resolution of the conflict, but came at a time in when both sides were very reluctant to prolong the fighting.

Tensions between the two main negotiators – Russia and the CSCE – were resolved at a CSCE-led summit in Budapest, in December 1994.[35] The OSCE elevated Russia's position in the negation process by making it one of the co-chairs of the Minsk Group.[36] It also secured a guarantee that no member state would provide more than 30 per cent of any future peacekeeping contingent should it be needed. While consent between Russia and the OSCE resulted in a strengthened negotiating position, it did little if anything to effect progress in the conflicting parties drawing closer to a resolution. With any resolution appearing to demand either a compromise of territory or recognition of Azerbaijani sovereignty of Nagorno-Karabakh, no middle ground appeared likely. This reality was further accentuated after the 1996 OSCE Summit in Lisbon, where the principle of Azerbaijani territorial integrity was upheld, a gesture which prompted the Armenians to veto the inclusion of any principles in the final document, and significantly slowed subsequent negotiations.[37]

Even when Armenia's President, Ter-Petrosian, and Aliyev appeared amenable to a new agreement prepared by the Minsk Group in 1997, domestic politics intervened. Ter-Petrosian responded positively to the Group's proposal of a multi-phase plan, which placed a greater emphasis on security concerns in Nagorno-Karabakh. Concerned that Armenia's dire economic situation could not sustain an indefinite impasse on the conflict, given the blockades from both Turkey and Azerbaijan,[38] he became more open to compromise. However, the Karabakh Armenians opposed the plan, provoking controversy within Armenia about the growing perception of Ter-Petrosian's apparent appeasement with Azerbaijan. Division within the government grew, and in early 1998 he was forced to resign. His successor, Robert Kocharian, was far

34 Croissant, *The Armenia-Azerbaijan Conflict,* pp. 110–111.

35 At the Summit, the CSCE changed its name to the Organization for Security and Cooperation in Europe (OSCE).

36 The other co-chair was Sweden. See de Waal, *Black Garden,* p. 255.

37 de Waal, *Black Garden,* p. 256.

38 Turkey closed its eastern border with Armenia in 1993 in response to Armenia's capture of Azerbaijani territory in Kelbajar.

more intransigent on the issue of Nagorno-Karabakh, and as such rejected the latest Minsk Group proposal.[39]

In Azerbaijan, Aliyev won a second election in 1998, underscoring the country's improved political stability. However, domestic politics in Azerbaijan was not absent of problems. Returns from the oil boom were much lower than anticipated, and had not translated into the alleviation of poverty and hardship for the vast majority of the population. Aliyev's hold on power was almost absolute, risking the possibility of future upheaval in the event that the regime collapsed, a prospect that in 1998 was not inconceivable, particularly in regards to his health, which in early 1997 prompted him to seek medical attention in Ankara for three months.[40] Moreover, given that the conflict in Nagorno-Karabakh had already claimed two presidents, Aliyev's scope for compromise was very limited.

The circumstances of political uncertainty in both countries meant that neither leader would risk a fall-out that compromises over Nagorno-Karabakh would provoke. Indeed, Robert Kocharian's pro-Karabakh stance yielded no desire to retreat from the territory's self-declared independence, an approach that strongly contrasted Ter-Petrosian's more conciliatory and economically pragmatic (and unpopular) approach to the conflict. In Azerbaijan, given that two presidents had fallen as a direct result of territorial losses during the conflict, any mediation plan that did not acknowledge and incorporate a full recognition of the country's sovereignty, including Nagorno-Karabakh itself, would not have any effect. As a result, tensions between Armenia and Azerbaijan continued to simmer with no prospect of resolution.

However, this had also had the effect of halting further atrocities. Although this impasse has not been beneficial for seeking a long-term resolution, atrocities have been avoided since the end of fighting in 1994. With neither side willing to return to conflict,[41] the ceasefire looked increasingly likely to hold, despite the impasse. By 1998 two things were apparent: the common ground needed for a resolution to the conflict seemed as elusive as ever, yet the political will not to resume fighting was strong on both sides.

39 de Waal, *Black Garden*, pp. 259–260.

40 Ibid, pp. 262–263.

41 Despite this, sporadic skirmishes between the soldiers on both sides continue to contribute to a modest casualty rate, amounting to approximately twenty per year. Nevertheless, the casualties were entirely combatants from the two armies, and did not include any targeting of civilians.

3.2 *Changed Demographics in Azerbaijan and the South Caucasus*

Since the advent of *glasnost* in the late 1980s, there have been profound demographic changes in Azerbaijan and Armenia as a result of the conflict over Nagorno-Karabakh. Rising tensions, massacres, ethnic cleansing and mass deportation in Azerbaijan (of Armenians), in Nagorno-Karabakh (of Azeris) and Armenia (of Azeris) have caused the displacement of more than one million people.[42] This dramatically reduced the population of minorities in both countries.[43] These demographic changes mean that with the exception of Nagorno-Karabakh, very few ethnic Armenians remain in Azerbaijan, and this has – perversely – lessened their salience as a perceived threat.

The violent displacement that occurred between 1988 and 1994 took place amidst riots and mass killing in some of Azerbaijan's key urban centres,[44] and during the phase of full-scale conflict in Nagorno-Karabakh. Between 1998 and 1990, Human Rights Watch estimated that 350,000 ethnic Armenians were compelled to leave Azerbaijan during the pogroms against them. Likewise, between 750,000 and 800,000 Azeris were violently displaced from Nagorno-Karabakh and Armenia, as well as seven other Azerbaijani provinces that were captured by the Armenian Karabakhs during the war. By 1989, it is estimated that 167,000 Azeris living in Armenia had fled. All of Nagorno-Karabakh's 40,000 Azeris were displaced from Nagorno-Karabakh as early as 1992, which meant that by the 1994 ceasefire, there were no Azeris living in this territory. However, the vast majority of displaced Azeris originated from the seven Azeri provinces that were captured by Armenian Karabakhs in the final year of the conflict. Approximately half a million Azeri civilians were forcibly displaced from Lachin, Kelbajar, Agdam, Fizuli, Jebrayil, Qubatli and Zangelan provinces.[45] The profound demographic changes that resulted from this mass displacement defines the current population distribution in Azerbaijan and Armenia. Displaced Azeri civilians from Nagorno-Karabakh and the seven other provinces have been unable to return due to continuation of the 1994 ceasefire and the unresolved status of the conflict. The displacement of minority groups from Armenia and Azerbaijan are highly unlikely to be reversed. As

---

42 Human Rights Watch, *Azerbaijan: Seven Years of Conflict in Nagorno-Karabakh* (Helsinki: Human Rights Watch Report, 1994), p. 99; Phil Gamaghelyan, 'Rethinking the Nagorno-Karabakh Conflict: Identity, Politics, Scholarship', *International Negotiation*, 15, 2010, p. 36.

43 Likewise, the territory of Nagorno Karabakh is currently absent of ethnic Azeris.

44 For example, in Baku and Sumgait.

45 Human Rights Watch, 'Azerbaijan', pp. 99–100.

a consequence, the populations of both countries have been dramatically homogenised.[46]

This has had an impact on the absence of atrocities from 1998 to 2008. The dramatically reduced numbers of Armenians in the major urban areas of Azerbaijan has meant a diminished likelihood of any violent targeting of the kind that occurred in the late 1980s. One of the preconditions of atrocities – social division, becomes more salient when the composition of diversity within a state has a particular character, according to some scholars. Paul Collier, for example, argued that states which have a situation where there is one dominant ethnic group yet other group/s that are still significant in population has 'some effect' on the occurrence of civil war.[47] Gregory Stanton claimed that 'bipolar' societies are the most likely to experience genocide.[48] Until the late 1980s, Azerbaijan clearly resembled a bipolar society, with its majority Azeri population and distinct Armenian minority. On a smaller scale, Nagorno-Karabakh also fit this characterization with its composition of 70 per cent Armenians and 30 per cent Azeris. However, between 1998 and 2008, this was no longer the case. The number of Armenians still living in Azerbaijan (not including Nagorno-Karabakh) is considerably less. Likewise, the territory of Nagorno-Karabakh is entirely absent of Azeris.[49] This does not mean that those ethnic Armenians who remained in Azerbaijan escaped reproach. Indeed, the small community of Armenians in the country (including people of mixed Armenian/Azeri heritage) continued to experience major discrimination. There have been numerous reports of local authorities denying them work, and access to

46 According to Minority Rights Group International, the 1999 census figures for Azerbaijan (the most recent to be cited) recorded a dramatic drop in the numbers of both Armenians and Russians. While the 1999 census puts the number of Armenians still living in Azerbaijan at 120,000 (1.5%), the CIA World Factbook points out this largely accounts for Armenians living in Nagorno Karabakh. See Minority Rights Group International, 'Azerbaijan Overview'. According to the CIA World Factbook, the current proportion of Armenians in Azerbaijan is 1.3% (see fn 7).

47 Paul Collier, *The Bottom Billion: Why the Poorest Countries are Failing and What Can Be Done About It* (Oxford: Oxford University Press, 2008), p. 25.

48 Gregory Stanton, *The Eight Stages of Genocide* (Cambridge, MA, 1996), accessed 6 June 2012, available at: http://www.genocidewatch.org/images/8StagesBriefingpaper.pdf.

49 While the territory of Nagorno Karabakh was in name still under Azerbaijani sovereignty, since 1992 it has operated as a de facto independent state, with Azerbaijan having no practical authority over it. For this reason, the social dynamics of this territory are distinguished from the rest of Azerbaijan.

both health and education.[50] Nevertheless, while systematic discrimination continued, the diminished population of Armenian population has given them a far less visible presence in the country.

However, this is not indicative of a reduced long-term risk of atrocities. The vast majority of Azeris who were displaced during the conflict remained that way between 1998 and 2008 – their anticipated resettlement delayed by the lack of a political resolution to the conflict. This displaced population remained in makeshift accommodation for most of this period, not far from the front lines where tensions continued to simmer dangerously.[51] While the homogenization of populations has made it more difficult for minorities to be targeted, between 1998 and 2008, the displaced populations from Nagorno-Karabakh and surrounding provinces have underscored the social and economic impact that the political impasse has had. Therefore, while the demographic shifts that have occurred since the late 1980s have reduced the risk of atrocities in some parts of Azerbaijan, they have prolonged tensions in the provinces close to the frontlines, and near Nagorno-Karabakh. Moreover, the scale of internal displacement in Azerbaijan has heightened tensions amongst different ethnic Azeri communities, creating new social divisions.[52] While many Armenians formerly residing in Azerbaijan fled permanently, the displacement of Azeris from Azerbaijani territory (currently comprising part of the Armenian-occupied frontline under ceasefire) is more temporary in character, not least because they were given temporary accommodation in displacement camps in anticipation of a return following a resolution to the conflict.

The conflict between Armenia and Azerbaijan that emerged during the late 1980s, resulted in widespread atrocities and mass displacement of minority Armenian and Azeri communities in each respective republic. This changed the demographic composition of both former Soviet republics, by dramatically homogenising their populations. One consequence of this has been the absence of a visible target group, upon which to inflict further violence. Therefore, although tensions over Nagorno-Karabakh remained high between 1998 and 2008, Azeri and Armenian communities no longer lived in close proximity, dramatically reducing the possibility of inter-group violence of the kind that erupted a decade earlier.

50 Minority Rights Group International, 'Azerbaijan Overview'.

51 International Crisis Group, 'Azerbaijan: Turning Over a New Leaf?' *ICG Europe Report No 156*, 13 May 2004, p. 30.

52 International Crisis Group, 'Nagorno-Karabakh: Risking War', *ICG Europe Report No 187*, 14 November 2007, pp. 16–17.

3.3 *Stable Autocratic Leadership*

Since the end of the war in 1994, Azerbaijan has experienced a relatively stable political environment, absent of the kind of political upheaval that preceded the most recent atrocities. Indeed, an overview of history in Azerbaijan and the South Caucasus reveals that conflict and atrocities have always occurred amidst profound political upheaval. The 1905 revolution, the 1917 revolution, and the weakening and collapse of the Soviet Union precipitated conflict and atrocities between Armenians and Azeris. Given this, the fact that the period between 1998 and 2008 was absent of political upheaval is in itself a protective factor against the possibility of mass atrocities. However, the absence of upheaval did not correspond to a diminishing of long-term risk. Rather, tensions between Azerbaijan and Armenia remained considerably high, with leaders from both countries not hesitant to engage in defamatory nationalist rhetoric to strengthen domestic support, especially during election campaigns. Even more significantly, the autocratic character of Azerbaijan's dynastic regime fostered an environment of repression, violently hostile to dissent, which gave it more than a passing resemblance to the style of rule typical during the Soviet Union.

During his presidency, Heydar Aliyev was instrumental in fostering positive relations with a broad range of international counterparts, effectively mitigating the real possibility of deepening geopolitical instability around the Nagorno-Karabakh conflict. This was in direct contrast to the turbulent nationalist phase of rule under Elchibey, which was marked by anti-Russian sentiment, and a forging of close ties with Turkey, mimicking the pan-Turkist ideology of the early twentieth century. Elchibey's pan-Turkism had further fuelled the conflict against Armenia at a time when that country was receiving increased military support from Russia. By contrast, Aliyev sought rapprochement with Russia by joining the CIS. This rebalancing of relations helped facilitate the Russian-initiated ceasefire of the conflict, which was the first ceasefire to be effective. He also reached out to the west – oil deposits were influential here. By 1998, the stability and continuity of the Azeri regime guaranteed continued lucrative investments in Azeri oil and natural gas. Thus, the absence of conflict was in the interest of many countries, not least some key OSCE members, such as France.[53]

However, Heydar Aliyev developed a highly centralized and rigid autocracy, which increasingly relied on violence and intimidation to assert authority as his popularity waned. Between 1993 and 2003, he developed a network of

53 Cornell, 'The Nagorno-Karabakh Conflict', pp. 38–42.

power around close friends and family.[54] First, he strengthened the office of the president and weakened the power of the parliament – the president's office controls both the national budget and the State Oil Fund. The president also personally appointed national executive authorities – those who administer at a district level. Within this network of power, Heydar Aliyev used his well-established patronage networks with the Nakhichevani and Yerazi clans to further cement his authority.[55]

Prominent positions within the president's Yeni Azerbaycan Party were given to close family members of Heydar Aliyev, including two of his brothers, his nephew and his son in law. Other relatives were given key portfolios in the government, including the Minister of Justice and the Minister of Communications. In addition to such personal appointments, the Aliyev family, relatives and friends have enjoyed enormous financial benefits through banking and the petroleum industry.[56]

Aliyev's decade in power brought an unprecedented stability to the country, but at great cost. This centralization of power intensified as Aliyev's popularity diminished, and as it did he relied more heavily on the security services to crush dissent. The interior ministry weakened political opposition by 'discrediting, intimidating or prosecuting political parties and journalists.'[57] The intolerance of opposition was particularly prescient during the 2003 election campaign and aftermath, where the ailing Aliyev secured a transfer of power to his son, Ilham. Opposition parties were regularly refused permits to hold rallies, or were given difficult conditions under which to conduct them.[58] In rallies that did take place, there were numerous instances of police intimidation, including severe beatings.[59] The election itself was marred by fraud so extensive it 'indicated national coordination.'[60] International monitors recorded a wide range of fraudulent practices, including pre-marked ballot papers and violent intimidation of opposition monitors. This led the OSCE to

54 Rasizade, 'Azerbaijan and the Transition to Democracy', p. 354.

55 Rasizade, 'Azerbaijan's Descent', pp. 201–204.

56 Ibid, pp. 201–204.

57 International Crisis Group, 'Azerbaijan: Turning Over a New Leaf?' (ICG Europe Report No 156, 13 May 2004), p. 13.

58 Such as assigning venues that accommodated very small numbers of people. See Human Rights Watch, *Crushing Dissent: Repression, Violence and Azerbaijan's Elections* Vol. 16 No. 1(D), January 2004, p. 12.

59 Ibid, p. 14.

60 Ibid, p. 20.

declare the results 'implausible'.[61] This provoked further unrest after the election, which was once again suppressed brutally by security forces. Since 2003, opposition leaders and supporters have endured frequent arrests and systematic torture in custody.[62]

Indeed, the style of Ilham Aliyev's presidency closely resembled that of his father. He continued the patronage networks that his father had established within government and the economy. He continued to intimidate opposition leaders and supporters, and engaged in comparable levels of fraud during the 2005 parliamentary elections, ensuring a favourable result for the Yeni Azerbaycan Party.[63] In addition, Ilham Aliyev entrenched his own autocratic style of rule by further restricting freedom of expression. Journalists and human rights advocates have frequently been the target of defamation charges brought against them by senior government officials, as well as being frequent targets of arrest, imprisonment and beatings. Between 2003 and 2008, Aliyev's government intensified its hostility against any form of journalistic expression not sanctioned by them.[64]

However, even with the autocratic character of Azerbaijan's regime, neither father nor son were able to formalize a resolution to the conflict over Nagorno-Karabakh. This was despite the fact that there was no political will within Azerbaijan for a return to conflict – the political risk associated with a resumption of fighting was on balance too great. But just as seeking a military solution had no political expediency, nor did making any concessions as part of a resolution agreement with Armenia, even though this almost occurred twice – once in 1997 and again in 2000. In 1997 the agreement that both Ter-Petrosian and Heydar Aliyev were in favour of was erased when Ter-Petrosian's support rapidly eroded and he was compelled to resign – making concessions on Nagorno-Karabakh had consequences for the Armenian leadership as well.[65] Despite this apparent intractability, particularly when Ter-Petrosian was replaced by Nagorno-Karabakh native and former combatant, Robert Kocharian, a resolution was very close to being formalized in 2000, with Heyder Aliyev agreeing to hand over sovereigny of Nagorno-Karabakh to Armenia. However, this time it was rejected by Aliyev's own inner circle.[66] As centralized and powerful as the

61 Ibid, p. 20; OSCE ODIHR, 'Republic of Azerbaijan Presidential Elections 15 October 2003', (Warsaw, 12 November 2003), pp. 1–2.

62 Human Rights Watch, 'Crushing Dissent', pp. 21–45.

63 International Crisis Group, 'Azerbaijan's 2005 Elections: A Lost Opportunity' *Baku/Brussels: ICG Europe Briefing No 40, 21* November 2005, p. 1.

64 Human Rights Watch, *Beaten, Blacklisted and Behind Bars: The Vanishing Space for Freedom of Expression in Azerbaijan* (New York, October 2010), pp. 1–2.

65 de Waal, *Black Garden*, pp. 259–260.

66 de Waal, *The Caucasus*, pp. 128–129.

office of the president had become in Azerbaijan, on the issue of Nagorno-Karabakh it was not omnipotent.

Subsequently, Kocharian's strong pro-Karabakh stance, as well as Ilham Aliyev's reluctance to progress mediation beyond verbal assurances, had the consequence of putting great strain on the ceasefire. In particular, the preference of both Heyder and Ilham Aliyev to crush dissent and suppress opposition parties made their regimes deeply unpopular. While it gathered strength through close-nit patronage, it also put itself at odds with the majority of the population through these brutal tactics and its economic policies, which favoured the very few and deprived most. This centralization of power and wealth has been effective in distancing Azerbaijan from the upheaval it endured in the early 1990s, but the rigid nature of governance made non-violent democratic regime change virtually impossible. This has raised the possibility that future regime change may again trigger the kind of upheaval that has historically coincided with war and atrocities. Given the continued tensions along the lines of ceasefire due to the failure to find a resolution, the social and political faultlines remain deep.

Adding to this tension is the fact that the unresolved conflict has been used by the Aliyev regime as a focal point for nationalist posturing, particularly during the presidential election campaigns of 2003 and 2008. This added further strain to the upholding of the ceasefire. Given that the frontlines over the years experienced sporadic exchange of fire – often resulting in dozens of casualties in any given year – these instances of heightened tension have on both occasions brought the two countries back to the brink of war.

The continuity of rule presided by Heydar Aliyev and his son Ilham, was effective in establishing relative stability following years of chaos and conflict during and following the deterioration of the Soviet Union. Given that all three major episodes of conflict and atrocities between Azeris and Armenians in the twentieth century occurred in the wake of major political upheaval, this point alone is significant in accounting for the absence of atrocities between 1998 and 2008. The Aliyev dynasty fostered greater investment in oil and gas, and in doing so established a more stable geopolitical environment where major regional stakeholders had an interest in the region's long term stability. However, the autocratic nature of the Aliyev regime also increased the long term risk of future atrocities, as it seemed unlikely that future regime change would occur peacefully and democratically. Given the continuing tensions and the unresolved conflict in Nagorno-Karabakh, any future violent regime overthrow could trigger another round of conflict and atrocities. Nevertheless, in the medium term, especially between 1998 and 2008, the absence of upheaval and reluctance to pursue a military solution to the conflict has sustained Azerbaijan's relative stability. However, it has not been Aliyev's regime alone that is responsible for the absence of atrocities – there have been times when the tension along the very tense frontline escalated into sporadic exchanges of fire, and these cases were badly managed by governments. In these times it was external mediation, and not the Azerbaijan (or Armenian) regime that prevented a return to war and atrocities.

3.4 *International Mediation Efforts*

The efforts of international mediators had mixed results between 1998 and 2008. As the chief mediators, the OSCE (through the Minsk Group) failed to bring the conflict to a resolution. However, they have been instrumental in the maintenance and strengthening of the ceasefire arrangements, and at times were the sole buffer against the resumption of conflict when tensions escalated to dangerous levels. This was particularly the case during the 2003 and 2008 election campaigns when nationalist rhetoric from Azerbaijan provoked tensions and sporadic fighting. If there has been a lack of success in bringing a permanent end to the conflict, the achievement of preventing a resumption of fighting and atrocities has been a product of the OSCE's commitment to facilitating ongoing communication between Armenian and Azerbaijani leaders.

The OSCE's initial attempts at mediation during fighting in 1992 (when it was the CSCE) were hopelessly inadequate. Their limited knowledge of the newly independent countries and the nature of the conflict being fought made their position as negotiators very tenuous. This provided Russia with an opportunity to persuade and pressure the parties into agreeing to a ceasefire in 1994. However, over the next few years, the OSCE forged a stronger presence in the region, developing a network of communication with key actors from Azerbaijan, Armenia as well as Nagorno-Karabakh. Although the Minsk Group had been created in 1992, it was not until Russia became co-chair in 1995 that mediation efforts became more coherent. Over numerous rounds of negotiations, a resolution was close to being reached three times – 1997, 1999 and 2001. Almost every conceivable solution had been tabled, but each time vetoed by either one party or both.[67]

However, the OSCE has been a key player in the prevention of a relapse of further violence, despite ongoing tensions and the occasional exchange of fire along the frontlines. This has occurred in three major ways. First, they have been instrumental in keeping the channel of communication between the two presidents open. Every year between 1998 and 2008, the OSCE facilitated meetings between the leaders – although a final agreement remained elusive, the frequent

67 Or, as mentioned earlier, agreed to by both but opposed by elites in either Azerbaijan or Armenia. See Gamaghelyan, 'Rethinking the Nagorno-Karabakh Conflict', pp. 37, 46–47.

communication provided the leaders with opportunities to develop a rapport with each other, and to negotiate the exchange of prisoners of war, which improved relations and at times diffused tensions along the frontlines.[68]

Second, they have been an effective source of early warning. Between 1998 and 2008 one significant development occurred, which enabled the OSCE to conduct effective early warning occurred. They established an office in Baku in 1999. One of the primary missions of the office was to foster cooperation with Armenia through the development of relations with key players in the region. The establishment of this office then enabled the OSCE to commence monthly monitoring of the front lines. This turned out to be an important confidence building measure, because soldiers on both sides were able to use OSCE radio equipment to communicate back and forth, and clear up any misunderstandings, particularly those which resulted in exchanges of fire.[69] Such action established trust in the OSCE monitors from both sides of the front lines, and gave OSCE the position of being a valued and objective third party. Consequently, from 2001, this monitoring was increased to twice a month.[70] It was this engagement along the lines of ceasefire that tension remained high, and at times threatened to escalate to a resumption of conflict. When such escalations occurred in 2003 and 2008, it was OSCE monitors that conveyed this early warning – on both occasions it was this early warning that directly led to timely diffusions of tensions.

Third, in response to this early warning, the OSCE's presence enabled them to be active in diffusing tension through the direct involvement of the Personal Representative (PR) of the Organization's Chairman in Office (CiO). This was significant because on both occasions that tensions and cross-border clashes intensified, Armenia and Azerbaijan were in the midst of election campaigns where the issue of Nagorno-Karabakh had heightened political currency – both governments engaged in dangerous posturing which led to increased activity along the ceasefire lines. At these times when the two national governments 'slowed down' talks and contributed to the risk of a return to conflict, the OSCE increased its involvement as the principle player involved in

---

68 OSCE, 'Annual Report 1998 on OSCE Activities 1 December 1997–30 November 1998' (Vienna, 2 December 1998), p. 20; OSCE 'Annual Report 1999 on OSCE Activities 1 December 1998–31 October 1999' (Vienna, 17 November 1999), pp. 3, 31; OSCE, 'Annual Report 2000 on OSCE Activities 1 November 1999–31 October 2000' (Vienna, 24 November, 2000), pp. 36–37; Gamaghelyan, 'Rethinking the Nagorno-Karabakh Conflict', pp. 46–47.

69 OSCE, 'Annual Report 1999,' pp. 3, 31.

70 OSCE, 'Annual Report 2001 on OSCE Activities 1 November 2000–31 October 2001' (Vienna, 26 November 2001), p. 39.

mitigating such tensions. In 2003, the PR personally conveyed the warning of the deterioration along the front lines between May and August to the co-chairs of the Minsk Group, which then led to the stabilization of those tensions.[71] When serious clashes broke out along the front line in 2008 – also during election campaigns in both countries – the PR personally intervened 'at the highest military and political levels,' which then helped to restore calm.[72] At these times, it was the diplomacy of the PR which was crucial to the maintenance of the ceasefire, and the avoidance of a return to full-scale conflict and possible atrocities.

Clearly mediation efforts have had a mixed record – they have not been effective in fostering a resolution to the conflict in Nagorno-Karabakh, although it is arguable that the OSCE has tried every conceivable option in order to reach an agreement. While this impasse is clearly the primary responsibility of the two main governments, it has resulted in the continuation of a volatile front-line, which – even though there appears to be little political will for a return to fighting – contains the real possibility that such violence will re-occur. Sustaining a ceasefire in such tense circumstances has been the greatest success of the mediation process. Maintaining these negotiations is crucial considering the investment that both states have put into enhancing their armies in order to keep alive a military solution if negotiations are abandoned.

Since the early 1990s, Azerbaijan has changed considerably. Mass deportation of ethnic minority populations in both countries has dramatically homogenized their populations, putting an end to centuries of co-existence. Perversely, this had the effect of dramatically lowering the visibility of these groups as potential targets of ethnic violence as they had been in the final years of the Soviet Union. Moreover, a combination of relative political stability and effective international mediation efforts ensured that the tense impasse between Armenia and Azerbaijan over the territory of Nagorno-Karabakh did not revert to violent conflict and atrocities between 1998 and 2008. While national and international actors did not manage to find consensus on a long term resolution to the conflict, there has been a developing competence in managing the current level of tension along the line of ceasefire. This has been relatively effective in the short to medium term, but it is doubtful that it will continue to mitigate the risk of atrocities in the long term. As both sides are building their military capacity, it is clear that a military solution to the long impasse is not entirely unfeasible. This risk is compounded by the character of

71 OSCE, 'Annual Report 2003 on OSCE Activities: Security and Cooperation for Europe' (Vienna, 2003), p. 28.

72 OSCE, 'Annual Report 2008' (Vienna: OSCE, 2009), pp. 11–12.

Azerbaijan's autocratic regime, which uses a complex network of patronage to consolidate its power, while not hesitating to use violence to crush dissent. Given the region's history of repressive autocracy and violent political upheaval, the combination of such upheaval, in an increasingly militarized environment amidst the ongoing impasse over Nagorno-Karabakh, the risk of future atrocities has not diminished.

4 Conclusion

An account of the historical dimensions of division and tension between Azeris and Armenians yield some key insights. Both groups experienced discrimination, although in the territory that corresponded roughly to the modern state of Azerbaijan, Armenians historically received greater economic and political favour. Despite this, Armenians were the victims of profound persecution, and the target of numerous atrocities between 1890 and 1917 in the neighbouring Ottoman Empire. The Azeris' perception of Armenian advantage in the Russian-controlled South Caucasus, and the Armenians' view of the absence of distinction between Azeris and Ottoman Turks fuelled tension, mistrust and hostility between the two groups. This tension materialized into violence during times of great upheaval. Moreover, the conflicting claims to Nagorno-Karabakh in particular remained unresolved for the duration of Soviet rule. The political upheaval that accompanied the collapse of the communist regime coincided with a reassertion of conflicting claims over Nagorno-Karabakh, and shifts in power which was characterized by extremist and exclusionary nationalist ideologies on both sides. This pattern of upheaval and atrocities emerged again in the late 1980s, and although a ceasefire to the conflict was achieved in 1994, no lasting resolution has been found.

In 1998, the tensions remained high – nearly one million Armenians and Azeris were displaced, and the frontline from the conflict continued to be volatile. However, the ceasefire held between 1998 and 2008 (and continues at the time of publication), despite these ongoing tensions. Stable regimes, buoyed by greater economic interdependency safeguarded the region against further upheaval, at least in the short term. Augmenting the stability was the extensive commitment to mediation by the OSCE – this maintained communication between the two armies, and was effective on a number of occasions in defusing situations arising from skirmishes along the frontline. The OSCE's mission in Baku also fostered a broad network of communication with key military and political leaders, and this enabled effective diplomacy during times of rising tension – especially during the election campaigns of 2003 and

2008. Although the forced deportation of minority Armenian and Azeri populations from either country (as well as Azeris from Nagorno-Karabakh) was indeed a negative outcome of the conflict, perversely, it had the result of diminishing the possibility of the kind of pogroms that occurred in both countries in the late 1980s and early 1990s.

The conflict over Nagorno-Karabakh remains unresolved. The period from 1998 to 2008 highlights just how volatile the situation continues to be. The ceasefire between the Azerbaijani and Armenian armies remains tense, and vulnerable to further outbreaks of violence. Indeed, were it not for the mediation efforts of the OSCE, it is arguable that a resumption of war would have occurred. Without a political solution to the solution, the area is left with a very tense stalemate, highly dependent on external actors (principally the OSCE) to put out spot fires.

Yet a political solution to the conflict seems a distant prospect. Both countries have, since the mid-1990s, avoided major profound political upheaval. However, nearly two decades of rule by Heydar Aliyev and his son Ilham Aliyev, have thwarted initial efforts of democratization. Their regimes have resorted increasingly to the use of force to maintain order. In addition, during election cycles, both leaders have provoked anti-Armenian sentiment to bolster their claims to power. This continues to raise tensions along the ceasefire line and further diminishes the possibility of a resolution to the conflict. Furthermore, Azerbaijan's growing authoritarianism has created a gulf between the generously rewarded elites and their cadres and the majority of the population who live close to or under the poverty line. This raises questions about the long-term sustainability of the current Aliyev regime – with most citizens experiencing political and economic marginalization, the possibility of future political upheaval remains high. This, combined with the ongoing stalemate over Nagorno-Karabakh, and Aliyev's readiness to scapegoat Armenia for domestic purposes, suggests that Azerbaijan's avoidance of atrocities between 1998 and 2008, and subsequently, has not diminished the high risk of future conflict and atrocities that remain.

Bibliography

Geneive Abdo, 'Ahmadinejad Shows No Signs of Going Quietly', Spotlight, Stimson Centre, 16 May (2013), http://www.stimson.org/spotlight/ahmadinejad-shows-no-signs-of-going-quietly/.

Geneive Abdo, 'The end of Rouhani's honeymoon', Aljazeera America, 18 February (2014), http://america.aljazeera.com/opinions/2014/2/hassan-rouhani-iranalikhamenei nuclearnegotiations.html.

Ervand Abrahamian, *A History of Modern Iran* (Cambridge: Cambridge University Press, 2008).

Adan Yusuf Abokor et al., *Further Steps to Democracy: The Somaliland Parliamentary Elections, September 2005* (London: Progressio, 2006).

Alice Ackermann, 'The Idea and Practice of Conflict Prevention,' *Journal of Peace Research*, 40/3: 339–347 (2003).

Friedrich Affolter, 'The Specter of Ideological Genocide: The Bahá'ís of Iran,' *War Crimes, Genocide, & Crimes against Humanity*, 1/1: 75–114 (2005).

Giorgio Agamben, *Homo Sacer: Sovereign Power and Bare Life*, tr. Daniel Heller-Roazen (Stanford, CA: Stanford University Press, 1998).

Feroz Ahmad, 'The Late Ottoman Empire,' in Marian Kent, ed., *The Great Powers and the End of the Ottoman Empire* (London: George Allen and Unwin, 1984).

Reuben Ahroni, *Jewish Emigration from the Yemen 1951–98* (Richmond, UK: Curzon Press, 2001).

April Longley Alley, 'Assessing (In)security after the Arab Spring: The Case of Yemen,' *Political Science and Politics*, 46/4: 721–726 (2013).

Mohammad Al-Momani, 'The Arab "Youth Quake": Implications on Democratization and Stability', *Middle East Law and Governance*, 3/1-2: 159–170 (2011).

Audrey L. Altstadt, *The Azerbaijani Turks: Power and Identity under Russian Rule* (Stanford, CA: Hoover Institution Press, 1992).

Jahangir Amuzegar, 'Khatami's First-Term Presidency: An Outsider's Assessment', *SAIS Review* 22/1: 1–21 (2002).

Jon Lee Anderson, 'Understanding Basij', The New Yorker, 19 June (2009), http://www.newyorker.com/news/news-desk/jon-lee-anderson-understanding-the-basij.

Kofi Annan, *Prevention of Armed Conflict: Report of the Secretary-General*, A/55/985, 7 June 2001.

Kofi Annan, *Interim Report of the Secretary-General on the Prevention of Armed Conflict*, A/58/365, 12 September 2003.

Kofi Annan, *Progress Report on the Prevention of Armed Conflict: Report of the Secretary-General*, A/60/891, 18 July 2006.

Ali M. Ansari, 'Iran and the United States in the shadow of 9/11: Persia and the Persian question revisited,' in *Iran in the 21st Century: Politics, economics and conflict*, eds. Homa Katouzian and Hossein Shahidi (London: Routledge, 2008).

Fionnuala Ni Aolain, 'Sex-based Violence and the Holocaust—A Reevaluaion of Harms and Rights in International Law,' *Yale Journal of Law and Feminism*, 12/1: 43–84 (2000).

Hannah Arendt, *The Origins of Totalitarianism* (New York: The World Publishing Co., 1951).

Ari Ariel, *Jewish-Muslim Relations and Migration from Yemen to Palestine in the Late Nineteenth and Twentieth Centuries* (Boston: Brill, 2014).

Bahá'í International Community, *The Bahá'í Question: Cultural Cleansing in Iran* (New York: Bahá'í International Community, 2008).

Bahá'í International Community, 'Current Situation of Bahá'ís in Iran', 27 January 2014, http://www.bic.org/media/Current-situation-Bahais-in-Iran, accessed 18 February 2014.

Ban Ki-moon, *Report of the Secretary-General on the Implementation of Security Council Resolution 1625 (2005), on Conflict Prevention, Particularly in Africa*, S/2008/18, 14 January 2008.

Ban Ki-moon, *Implementing the Responsibility to Protect: Report of the Secretary-General*, A/63/677, 12 January 2009.

Ban Ki-moon, *Report of the Secretary General on the protection of civilians in armed conflict*, S/2012/376, 22 May 2012.

Ban Ki-moon, *Responsibility to Protect: State Responsibility and Prevention*, A/67/929-S/2013/399, 9 July 2013.

Ban Ki-moon, *Fulfilling our Collective Responsibility: International Responsibility and the Responsibility to Protect*, A/68/946-S/2014/449, 11 July 2014.

Erin Baines and Emily Paddon, 'This is How we Survived: Civilian Agency and Humanitarian Protection,' *Security Dialogue*, 43/3: 231–47 (2012).

Anne Barnard, 'Syria Death Toll Reported to Rise by 10,000 in Less Than 2 Months,' *New York Times*, 19 May 2014.

Casey Barrs, *How Civilians Survive Violence: A Preliminary Inventory*, The Cuny Center, November 2010.

Andrea Bartoli, Tetsushi Ogata and Gregory H. Stanton, 'Emerging Paradigms in Genocide Prevention,' *Genocide Prevention* (Bern: Federal Department of Foreign Affairs, Confederation of Switzerland, 2009).

Paul Bartrop and Samuel Totten, '*Realpolitik:* The *Major* Impediment to the Prevention and Intervention of Genocide' in *Impediments to the Prevention and Intervention of Genocide: Genocide: A Critical Bibliographic Review Volume 9*, ed. Samuel Totten (New Brunswick, NJ: Transaction, 2013).

Matthias Basedau and Jann Lay, 'Resource Curse or Rentier Peace? The Ambiguous Effects of Oil Wealth and Oil Dependence on Violent Conflict,' *Journal of Peace Research*, 46/6: 757–776 (2009).

Stephen K. Batalden and Sandra L. Batalden, *The Newly Independent States of Eurasia: Handbook of Soviet Republics* (Phoenix: Oryx, 1997).

Yehuda Bauer, *A History of the Holocaust* (New York: Franklin Watts, 1982).

BBC News, 'Iran hangs 11 Jundullah Sunni militants', 20 December 2010. http://www.bbc.co.uk/news/world-middle-east-12039745, accessed 20 December 2010.

BBC News, 'Six Days that shook Iran', 11 July 2000, http://news.bbc.co.uk/2/hi/middle_east/828696.stm.

Alex J. Bellamy and Paul D. Williams, 'The New Politics of Protection? Côte d'Ivoire, Libya and the Responsibility to Protect,' *International Affairs* 87/4: 825–850 (2011).

Alex J. Bellamy, 'The Responsibility to Protect and the Problem of Military Intervention', *International Affairs* 84/4: 615–39 (2008).

Alex J. Bellamy, *Responsibility to Protect: The Global Effort to End Mass Atrocities* (Cambridge: Polity, 2009).

Alex J. Bellamy, *Mass Atrocities and Armed Conflict: Links, Distinctions, and Implications for the Responsibility to Prevent*, Policy Analysis Brief (Muscatine: The Stanley Foundation, 2011).

Eva Bellin, 'Reconsidering the Robustness of Authoritarianism in the Middle East: Lessons from the Arab Spring,' *Comparative Politics*, 44/2: 127–149 (2012).

Milton Bearden, 'Afghanistan, Graveyard of Empires,' *Foreign Affairs*, 80/6: 17–30 (2001).

Fikret Berkes and Carl Folke, 'Linking Social and Ecological Systems for Resilience and Sustainability' in *Linking Social and Ecological Systems. Management Practices and Social Mechanisms for Building Resilience,* eds. Fikret Berkes and Carl Folk (Cambridge: Cambridge University Press, 1998).

Catherine Besteman, 'Primordialist Blinders: A Reply to I.M. Lewis,' *Cultural Anthropology,* 13/1: 109–120 (1998).

Katharine Bigelow, 'A Campaign to Deter Genocide: The Bahá'í Experience' in *WatchGenocide,* ed. Helen Fein (New Haven, CT: Yale University Press, 1992).

Cyrus Bina, 'The Hot Summer of Defiance: The Student Protests for Freedom and Democracy in Iran', *Journal of Iranian Research and Analysis* 15/2: 47–62 (1999), p. 49.

Lisa Blaydes, *Elections and Distributive Politics in Mubarak's Egypt,* (New York: Cambridge University Press, 2011).

Berit Bliesemann de Guevara and Florian P. Kühn, 'The International Community Needs to Act': Loose Use and Empty Signalling of a Hackneyed Concept,' *International Peacekeeping*, 18/2: 135–151 (2011).

Edwin Bliss, *Turkey and the Armenian Atrocities* (Boston: H.L. Hastings, 1896).

Suha Bolukbasi, *Azerbaijan: A Political History* (London: I.B. Tauris, 2011).

Boutros Boutrous Ghali, 'An Agenda for Peace. Preventive Diplomacy, Peacemaking and Peace-keeping', *International Relations*, 11/3: 201–218 (1992).

Mark Bradbury, *The Somali Conflict: Prospects for Peace* (Oxford: Oxfam, 1994).

Mark Bradbury, *Somaliland Country Report* (London: Catholic Institute for International Relations, 1997).

E.A. Brayley Hodgetts, *Round About Armenia: The Record of a Journey across the Balkans through Turkey, the Caucasus and Persia in 1895* (London: Sampson Low Marston, 1896).

F.R. Bridge, 'The Habsburg Monarchy and the Ottoman Empire, 1900–18' in *The Great Powers and the End of the Ottoman Empire*, ed. Marian Kent (London: George Allen and Unwin, 1984).

Christopher R. Browning, *The Origins of the Final Solution: The Evolution of Nazi Jewish Policy, September 1939–March 1942* (Jerusalem: Yad Vashem and Lincoln: University of Nebraska Press, 2004).

Jason Brownlee, *Authoritarianism in an Age of Democratization* (Cambridge: Cambridge University Press, 2007).

Jason Brownlee, 'Executive Elections in the Arab World: When and How Do They Matter?' *Comparative Political Studies*, 44/7: 807–828 (2011).

Rogers Brubaker and David Laitin, 'Ethnic and Nationalist Violence' *Annual Review of Sociology*, 24/1: 423–452 (1998).

Matt Bryden and Dr. Ahmed Yusuf Farah, *The Peace Committee for Somaliland: Case Study of a Grassroots Peace Making Initiative* (Addis Ababa: UNDP Emergencies Unit for Ethiopia, 1996).

Halvard Buhaug and Scott Gates, 'The Geography of Civil War,' *Journal of Peace Research*, 39/4: 417–433 (2002).

Halvard Buhaug and Päivi Lujala, 'Accounting for scale: Measuring geography in quantitative studies of civil war,' *Political Geography*, 24/4: 399–418 (2005).

Halvard Buhaug, Scott Gates, and Päivi Lujala, 'Geography, Rebel Capability, and the Duration of Civil Conflict,' *Journal of Conflict Resolution*, 53/4: 544–569 (2009).

Philippe Burrin, *Hitler and the Jews: The Genesis of the Holocaust*, trans. Patsy Southgate (London: Edward Arnold, 1994).

Nicholas Canny, 'Early Modern Ireland, c. 1500–1700' in *The Oxford Illustrated History of Ireland*, ed. R.F. Foster (Oxford: Oxford University Press, 1991).

David Carment and Albrecht Schnabel, 'Conflict Prevention – Taking Stock' in *Conflict Prevention: Path to Peace or Grand Illusion?* eds. David Carment and Albrecht Schnabel (Tokyo: United Nations University Press, 2003).

David Carment and Albrecht Schnabel (eds.), *Conflict Prevention: From Rhetoric to Reality* (Lanham: Lexington Books, 2003).

Antonio Cassese, *Cassese's International Criminal Law*, Third Edition (Oxford: Oxford University Press, 2013).

Central Intelligence Agency, 'Azerbaijan', in *The World Factbook*, 2012, https://www.cia.gov/library/publications/the-world-factbook/geos/aj.html, accessed 5 July 2012.

David Chandler, 'The People-Centred Approach to Peace Operations: The New UN Agenda,' *International Peacekeeping*, 8/1: 1–9 (2001).

Lorraine Charles and Kate Denman, Syrian and Palestinian Syrian Refugees in Lebanon: the Plight of Women and Children,' *Journal of International Women's Studies*, 14/5: 96–111 (2013).

Frederick Chary, *The Bulgarian Jews and the Final Solution, 1940–1944* (Pittsburgh: University of Pittsburgh Press, 1972).

Daniel Chirot and Clark McCauley *Why Not Kill Them All?* (Princeton: Princeton University Press, 2006).

Christopher S. Chivvis, 'Libya and the Future of Liberal Intervention,' *Survival: Global Politics and Strategy*, 54/6: 69–92 (2012).

Norman Cigar, *Genocide in Bosnia: The Policy of 'Ethnic Cleansing'* (College Station, Texas: Texas A&M University Press, 1995).

Patrick Clawson and Michael Rubin, *IranEternal: Continuity and Chaos* (New York: Palgrave Macmillan, 2005).

Richard Clogg, 'The Greek *Millet* in the Ottoman Empire' in *Christians and Jews in the Ottoman Empire: The Functioning of a Plural Society*, eds. Benhamin Braude and Bernard Lewis (New York: Holmes and Meier, 1982).

John G. Cockell, 'Early Warning Analysis and Policy Planning in UN Preventive Action' in *Conflict Prevention: Path to Peace or Grand Illusion?* eds. David Carment and Albrecht Schnabel (Tokyo: United Nations University Press, 2003).

Paul Collier, 'Rebellion as Quasi-Criminal Activity,' *Journal of Conflict Resolution*, 44/6: 839–853 (2000).

Paul Collier, Lani Elliot, Håvard Hegre, Anke Hoeffler, Marta Reynal-Querol and Nicholas Sambanis, *Breaking the Conflict Trap. Civil War and Development Policy. World Bank Policy Research Report* (Washington, D.C.: World Bank, 2003).

Paul Collier, *Development and Conflict* (Oxford: Oxford University, 2004).

Paul Collier, *The Bottom Billion: Why the Poorest Countries are Failing and What Can Be Done About It* (Oxford: Oxford University Press, 2008).

Committee on the Elimination of Racial Discrimination (CERD), 'Consideration of reports submitted by States parties under article 9 of the convention. Concluding observations of the Committee on the Elimination of Racial Discrimination - Islamic Republic of Iran', Advanced Unedited Version, Seventy-seventh session, CERD/C/IRN/CO/18–19, 27 August 2010.

Roger Cooper, 'The Bahá'ís of Iran: A Minority Rights Group Report' (London: Minority Rights, 1985).

Theodore A. Couloumbis, John A. Petropulos, and Harry J. Psomiades, *Foreign Interference in Greek Politics: A Historical Perspective* (New York: Pella Publishing Co., 1976).

Michael P. Croissant, *The Armenia-Azerbaijani Conflict: Causes and Implications* (Westport, CT: Praeger, 1998).

Thomas Cushman, 'Is Genocide Preventable? Some Theoretical Considerations,' *Journal of Genocide Research*, 5/4: 523–542 (2003).

Uri Dadush and Michele Dunne, 'American and European Responses to the Arab Spring: What's the Big Idea?' *The Washington Quarterly*, 34/4: 131–145 (2011).

Sam Dagher, 'Kurds', *New York Times*, 3 May 2010, http://topics.nytimes.com/top/reference/timestopics/subjects/k/kurds/index.html?scp=2&sq=iran%20 kurdistan&st=cse.

Norman Davies, *God's Playground: A History of Poland in Two Volumes, Volume 1: The Origins to 1795* (New York: Columbia University Press, 1982).

Thomas de Waal, *Black Garden: Armenia and Azerbaijan Through Peace and War* (New York: New York University Press, 2003).

Thomas de Waal, *The Caucasus: An Introduction* (Oxford: Oxford University Press, 2010).

John Dippel, *Bound upon a Wheel of Fire: Why So Many German Jews made the Tragic Decision to Remain in Nazi Germany* (New York: Basic Books, 1996).

Rasheed Draman, 'Conflict Prevention in Africa: Establishing Conditions and Institutions conducive to durable Peace' in *Conflict Prevention: Path to Peace or Grand Illusion?* eds. David Carment and Albrecht Schabel (Tokyo: United Nations University Press, 2003).

Tobi P. Dress and Gay Rosenblum-Kumar, 'Deconstructing Prevention: A Systems Approach to Mitigating Violent Conflict' in *From Reaction to Conflict Prevention: Opportunities for the UN System,* eds. Fen Osler Hampson and David M. Malone (Boulder: Lynne Rienner, 2003).

Philippe Droz-Vincent, '"State of Barbary" (Take Two): From the Arab Spring to the Return of Violence in Syria,' *The Middle East Journal*, 68/1: 33–58 (2014).

Shirin Ebadi, *AwakeningIran: A Memoir of Revolution and Hope* (New York: Random House, 2006).

The Economist 2011, 'The Arab Spring Death Toll, The Price of Protest, So far,' http://www.economist.com/blogs/dailychart/2011/07/arab-spring-death-toll, accessed 4 June 2014.

Jan Eliasson, 'Establishing Trust in the Healer: Preventive Diplomacy and the Future of the United Nations' in *Stopping Wars Before they Start: Preventive Diplomacy*, ed. Kevin Cahill (New York: Basic Books, 1996).

Rebecca Jean Emigh, 'The Power of Negative Thinking: The Use of Negative Case Methodology in the Development of Sociological Theory,' *Theory and Society* 26: 649–684 (1997).

David Engel, *The Holocaust: The Third Reich and the Jews* (Essex, UK: Longman: 2000).

Bat-Zion Eraqi-Klorman, 'The Forced Conversion of Jewish Orphans in Yemen,' *International Journal of Middle Eastern Studies* 33: 23–47 (2001).

Joan Esteban and Debraj Ray, 'Linking Conflict to Inequality and Polarization,' *The American Economic Review*, 101/4: 1345–1374 (2011).

Helen Fein, 'Accounting for Genocide after 1945: Theories and Some Findings,' *International Journal on Group Rights*, 1: 79–106 (1993).

Yi Feng, 'Democracy, Political Stability and Economic Growth,' *British Journal of Political Science*, 27/39: 401–418 (1997).

Keitha Sapsin Fine, 'Fragile Stability and Change: Understanding Conflict during the Transitions in East Central Europe' in *Preventing Conflict in the Post-Communist World: Mobilizing International and Regional Organizations*, eds. Abram Chayes and Antonia Handler Chayes (Washington, D.C.: The Brookings Institution, 1996).

Samuel Fiszman, ed., *Constitution and Reform in Eighteenth-Century Poland: The Constitution of 3 May 1791* (Bloomington: Indiana University Press, 1997).

R.F. Foster, 'Ascendancy and Union' in *The Oxford Illustrated History of Ireland*, ed. R.F. Foster (Oxford: Oxford University Press, 1991).

Lee Ann Fujii, *Killing Neighbors: Webs of Violence In Rwanda* (Ithaca: Cornell University Press, 2009).

Fund for Peace, 'The Methodology Behind the Index,' http://ffp.statesindex.org/methodology, accessed 7 June 2014.

Fund for Peace, 'Failed States Index 2013,' http://ffp.statesindex.org/rankings-2013-sortable, accessed 7 June 2014.

Fund for Peace, 'Failed States Index 2013: Five-Year Trends, 2008–2013,' http://ffp.statesindex.org/fsi-trends-2013, accessed 7 June 2014.

Kathleen Gallagher Cunningham and Nils B. Weidman, 'Shared Space: Ethnic Groups, State Accommodation, and Localized Conflict,' *International Studies Quarterly*, 54/4: 1035–1954, (2010).

Florence Gaub, 'A Libyan Recipe for Disaster,' *Survival: Global Politics and Strategy*, 56/1: 101–120 (2014).

Gregory Gause III, 'Why Middle East Studies Missed the Arab Spring,' *Foreign Affairs*, 90/4: 81–90 (2011).

Genocide Prevention Advisory Network, 'Genocides, Politicides, and Other Mass Murder Since 1945 With Stages in 2008,' 2009, www.gpanet.org/content/genocides-politicides-and-other-mass-murder-1945-stages-2008, accessed 24 November 2012.

Genocide Prevention Task Force, 'Preventing Genocide: A Blueprint for U.S. Policymakers,' 2008, http://media.usip.org/reports/genocide_taskforce_report.pdf, accessed May 30, 2014.

N. Gergel, 'The Pogroms in the Ukraine in 1918–1921,' *YIVO Annual of Jewish Social Science*, 6.

Nazila Ghanea, *Human Rights, the UN and the Bahá'ís in Iran* (Oxford: George Ronald, 2002).

Vatche Ghazarian (ed.), *Armenians in the Ottoman Empire: An Anthology of Transformation 13th–19th Centuries* (Waltham: Mayreni Publishing, 1997).

Aleksander Gieysztor, Stefan Kieniewicz, Emanuel Rostworowski, Janusz Tazbir, and Henryk Wereszycki, *History of Poland*, 2nd ed. (Warsaw: PWN-Polish Scientific Publishers, 1979).

Martin Gilbert, *The Straits of War: Gallipoli Remembered* (Stroud UK: Sutten, 2000).

Benjamin E. Goldsmith, Charles R. Butcher, Dimitri Semenovich, and Arcot Sowmya, 'Forecasting the onset of genocide and politicide: Annual out-of-sample forecasts on a global dataset, 1988–2003,' *Journal of Peace Research*, 50/4: 437–452 (2013).

Benjamin E. Goldsmith, Dimitri Semenovich, and Arcot Sowmya, 'Political Instability and Genocide. Comparing causes in Asia and the Pacific and globally' in *Genocide and Mass Atrocities in Asia: Legacies and prevention*, eds. Deborah Mayersen and Annie Pohlman (New York: Routledge, 2013).

Jack A. Goldstone and Jay Ulfelder (2004) 'How to Construct Stable Democracies,' *The Washington Quarterly*, 28/1: 9–20 (2004).

Jack A. Goldstone, Robert H. Bates, David L. Epstein, Ted Robert Gurr, Michael B. Lustik, Monty G. Marshall, Jay Ulfelder, and Mark Woodward, 'A Global Forecasting Model of Political Instability,' *American Journal of Political Science*, 54/1: 190–208 (2010).

Mark Gollom, 'Why Ahmadinejad's greatest enemies may be in Tehran', CBC News, 15 March (2013), http://www.cbc.ca/news/world/why-ahmadinejad-s-greatest-enemies-may-be-in-iran-1.1341886.

Robert Grenier, 'Iraq: Threats of foreign influence', *Al Jazeera* 11 January 2011, http://english.aljazeera.net/indepth/opinion/2011/01/2011110142254749996.html.

Ted Robert Gurr, *Why Men Rebel* (Princeton: Princeton University Press, 1970).

Yisrael Gutman, *The Jews of Warsaw, 1939–1943: Ghetto, Underground, Revolt*, trans. Ina Friedman (Bloomington: Indiana University Press, 1982).

Franz Halder, *The Halder Way Diary: 1939–1942*, eds. Charles Burdick and Hans-Adolf Jacobson, eds. (Novalto, CA: Presidio, 1988).

David Hamburg and Cyrus R Vance, *Preventing Deadly Conflict – Final Report* (Washington, D.C.: Carnegie Commission on Preventing Deadly Conflict, 1997).

David A Hamburg, *Preventing Genocide: Practical Steps Toward Early Detection and Effective Prevention* (Boulder: Paradigm, 2008).

Ayman Hamidi, 'Inscriptions of Violence in Northern Yemen: Haunting Histories, Unstable Moral Spaces,' *Middle Eastern Studies*, 45/2: 165–187 (2009).

Fen Osler Hampson and David M. Malone (eds.), *From Reaction to Conflict Prevention: Opportunities for the UN System* (Boulder: Lynne Rienner, 2003).

Fen Osler Hampson, Fen Osler, Karin Wermester & David M. Malone, 'Introduction: Making Conflict Prevention a Priority' in *From Reaction to Conflict Prevention: Opportunities for the UN System*, eds. Fen Osler Hampson and David M. Malone (Boulder: Lynne Rienner, 2003).

Roger Hardy, 'Profile: Iran's Jundullah militants', *BBC News* 20 June 2010. http://news.bbc.co.uk/2/hi/middle_east/8314431.stm.

Barbara Harff, 'No Lessons Learned from the Holocaust? Assessing the Risks of Genocide and Political Mass Murder since 1955,' *The American Political Science Review*, 97/1: 57–73 (2003).

Barbara Harff, 'Assessing Global Risks of Genocide and Politicide,' in *Peace and Conflict 2012*, eds. Joseph J. Hewitt, Jonathan Wilkenfeld, and Ted Robert Gurr (Boulder, CA: Paradigm, 2012).

Harff, Assessing Risks of Genocide and Politicide; 'Common' and 'Specific' risk terms used in UN Office on Genocide Prevention and the Responsibility to Protect, 'Framework of Analysis for Atrocities Crimes: A Tool for Prevention', July 2014. http://www.un.org/en/preventgenocide/adviser/pdf/framework%20of%20analysis%20for%20atrocity%20crimes_en.pdf.

Hussein D. Hassan, 'Iran: Ethnic and Religious Minorities,' *CRS Report for Congress*, updated 25 November 2008 (Washington: Congressional Research Service, 2008).

Keren Hayesod, *The Exodus from Yemen* (Jerusalem: Keren Hayesod, [1950]).

Havard Hegre, Tanja Ellingsen, Scott Gates and Nils Petter Gleditsch, 'Toward a Democratic Civil Peace? Democracy, Political Change, and Civil War, 1816–1992,' *The American Political Science Review*, 95/1: 33–48 (2001).

Andreas Heinemann-Grüder, 'Konfliktprävention – Alternative zu Militäreinsätzen?' in *Friedensgutachten*, eds. Bruno Schoch, Andreas Heinemann-Grüder, Jochen Hippler, Markus Weingardt, and Reinhard Mutz (Münster: LIT-Verlag, 2007).

Birger Heldt, 'Mass Atrocity Early Warning Systems: Data Gathering, Data Verification and Other Challenges,' 2012, http://papers.ssrn.com/sol3/papers.cfm?abstract_id=2028534, accessed 18 March 2014.

Elissa Helms, *Innocence and Victimhood: Gender, Nation and Women's Activism in Postwar Bosnia-Herzegovina* (Madison, WI: University of Wisconsin Press, 2013).

Elliot Hen-Tov, 'Understanding Iran's New Authoritarianism,' *The Washington Quarterly* 30/1: 163–179 (2007).

Raul Hilberg, *The Destruction of the European Jews* (New York: Holmes and Meier Publishers, 1985).

Raul Hilberg, *Perpetrators, Victims, Bystanders: The Jewish Catastrophe 1933–1945* (New York: HarperCollins, 1992).

Raymond Hinnebusch, 'Syria: from 'authoritarian upgrading' to revolution?' *International Affairs*, 88/1: 95–113 (2012).

Herbert Hirsch, '"Paved with Good Intentions": Attempts to Design Mechanisms to Prevent Genocide in the Twenty-First Century and Why They Have Not Succeeded' in *Impediments to the Prevention and Intervention of Genocide: Genocide: A Critical Bibliographic Review Volume 9*, ed. Samuel Totten (New Brunswick, NJ: Transaction, 2013).

Richard Hovannisian, 'The Historical Dimensions of the Armenian Question, 1878–1923' in *The Armenian Genocide in Perspective*, ed. Richard Hovannisian (New Brunswick: Transaction Books, 1986).

Michael Howard, 'Kurds flee homes as Iran shells Iraq's northern frontier', *The Guardian*, 18 August 2006. http://guardian.co.uk/world/2006/aug/18/iraq.iran.html, accessed 14 January 2011.

Ben Hubbard, 'Lebanon Hosts Over a Million Who Fled Syria, U.N. Reports,' *New York Times*, 3 April 2014.

Lisa Hultman, Jacob Kathman, and Megan Shannon, 'United Nations Peacekeeping and Civilian Protection in Civil War,' *American Journal of Political Science*, 57/4: 875–891 (2013).

Human Rights Watch, *Azerbaijan: Seven Years of Conflict in Nagorno-Karabakh* (Helsinki: Human Rights Watch Report, 1994).

Human Rights Watch, *Beaten, Blacklisted and Behind Bars: The Vanishing Space for Freedom of Expression in Azerbaijan* (New York, October 2010).

Human Rights Watch, *Crushing Dissent: Repression, Violence and Azerbaijan's Elections* Vol. 16 No. 1(D), January 2004.

Human Rights Watch, *Harsh War, Harsh Peace: Abuses by al-Shabaab, the Transitional Federal Government, and AMISOM in Somalia*, April 2010.

Human Rights Watch, 'Iran,' *World Report 2012: Time to Abandon the Autocrats and Embrace Rights*, 2012, http://www.hrw.org/sites/default/files/iran_2012.pdf.

Human Rights Watch, 'The Islamic Republic at 31: Post-election Abuses Show Serious Human Rights Crisis' (2010). Accessed at: http://www.hrw.org/sites/default/files/reports/irano210web.pdf.

Human Rights Watch, *'The Power These Men Have Over Us': Sexual Exploitation and Abuse by African Union Forces in Somalia*, September 2014.

Human Security Report Project. *Human Security Report 2009/2010: The Causes of Peace and the Shrinking Costs of War* (New York: Oxford University Press, 2011).

Macartan Humphreys, 'Natural Resources, Conflict, and Conflict Resolution: Uncovering the Mechanisms,' *Journal of Conflict Resolution*, 49/4: 508–537 (2005).

Paula E. Hyman, *The Jews of Modern France* (Berkeley: University of California Press, 1998).

Lee Igel, 'The Fate of the Jews in Austria, 1933–39' in *The Routledge History of The Holocaust*, ed. Jonathan Friedman (New York: Routledge, 2012).

International Commission on Intervention and State Sovereignty (ICISS). *The Responsibility to Protect* (Ottawa: IDRC, 2001).

International Crisis Group, 'Azerbaijan's 2005 Elections: A Lost Opportunity' *Baku/Brussels: ICG Europe Briefing No 40*, 21 November 2005.

International Crisis Group, 'Azerbaijan: Turning Over a New Leaf?' *ICG Europe Report No 156*, 13 May 2004.

International Crisis Group, 'Nagorno-Karabakh: Risking War', *ICG Europe Report No 187*, 14 November 2007.

International Crisis Group, 'Yemen: Coping with Terrorism and Violence in a Fragile State,' *Middle East Report No. 8*, 8 January 2003.

International Crisis Group, 'Egypt's Muslim Brothers: Confrontation or Integration?' *Middle East/North Africa Report No. 76*, 18 June 2008.

International Crisis Group, 'Yemen: Defusing the Saada Time Bomb,' *Middle East Report No. 86*, 27 May 2009.

International Crisis Group, 'Reshuffling the Cards (I)? Syria's Evolving Strategy,' *Middle East Report No. 92*, 14 December 2009.

International Crisis Group, 'Popular Protest in North Africa and the Middle East (I): Egypt Victorious?' *Middle East/North Africa Report No. 101*, 24 February 2011.

International Crisis Group, 'Libya,' http://www.crisisgroup.org/en/regions/middle-east-north-africa/north-africa/libya.aspx, accessed 22 February 2014.

International Crisis Group, 'CrisisWatch Database Libya,' http://www.crisisgroup.org/en/publication-type/crisiswatch/crisiswatch-database.aspx?CountryIDs={28685262-BE79-473E-B18E-ED22761A0F17}, accessed 22 February 2014.

International Crisis Group, 'CrisisWatch Database Tunisia,' http://www.crisisgroup.org/en/publication-type/crisiswatch/crisiswatch-database.aspx?CountryIDs={684E8DDD-7048-41F2-A1D0-8D34F565C336}#results, accessed 22 February 2014.

International Republican Institute, *Strategy for International Democratisation Support to Somaliland* (London/Washington, D.C.: DFID/International Republican Institute, 2014).

Charles Issawi, *The Economic History of Turkey: 1800–1914* (Chicago: University of Chicago Press, 1980).

Bruce W. Jentleson, (2000) 'Preventive Diplomacy: a conceptual and analytic framework' in *Opportunities Missed, Opportunities Seized: Preventive Diplomacy in the Post-Cold War World*, ed. Bruce W Jentleson (Lanham MD: Rowman & Littlefield, 2000).

Bruce Jentleson, 'The Obama Administration and R2P: Progress, Problems and Prospects,' *Global Responsibility to Protect*, 4/4: 399–423 (2012).

George Joffé, 'The End of Autocracy? The Seeds of Libya's Civil War,' *The RUSI Journal*, 156/3: 12–19 (2011).

Adam Jones, *Genocide: A Comprehensive Introduction* (Oxon: Routledge, 2006).

Stathis Kalyvas, *The Logic of Violence in Civil War* (New York: Cambridge University Press, 2006).

Stathis N. Kalyvas and Laia Balcells, 'International System and Technologies of Rebellion: How the End of the Cold War Shaped Internal Conflict,' *American Political Science Review*, 104/3: 415–429 (2010).

Mukesh Kapila and Karin Wermester, 'Development and Conflict: New Approaches in the United Kingdom' in *From Reaction to Conflict Prevention: Opportunities for the*

UN System, eds. Fen Osler Hampson and David M. Malone (Boulder: Lynne Rienner, 2003).

Marion Kaplan, 'Persecution and Gender: German-Jewish Responses to Nazism, 1933–39' in *The Routledge History of the Holocaust*, ed. Jonathan Friedman (London: Routledge, 2012).

Michael Karlberg, 'Constructive Resilience: The Bahá'í Response to Oppression,' *Peace and Change*, 35/2: 222–256 (2010).

Kemal H. Karpat, *The Politicization of Islam: Reconstructing Identity, State, Faith, and Community in the Late Ottoman State* (Oxford: Oxford University Press, 2001).

Stuart J. Kaufman, *Modern Hatreds: The Symbolic Politics of Ethnic War* (Ithaca: Cornell University Press, 2001).

Nikki R. Keddie, *Modern Iran: Roots and Results of Revolution. Updated Edition*, with section by Yann Richard (New Haven: Yale University Press, 2006).

Nikki R. Keddie and Yann Richard. *Modern Iran: Roots and Results of Revolution* (New York: Yale University Press, 2003).

Jeffrey T. Kenney, 'Movement Activism: The Society of Muslim Brothers After Egypt's Arab Spring,' *Nova Religio*, 16/3: 95–104 (2013).

Ben Kiernan, *Blood and Soil: A World History of Genocide and Extermination from Sparta to Darfur* (Melbourne: Melbourne University Press, 2007).

Kevin Köhler, 'Authoritarian Elections in Egypt: Formal Institutions and Informal Mechanisms of Rule,' *Democratization*, 15/5: 974–990 (2008).

Farideh Koohi-Kamali, *The Political Development of the Kurds in Iran: Pastoral Nationalism* (Hampshire: Palgrave Macmillan 2003).

David Kopel, Paul Gallant and Joanne Eisen, 'Is Resisting Genocide a Human Right?' *Notre Dame Law Review*, 81/4: 1275–1346 (2005–2006).

Yorgos A. Kourvetaris and Betty A. Dobratz, *A Profile of Modern Greece in Search of Identity* (Oxford: Clarendon Press, 1987).

Matthew Krain, "State-Sponsored Mass Murder The Onset and Severity of Genocides and Politicides." *Journal of Conflict Resolution* Vol. 41 (3) (1997): 331–360.

Matthew Krain, 'Democracy, Internal War, and State-Sponsored Mass Murder,' *Human Rights Review*, 1/3: 1–24 (2000).

Leo Kuper, *Genocide: Its Political Use in the Twentieth Century* (New Haven, CT: Yale University Press, 1981).

Leo Kuper, *The Prevention of Genocide* (New Haven, CT: Yale University Press, 1985).

Leo Kuper, 'Reflections on the Prevention of Genocide' in *Genocide Watch*, ed. Helen Fein (New Haven, CT: Yale University Press, 1992).

David D. Laitin and Said S. Samatar, *Somalia: Nation in Search of a State* (Boulder: Westview Press, 1987).

Arnim Langer, 'When do Horizontal Conflicts Lead to Conflict? Lessons from a Comparative Study of Ghana and Côte d'Ivoire' in *Horizontal Inequalities and Conflict:*

Understanding Group Violence in Multiethnic Societies, ed. Frances Stewart (Basingstoke: Palgrave, 2008).

Lawrence Langer, 'Gendered Suffering? Women in Holocaust Testimonies' in *Women and the Holocaust*, ed. D. Ofer and L.J. Weitzman (New Haven, CT: Yale University Press, 1998).

Miles Larmer, 'Zambia Since 1990: Paradoxes of Democratic Transition' in *Turning Points in African Democracy,* eds. Abdul Raufu Mustapha and Lindsay Whitfield (Cumbria: James Currey, 2009).

Peter T. Leeson, 'Better off stateless: Somalia before and after government collapse,' *Journal of Comparative Economics,* 35/4: (2007).

Laurel Leff, *Buried by the Times: The Holocaust and America's Most Important Newspaper* (New York: Cambridge University Press, 2005).

Raphael Lemkin, *Axis Rule in Occupied Europe* (Washington, D.C.: Carnegie Endowment for International Peace, 1944).

E. Leonard and G. Ramsay, (eds.) *Globalising Somalia: Multilateral, international, and transnational repercussions of conflict.* (New York: Bloomsbury, 2013).

Hillel Levine, *Economic Origins of Antisemitism: Poland and Its Jews in the Early Modern Period* (New Haven, CT: Yale University Press, 1991).

Ioan M. Lewis, *A Pastoral Democracy: A Study of Pastoralism and Politics among the Northern Somali of the Horn of Africa* (Oxford: International African Institute/ Oxford University Press, 1961).

Ioan M. Lewis, 'Sufism in Somaliland: A study in tribal Islam' in *Islam in Tribal Societies: From the Atlas to the Indus*, eds. Akbar S. Ahmed and David M. Hart (London: Routledge and Kegan Paul, 1984).

Ioan M. Lewis, 'Doing Violence to Ethnography: A Response to Catherine Besteman's "Representing Violence and 'Othering' Somalia",' *Cultural Anthropology,* 13/1: 100–108 (1998).

L.R. Lewitter, 'The Partitions of Poland' in *The New Cambridge Modern History*, vol. 8, ed. A. Goodwin (Cambridge: Cambridge University Press, 1965).

Albert S. Lindemann, *Esau's Tears: Modern Anti-Semitism and the Rise of the Jews* (New York: Cambridge University Press, 1997).

John B. Londregan and Keith T. Poole, 'Poverty, the Coup Trap, and the Seizure of Executive Power,' *World Politics,* 42/2:151–183 (1990).

Peter Longerich, *Holocaust: The Nazi Persecution and Murder of the Jews* (Oxford: Oxford University Press, 2010).

Ivan Lovrenovic, *Bosnia: A Cultural History* (New York: New York University Press, 2001).

Edward Luck 'Prevention, Theory and Practice' in *From Reaction to Conflict Prevention: Opportunities for the UN System,* eds. Fen Osler Hampson and David M. Malone (Boulder, CA: Lynne Rienner Publishers, 2002).

Jerzy Lukowski, *The Partitions of Poland 1772, 1793, 1795* (London: Longman, 1999).
Michael S. Lund, 'Underrating Preventive Diplomacy,' *Foreign Affairs*, July/August 1995.
Michael S. Lund, 'Conflict Prevention: Theory in Pursuit of Policy and Practice' in *The SAGE Handbook of Conflict Resolution*, eds. Jacob Bercovitch, Victor Kremenyuk, and William Zartman (London: SAGE Publications, 2009).
Ellen Lust-Okar, *Structuring Conflict in the Arab World. Incumbents, Opponents, and Institutions* (Cambridge: Cambridge University Press, 2005).
Donald M. MacRaild, *Irish Migrants in Modern Britain, 1750–1922* (New York: St. Martin's Press, 1999).
Ali Akbar Mahdi, 'The Student Movement in the Islamic Republic of Iran', *Journal of Iranian Research and Analysis* 15/2: 5–46 (1999).
Raphael Mahler, *A History of Modern Jewry 1780–1815* (New York: Schocken Books, 1971).
Mahmood Mamdani, *When Victims Become Killers: Colonialism, Nativism, and Genocide in Rwanda* (Princeton: Princeton University Press, 2001).
Monty G. Marshall, *Fragility, Instability, and the Failure of States. Assessing Sources of Systemic Risk* (New York: Center for Preventive, 2008).
Greg Martin, 'Conceptualizing Cultural Politics in Subcultural and Social Movement Studies,' *Social Movement Studies: Journal of Social, Cultural, and Political Protest*, 1/1: 73–88 (2002).
Volker Matthies, *Krisenprävention. Vorbeugen ist besser als Heilen* (Opladen: Leske + Budrich, 2000).
Volker Matthies, 'Eine Welt voller neuer Kriege? Der vernachlässigte Blick auf den Frieden,' *Der Bürger im Staat*, 54/4: 185–190 (2004).
Deborah Mayersen and Stephen McLoughlin, 'Risk and Resilience to Mass Atrocities in Africa: A Comparison of Rwanda and Botswana,' *Journal of Genocide Research*, 13/3: 247–269 (2011).
Kieran McEvoy and Kirsten McConnachie, 'Victim and Transitional Justice: Voice, Agency and Blame,' *Social and Legal Studies*, 22/4: 489–513 (2013).
Stephen McLoughlin and Deborah Mayersen, 'Reconsidering Root Causes: A New Framework for the Prevention of Genocide and Mass Atrocities' in *Genocide, Risk and Resilience: An Interdisciplinary Approach*, eds. Bert Engelaere, Stephan Parmentier, Jacques Haers and Barbara Segaert (Basingstoke: Palgrave, 2013).
Stephen McLoughlin, *The Structural Prevention of Mass Atrocities* (Oxon: Routledge, 2014).
Frédéric Mégret, 'Beyond the "Salvation" Paradigm: Responsibility to Protect (Others) vs the Power of Protecting Oneself,' *Security Dialogue*, 40/6: 575–95 (2009).
Stanley Meisler, *AnnanKofi: A Man of Peace in a World of War* (London: Wiley, 2007).
Robert Melson, *Revolution and Genocide: On the Origins of the Armenian Genocide and the Holocaust* (Chicago: University of Chicago Press, 1992).

Manus Midlarsky, *The Killing Trap: Genocide in the Twentieth Century* (Cambridge: Cambridge University Press, 2005).

Manus Midlarsky, *Origins of Political Extremism: Mass Violence in the Twentieth Century and Beyond* (Cambridge: Cambridge University Press, 2011).

Abbas Milani, 'Is Ahmadinejad Islamic Enough for Iran', *Foreign Policy* 29 (2011), https://abbasmilani.stanford.edu/wp-content/uploads/2014/10/Is-Ahmadinejad-Islamic-Enough-for-Iran.pdf.

Minority Rights Group International, 'Azerbaijan Overview', in *World Directory of Minorities and Indigenous Peoples,* 2012, http://www.minorityrights.org/1922/azerbaijan/azerbaijan-overview.html.

Minority Rights Group International, 'Iran', *World Directory of Minorities and Indigenous Peoples,* July 2014. http://www.minorityrights.org/?lid=5092#minorities.

Gelijn Molier, 'Humanitarian Intervention and The Responsibility to Protect after 9/11,' *Netherlands International Law Review,* 53/1: 37–62 (2006).

Moojan Momen, 'The Babi and Bahá'í community of Iran: A case of "suspended genocide"?' *Journal of Genocide Research,* 7/ 2: 221–241 (2005).

The Montreal Institute for Genocide and Human Rights Studies, *Mobilizing the Will to Intervene: Leadership and Action to Prevent Mass Atrocities* (Montreal: Concordia University, 2009).

Mehdi Moslem, *Iran: Factional Politics in Post-Khomeini* (NewYork: Syracuse University Press, 2002).

Witold Mucha, 'Prone to Conflict, but Resilient to Violence. Why Civil Wars Sometimes Do Not Happen: Insights from Peru and Bolivia,' *Journal of Peace, Conflict and Development,* 20: 97–114 (2013).

Robert Muggah with Natasha White, 'Is there a Preventive Action Renaissance? The Policy and Practice of Preventive Diplomacy and Conflict Prevention,' Norwegian Peacebuilding Resource Centre, Report February 2013, http://www.peacebuilding.no/var/ezflow_site/storage/original/application/00175abccdb1df5f006c8e4 0da206643.pdf, accessed 23 July 2014.

J. Murphy and A. Cohn, 'Mental Health Innovations with the Australian Defence Force,' *Journal of Occupational Health and Safety in Australia and New Zealand,* 24/6 (2008).

S. Mansoob Murshed and Mohammad Zulfan Tadjoeddin, 'Revisiting the Greed and Grievance Explanations for Violent Internal Conflict,' *Journal of International Development,* 21/1: 87–111 (2009).

S. Mansoob Murshed, *Explaining Civil War: A Rational Choice Approach* (Cheltenham: Edward Elgar, 2010).

Vali Nasr, 'When the Shiites Rise,' *Foreign Affairs* 85 (4) 2006.

Sharon Erickson Nepstad, 'Nonviolent Resistance in the Arab Spring: The Critical Role of Military-Opposition Alliances', *Swiss Political Science Review,* 17/4: 485–491 (2011).

Brett R. O'Bannon, 'Monitoring the Frog in Africa: Conflict Early Warning with Structural Data,' *Global Responsibility to Protect*, 4/4: 449–474 (2012).

Pat O'Malley, (2010) 'Resilient Subjects: Uncertainty, Warfare and Liberalism,' *Economy and Society*, 39/4: 488–509 (2010).

OECD, 'Concepts and Dilemmas of State Building in Fragile Situations: From Fragility to Resilience', OECD Discussions Paper (2008), http://www.oecd.org/dac/governance-peace/conflictandfragility/docs/41100930.pdf.

Mariya Y. Omelicheva, 'Natural Disasters: Triggers of Political Instability?' *International Interactions: Empirical and Theoretical Research in International Relations*, 37/4: 441–465 (2011).

Norimitsu Onishi, 'Lebanon Worries That Housing Will Make Syrian Refugees Stay,' *New York Times*, 11 December 2013.

Ilber Ortayli, 'Greeks in the Ottoman Administration During the Tanzimat Period' in *GreeksOttoman in the Age of Nationalism: Politics, Economy, and Society in the Nineteenth Century*, eds. Dimitri Gondicas and Charles Issawi, eds (Princeton, NJ: Darwin Press, 1999).

OSCE, 'Annual Report 1998 on OSCE Activities 1 December 1997–30 November 1998' (Vienna, 2 December 1998).

OSCE 'Annual Report 1999 on OSCE Activities 1 December 1998–31 October 1999' (Vienna, 17 November 1999).

OSCE, 'Annual Report 2000 on OSCE Activities 1 November 1999–31 October 2000, (Vienna, 24 November, 2000).

OSCE, 'Annual Report 2001 on OSCE Activities 1 November 2000–31 October 2001' (Vienna, 26 November 2001).

OSCE, 'Annual Report 2003 on OSCE Activities: Security and Cooperation for Europe' (Vienna, 2003).

OSCE, 'Annual Report 2008' (Vienna: OSCE, 2009).

OSCE ODIHR, 'Republic of Azerbaijan Presidential Elections 15 October 2003', (Warsaw, 12 November 2003).

Gudrun Østby, 'Polarization, Horizontal Inequalities and Violent Civil Conflict,' *Journal of Peace Research*, 45/2: 143–162 (2008).

Adam Pain and Simon Levine, 'A conceptual analysis of livelihoods and resilience: addressing the 'insecurity of agency,' Humanitarian Policy Working Group, HPG Working Paper, November 2012, http://www.odi.org.uk/publications/6976-resilience-livelihoods-agency-socio-economic-security, accessed 30 May 2014.

Emanuela Paoletti, 'Libya: Roots of a Civil Conflict,' *Mediterranean Politics*, 16/2: 313–319 (2011).

Tudor Parfitt, *The Road to Redemption: The Jews of Yemen 1900–1950* (New York: EJ Brill, 1996).

Susan Pedersen, 'Back to the League of Nations', *The American Historical Review*, 112/4: 1091–117 (2007).

Margot Phaneuf, 'Resilience: Abstract Concept of Survival Skill,' 2007. http://www.infiressources.ca/fer/Depotdocument_anglais/Resilience_abstract_concept_or_survival_skill.pdf, accessed 30 May 2014.

Christopher Phillips, *After the Arab Spring: power shift in the Middle East? Syria's bloody Arab Spring* (London: London School of Economics and Political Science, 2012).

David Pinault 'Hidden Prayer in Yemen: Islam and the Problem of Religious Intolerance,' *America*, 201/17: 10–14 (2009).

Polity IV, 'Country Reports 2010,' http://www.systemicpeace.org/polity/polity06.htm, accessed 7 June 2014.

Public Broadcasting Service (PBS), 'Mahmoud Ahmadinejad's Victory in Iran's Presidential Runoff Election', *Online NewsHour*, 27 June 2005, http://www.pbs.org/newshour/bb/middle_east/jan-june05/ahmadinejad_6-27.html.

Jacques Ranciere, 'Who is the Subject of the Rights of Man?' *South Atlantic Quarterly*, 103/2-3: 297–310, (2004).

Lissi Rasmussen, *Christian-Muslim Relations in Africa: The Cases of Northern Nigeria and Tanzania Compared* (London: British Academic Press, 1993).

Alec Rasizade, 'Azerbaijan after Heydar Aliev,' *Nationalities Papers: The Journal of Nationalism and Ethnicity* 32/1: 137–164 (2004).

Alec Rasizade, 'Azerbaijan Descending into the Third World after a Decade of Independence,' *Journal of Third World Studies*, 21/1: 191–219 (2004).

Alec Rasizade, 'Azerbaijan's Prospects in Nagorno-Karabakh,' in *Mediterranean Quarterly* 22/3: 72–94 (2011).

Patrick M. Regan and Daniel Norton, 'Greed, Grievance, and Mobilization in Civil Wars', *Journal of Conflict Resolution*, 49/3: 319–336 (2005).

Rubin Reike, Serena Sharma and Jennifer Welsh, 'A Strategic Framework for Mass Atrocity Prevention,' March 2013, http://acmc.gov.au/wp-content/uploads/2013/11/3-2013-A-Strategic-Framework-for-Mass-Atrocity-Prevention.pdf, accessed 12 February 2014.

Ben Reilly, 'Institutional Designs for Diverse Democracies: Consociationalism, Centripetalism and Communalism Compared,' *European Political Science*, 11: 259–270 (2012).

David Roberts, 'Post-Conflict Peacebuilding, Liberal Irrelevance and the Locus of Legitimacy,' *International Peacekeeping*, 18/4: 410–424 (2011).

Hugh Roberts, 'Who Said Gaddafi Had to Go?' *London Review of Books*, 33/22: 8–18 (2011).

Nicolas Rost, 'Will it happen again? On the possibility of forecasting the risk of genocide,' *Journal of Genocide Research*, 15/1: 41–67 (2013).

Donald Rothchild, 'Third-party incentives and the phases of conflict prevention' in *From Promise to Practice: Strengthening UN Capacities for the Prevention of Violent Conflict*, eds. Chandra Lekha Sriram and Karin Wermester (Boulder, London: Lynne Rienner, 2003).

Barnett R. Rubin and Bruce D. Jones, 'Prevention of Violent Conflict: Tasks and Challenges for the United Nations,' *Global Governance*, 13/3: 391–408 (2007).

Michael Rubin, 'Are Kurds a Pariah Minority?' *Social Research* 70/1: 295–330 (2003).

Rudolph Rummel, *Death By Government* (New Brunswick: Transaction Publishers, 1994).

Rudolph Rummel, *Power Kills: Democracy as a Method of Nonviolence* (New Brunswick, NJ: Transaction Publishers, 1997).

Anastasyia Ryabchuk, 'Right Revolution? Hopes and Perils of the Euromaidan Protests in Ukraine,' *Debate: Journal of Contemporary Central and Eastern Europe*, forthcoming.

Djavad Salehi-Isfahani, 'Poverty, inequality, and populist politics in Iran,' *Journal of Economic Inequality* 7/1: 5–28 (2009).

Said S. Samatar, 'Genius as Madness: King Tewodros of Ethiopia and Sayyid Muhammad of Somalia in Comparative Perspective,' *Northeast African Studies*, 10/3: 27–32 (2003).

Nicholas Sambanis and Moses Shayo, 'Social Identification and Ethnic Conflict,' *American Political Science Review*, 107/2: 294–325 (2013).

Eliz Sanasarian and Avi Davidi, 'Domestic Tribulations and International Repercussions: The State and The Transformation of Non-Muslims in Iran', *Journal of International Affairs*, 60/2: 55–69 (2007).

William Schabas, 'Groups Protected by the Genocide Convention: Conflicting Interpretations from the International Criminal Tribunal for Rwanda,' *ILSA Journal of International and Comparative Law*, 6/1: 375–388 (1999).

Jules Schelvis, *Sobibor: A History of a Nazi Death Camp*, trans. Karin Dixon, (Oxford: Berg, 2007).

Thomas Schirrmacher, 'Iran: Suppression of religious freedom and persecution of religious minorities,' *International Journal for Religious Freedom*, 2/1: 111–130 (2009).

Oliver Schlumberger, *Debating Arab authoritarianism. Dynamics and durability in non-democratic regimes* (Stanford California: Stanford University Press, 2007).

Susanne Schmeidl, 'Early Warning at the Grass-Roots Level: Fine-tuning Early Warning to Context and User-Needs,' paper presented at the Annual Convention of the International Studies Association, San Francisco, 26 March 2008.

Asghar Schirazi, *The Constitution of Iran: Politics and the State in the Islamic Republic*, translation by John O'Kane (London: I.B.Tauris, 1997).

Albrecht Schnabel, 'Human Security and Conflict Prevention' in *Conflict Prevention from Rhetoric to Reality, Volume 2: Opportunities and Innovations*, eds. David Carment and Albrecht Schnabel (Lanham: Lexington Books, 2004).

Jacques Semelin, *Purify and Destroy: The Political Uses of Massacre and Genocide* (London: C. Hurst & Co, 2007).

Stanford J. Shaw and Ezel Kural Shaw, *History of the Ottoman Empire and Modern Turkey, Volume II: Reform, Revolution, and Republic: The Rise of Modern Turkey, 1808–1975* (Cambridge: Cambridge University Press, 1977).

Noha Shawki, 'Responsibility to Protect: The Evolution of an International Norm,' *Global Responsibility to Protect*, 3/2: 172–96 (2011).

Sujai Shivakumar, *ActionAid Somaliland: Programme Review – Institutional Analysis* (London: ActionAid, 1998).

C.J. Shivers and David M. Herszenhorn, 'Separatists Defy Kiev and Putin on Referendum,' *New York Times*, 8 May 2014.

Hugo Slim, *Civilians Killing: Method, Madness and Morality in War* (New York: Columbia University Press, 2008).

Michael Llewellyn Smith, *Ionian Vision: Greece in Asia Minor, 1919–1922* (Ann Arbor: University of Michigan Press, 1998).

Richard Snyder and Ravi Bhavnani, 'Diamonds, Blood, and Taxes. A Revenue-Centered Framework for Explaining Political Order', *Journal of Conflict Resolution*, 49/4: 563–597 (2005).

Israel Solomons, 'Lord George Gordon's Conversion to Judaism,' paper read before the Jewish Historical Society of England, June 2, 1913.

Ashley South and Simon Harragin, with Justin Corbett, Richard Horsey, Susanne Kempel, Henrik Fröjmark and Nils Carstensen, *Local to Global Protection in Myanmar (Burma), Sudan, South Sudan and Zimbabwe*, Humanitarian Practice Network at the Overseas Development Institute, Number 72, February 2012.

S. Southwick, M. Vyhiligan and D. Charney, 'The Psychobiology of Depression and Resilience to Stress: Implications for Prevention and Treatment,' *Annual Reviews of Clinical Psychology*, 1: 255–291 (2005).

William Spry, *Life on the Bosphorus-Doings in the City of the Sultan. Turkey Past and Present, Including Chronicles of the Caliphs from Mahomet to Abdul Hamid II* (London: H.S. Nichols, 1895).

Chandra Likha Sriram and Karin Wermester eds., *From Promise to Practice: Strenghtening UN Capacities for the Prevention of Violent Conflict* (Boulder CO: Lynne Rienner, 2003).

Chandra Likha Sriram and Karin Wermester 'Preventive Action at the United Nations: From Promise to Practice?' in *From Reaction to Conflict Prevention*, eds. Fen Osler Hampson and David M Malone (Boulder CO: Lynne Rienner, 2003).

V.V. Stanciu, 'Reflections on the Congress for the Prevention of Genocide,' *Yad Vashem Studies*, 7: 185–187 (1968).

Gregory H. Stanton, *The 8 Stages of Genocide*, 1996, http://www.genocidewatch.org/images/8StagesBriefingpaper.pdf, accessed 23 November 2012.

Stephen John Stedman, 'Alchemy for a new world order: overselling "preventive diplomacy",' *Foreign Affairs*, 74/3: 14–20 (1995).

Maria Stephan and Erica Chenoweth, 'Why Civil Resistance Works: The Strategic Logic of Nonviolent Conflict,' *International Security*, 33/1: 7–44 (2008).

Emma J. Stewart, *The European Union and Conflict Prevention: Policy Evolution and Outcome* (New Brunswick USA: Transaction, 2005).

Frances Stewart, 'Horizontal Inequalities and Conflict: An Introduction and some Hypotheses' in *Horizontal Inequalities and Conflict: Understanding Group Violence in Multiethnic Societies*, ed. Frances Stewart (New York: Palgrave Macmillan, 2008).

Daniel Stone, *Polish Politics and National Reform, 1775–1788* (Boulder, CO: East European Monographs, Distributed by Columbia University Press, 1976).

Scott Straus, 'Darfur and the Genocide Debate,' *Foreign Affairs*, 84/1: 123–133 (2005).

Scott Straus, 'Retreating from the Brink: Theorizing Mass Violence and the Dynamics of Restraint,' *Perspectives on Politics*, 10/2: 343–362 (2012).

Andrea Kathryn Talentino, 'Evaluating Success and Failure: Conflict Prevention in Cambodia and Bosnia' in *Conflict Prevention: Path to Peace or Grand Illusion?* eds. David Carment and Albrecht Schnabel (Tokyo: United Nations University Press, 2003).

Marcus Tanner, *Ireland's Holy Wars: The Struggle of a Nation's Soul, 1500–2000* (New Haven: Yale University Press, 2001).

Kamran Taremi, 'Iranian Foreign Policy Towards Occupied Iraq, 2003–2005,' *Middle East Policy* 12 (4) 2005, pp. 28–47.

Adam Tarock, 'The Politics of the Pipeline: The Iran and Afghanistan Conflict,' *Third World Quarterly*, 20/4: 801–819 (1999).

Tzvetan Todorov, *The Fragility of Goodness: Why Bulgaria's Jews Survived the Holocaust*, trans. Arthur Denner (Princeton, NJ: Princeton University Press, 2001).

Michelle Tusan, *Smyrna's Ashes: Humanitarianism, Genocide, and the Birth of the Middle East* (Berkeley: University of California Press, 2012).

Nsongurua J. Udombana, 'When Neutrality is a Sin: The Darfur Crisis and the Crisis of Humanitarian Intervention in Sudan,' *Human Rights Quarterly*, 27/4: 1149–1199 (2005).

Jay Ulfelder and Benjamin Valentino, 'Assessing Risks of State-Sponsored Mass Killing,' February 2008. Available at http://ssrn.com/abstract=17033426. Retrieved 23 October 2013.

UNHCR, 'Islamic Republic of Iran', 2014 UNHCR Country Operations Profile. http://www.unhcr.org/pages/49e486f96.html.

United Nations, 'Letter Dated 12 July 2004 from the Secretary-General Addressed to the Security Council,' S/2004/567, 13 July 2004.

United Nations, *Basic Principles and Guidelines on the Right to a Remedy and Reparation for Victims of Gross Violations of International Human Rights Law and Serious Violations of International Humanitarian Law*, A/RES/60/147, 16 December 2005.

United Nations, *Charter of the United Nations*, https://www.un.org/en/documents/charter/, accessed 26 March 2014.

United Nations, 'Letter dated 9 November 2011 from the Permanent Representative of Brazil to the United Nations addressed to the Secretary-General,' /A/66/551; paragraph 10.

United Nations, *Report of the Independent Inquiry into the Actions of the United Nations during the 1994 Genocide in Rwanda*, S/1999/1257, 15 December 1999.

United Nations, 'United Nations and the Rule of Law', 2014, http://www.un.org/en/ruleoflaw/, accessed 19 May, 2014.

United Nations High Commissioner for Refugees, 'Refugee Figures', http://www.unhcr.org/pages/49c3646c1d.html, accessed 19 February 2014.

United Nations General Assembly, '2005 World Summit Outcome', UNGA Res. 60/1, 16 September 2005.

The United Nations Office for Disaster Risk Reduction, 'Terminology', http://www.unisdr.org/we/inform/terminology#letter-r, (2013), accessed 4 March 2013.

United Nations Office of the United Nations Special Adviser on the Prevention of Genocide, 'Preventing Genocide', 2012, http://www.un.org/en/preventgenocide/adviser/genocide_prevention.shtml, accessed 5 January 2013.

United Nations Office of the United Nations Special Adviser on the Prevention of Genocide, 'Preventing Genocide, Crimes Against Humanity, Ethnic Cleansing and War Crimes', 2012, http://www.un.org/en/preventgenocide/adviser/un_role.shtml, accessed 5 January 2013.

Office of the Special Adviser on the Prevention of Genocide, 'Work of the Office', 2014, http://www.un.org/en/preventgenocide/adviser/engagement_partners.shtml, accessed 14 May 2014.

United Nations Security Council, S/RES/1366, 30 August 2001.

United States Holocaust Memorial Museum, 'Austria', in *Holocaust Encyclopedia*, http://www.ushmm.org/wlc/en/article.php?ModuleId=10005447, accessed 14 February 2014.

K.E. Vaidyanathan, *Population Statistics of Somalia* (Nairobi: UNDP Somalia, 1997).

Sanam Vakil, 'Iran: Balancing east against west,' *The Washington Quarterly* 29/4 (2006): 51–65.

Benjamin Valentino, *Final Solutions: Mass Killing and Genocide in the Twentieth Century* (Ithaca, NY: Cornell University Press, 2004).

Benjamin A. Valentino, 'Why We Kill: The Political Science of Political Violence against Civilians', *Annual Review of Political Science*, Vol. 17 (2014): 89–103.

Charles van der Leeuw, *Azerbaijan: A Quest for Identity* (Surrey: Curzon, 2000).

Katherine Verdery, *The Political Lives of Dead Bodies: Reburial and Postsocialist Change* (New York: Columbia University Press, 1999).

David Vital, *A People Apart: The Jews in Europe 1789–1939* (Oxford: Oxford University Press, 1999).

James Raymond Vreeland, 'The Effect of Political Regime on Civil War: Unpacking Anocracy,' *Journal of Conflict Resolution*, 52/3: 401–425 (2008).

Alex de Waal and Bridget Conley-Zilkic, 'Reflections on How Genocidal Killings are Brought to an End,' Social Science Research Council, 22 December 2006, http://howgenocidesend.ssrc.org/de_Waal/, accessed 30 May 2014.

Peter Wallensteen, 'Reassessing Recent Conflicts: Direct vs Structural Prevention' in *From Reaction to Conflict Prevention: Opportunities for the UN System,* eds. Fen Osler Hampson and David M Malone (eds.) (Boulder CO: Lynne Rienner Publishers, 2003).

James Waller *Becoming Evil: How Ordinary People Commit Genocide* (New York: Oxford University Press, 2002).

Michael Walls, 'The Emergence of a Somali State: Building Peace from Civil War in Somaliland,' *African Affairs,* 108/432: 371–389 (2009).

Michael Walls, 'Somaliland: Democracy Threatened - Constitutional Impasse as Presidential Elections are Postponed,' *Chatham House Briefing Note* (2009).

Michael Walls, *A Somali Nation-State: History, Culture and Somaliland's Political Transition* (Pisa: Ponte Invisibile, 2014).

Michael Walls et al, *Peace in Somaliland: An Indigenous Approach to State-Building. The Search for Peace Series* (Geneva/Hargeysa: Interpeace/Academy for Peace and Development, 2008).

Michael Walls and Steve Kibble, *Somaliland: Change and Continuity: Report by International Election Observers on the June 2010 Presidential Elections in Somaliland,*(London: Progressio, 2011).

Michael D. Ward, Nils W. Metternich, Cassy L. Dorff, Max Gallop, Florian M. Hollenbach, Anna Schultz, and Simon Weschle, 'Learning from the Past and Stepping into the Future: Toward a New Generation of Conflict Prediction,' *International Studies Review,* 15/4: 473–490 (2013).

Thomas G. Weiss Jr., 'New Challenges for UN Military Operations: Implementing an Agenda for Peace,' *The Washington Quarterly,* 16/1: 51–66 (1993).

Gilbert H. Welch, *Overdiagnosed: Making People Sick in the Pursuit of Health* (Boston: Beacon Press, 2011).

Gilbert H. Welch and William C. Black, 'Overdiagnosis in Cancer,' *Journal of the National Cancer Institute,* 10, pp. 605–613 (2010).

Jennifer M. Welsh, 'Turning Words Into Deeds? The Implementation of the "Responsibility to Protect",' *Global Responsibility to Protect,* 2/1-2: 149–154 (2010).

Jon Western and Joshua S. Goldstein, 'Humanitarian Intervention Comes of Age: Lessons from Somalia to Libya,' *Foreign Affairs,* 90/6: 48–59 (2011).

The White House, 'Fact Sheet: A Comprehensive Strategy and New Tools to Prevent and Respond to Atrocities,' 23 April 2012, http://www.whitehouse.gov/the-press-office/

2012/04/23/fact-sheet-comprehensive-strategy-and-new-tools-prevent-and-respond-atro, accessed 12 December 2012.

Paul D. Williams and Alex J. Bellamy, 'The Responsibility to Protect and the Crisis in Darfur,' *Security Dialogue*, 36/1: 27–47 (2005).

The World Bank, *Social Assessments for Better Development: Case Studies from Albania, Azerbaijan and Moldova* (Washington: World Bank, 2002).

The World Bank, *Islamic Republic of Iran.* http://data.worldbank.org/country/iran-islamic-republic.

The World Bank, 'Lower Middle Income,' http://data.worldbank.org/income-level/LMC, accessed 27 February 2014.

Lawrence Woocher, *Preventing Violent Conflict: Assessing Progress, Meeting Challenges* (Washington, D.C.: United States Institute of Peace, 2009).

Herbert Wulf and Tobias Debiel, *Conflict Warning and Response Mechanisms: Tools for Enhancing the Effectiveness of Regional Organisations? A Comparative Study of the AU, ECOWAS, IGAD, ASEAN/ARF and PIF* (London: Development Studies Institute, 2009).

W.B. Yeats, *Essays and Introductions* (New York: MacMillan, 1961).

Index

www.ingramcontent.com/pod-product-compliance
Lightning Source LLC
Chambersburg PA
CBHW031323230926
51848CB00001B/60
9789004299863